Masonry is ". . . the most powerful organization in the land."

"It is an ordainer of kings. Its hand has shaped the destinies of worlds."

From the writings of Manly P. Hall,
one of the greatest Masons of all time

CONSPIRACY
AGAINST
CHRISTIANITY

published by
PUBLIUS PRESS
3100 S. Philamena Place (ste. B3)
Tucson, Arizona Republic 85730
the united States of America
telephone (520) 886-4380

It is the intent of the publisher to make
this vital information available to as
large an audience as is possible.

International Standard Book Number
0 - 96 14 13 5 - 4 - 9

Printed in the united States of America

WRITE OR CALL THE PUBLISHER
for a catalog of other books and videos
written and produced by
Ralph Epperson
including his other two books
The Unseen Hand and *The New World Order*

Conspiracy
Against
Christianity

by
A. Ralph Epperson

SYMBOLS USED
ON THE COVER

I have attempted to portray the symbolic world of the Masons on the cover of this book by making up my own symbols. (The Masonic terms that I will use in this section, like "the Blue Lodge," "the layer inside the layer," and the "written record of the Masons," will all be discussed in further detail later in this book.)

The blue background on the cover is symbolic of the "Blue Lodge" of Freemasonry. The font for the word "Masonry," the first word of the title, was selected because the black and white area behind the letter, and the white letter itself, symbolically represent the "two layers" that exist inside the Blue Lodge, the one visible and the other invisible. The words inside the bordered areas on both sides of the cover symbolically represent the "written record of the Masons" that one is to "read, study and reflect upon." More specifically, the words shown inside the third border on the front cover are "the secret" of "the worldwide Masonic movement" that the Masonic writers refer to.

These lines around the words are the "intentionally misleading" explanations offered by the "Adept Masons," the members of the second layer, who are keeping their true meaning from the "initiate Mason," the first layer.

TABLE OF CONTENTS

INTRODUCTION

The two quotations by Manly P. Hall, cited on one of the previous pages, present a completely different view of Masonry than most of the American people have, if they have any view about the lodge at all. I believe it is fair to say that most Americans who are not members of the Masonic Lodge know little or nothing about this group, especially the conclusion that they are as powerful as Mr. Hall has stated. Some of the remainder of the American people know a little, possibly because they know a friend, family member or business associate who is a member. But, even these people know very little about the Masons because they are a "secret" organization, choosing not to reveal what they stand for to non-members.

Those Americans who are Masons know a great deal more, but even then only a small percentage of these men truly know that Masonry is as powerful as Mr. Hall reported.

So, basically the overwhelming majority of the American people do not know much about the Masonic Lodge. Yet many have seen their symbols on the backs of cars, on buildings the Masons call "temples," and on signs outside of cities advertising their meeting places and times.

If you have seen a "square and a compass," a "star with one point down and two points up," or "a crescent moon and a scimitar [a curved sword,]" you have seen a Masonic symbol. If you have ever seen men in one of your city's parades dressed as clowns, or performing a precision routine in a street parade on horses, motorcycles or in small cars, you have seen the Masons. If you have ever attended a function in a "Shriners Hall," you have seen the Masons. If you have ever tuned in or watched the "East-West football game," you have seen the Masons. If you have gone to the Shriners Circus, you have seen the Masons. If you have ever seen a man in a red hat that looks like an inverted clay pot, you have seen the Masons.

But to stretch these visible, non-controversial images that the American people have of the Masons to an organization that "shapes the destinies of worlds," is almost totally unreasonable to most Americans.

But, Mr. Hall, a leading Masonic writer, said that they "are the most powerful organization in the land." And if he doesn't know, one might ask just who does?

So, a good place to start as to whether or not Mr. Hall is correct is with a quotation on their "overall mission" taken from a book written by Henry C. Clausen, a Past Sovereign Grand Commander of the Supreme Council, 33rd Degree, the Masonic equivalent of a President. This is what he wrote in response to his own question: "What is the Scottish Rite? [a branch of the Masons, to be discussed more in detail a little later in this book.]"

> "Our overall mission can be summarized thus; To seek that which is the most worth in the world;
>   To exalt the dignity of every person, the human side of our daily activities and the maximum service to humanity;
>   To aid mankind's search in God's Universe for identity, for development, and for destiny;
>   And thereby achieve better men in a better world, happier men in a happier world, and wiser men in a wiser world." [1]

If the American people know anything at all about Masonry, this is about all that they know: the Masons appear to be a group of good men with noble causes.

A similar position was taken by the Masons in Tucson, Arizona when their leaders placed an advertisement in the Arizona Daily Star, Tucson's morning newspaper. This advertisement appeared in 1983, and contained a statement of their purposes and goals, and it read, in part:

"No organization of human origin, in all probability, has ever exercised a greater influence over the affairs of mankind than that which is known under the general name of Freemasonry [notice that they here agree with Manly P. Hall's assessment that they "are the most powerful organization in the land."]

The teachings and symbols [in the Masonic rituals and in their writings] precede the formal organization by thousands of years. They go deep into ancient ages [this thought will be confirmed later in this book by other key Masonic writers.] The members are taught the highest ethics, the wise expositions of philosophy and religion and the blessings of charity.

The code of personal conduct stems from the precepts of chivalry, the Ten Commandments and the Golden Rule.

Members gain a comprehensive knowledge of the heritage of history, philosophy, religion, morality, freedom and toleration, and the relationship of their Creator, their country, their family and themselves.

The mission of the Scottish Rite is carried out in a series of spiritual, charitable and moral programs.

Thus the order has been a strong voice for human dignity, justice, morality and civic responsibility.
The Scottish Rite Creed is:

The cause of human progress is our cause, the enfranchisement of human thought our supreme wish, the freedom of human conscience our mission and the guarantee of equal rights to all peoples everywhere, the end of our contention." [2]

This book will reveal to the reader just what those words mean, because they conceal a very frightening truth. Because they conceal the hidden agenda of the Masons that has been kept from the people of the world.

I love to ask the Mason the following question after he tells me that these noble causes are the goals of the Masons:

> "If all of these worthy goals are why the Masons have organized, why not just come out from behind all of this secrecy and publicly tell the whole world of your purposes?"

And the answer to this question is obvious: because they are concealing a hidden agenda, one that they will not make public until they wish it to become known.

And the date of that revealing is very near.

We shall soon know for certain what this hidden agenda is.

So it is understandable that most Americans are not aware of the powerful influence of the Masons in the affairs of the world. Because the general perception of what the Masons believe in, to those who have any idea at all as to who they are and what they stand for, is that these statements are correct.

But, after thirty-four years of research into this field, I can assure you that Mr. Hall's quotations are completely accurate. The perception of the average American is wrong.

Masonry is "powerful." Masonry does indeed "ordain kings and shape the destinies of worlds."

And it is certain that only a few members of the Masonic Lodge know that Mr. Hall's statements are true.

And that is why I have chosen to write this book.

It is time that all of us understand exactly what the Masons believe in.

Because what you are about to read has never been put into written form by anyone in the history of mankind, at least as far as I have been able to determine in my thirty-four years of research. I have read hundreds of books on Masonry, and some have more information about the Masonic puzzle than others, but none of the books that I have read that were written by what the Masons call "an Anti-Mason" have revealed "THE SECRET" of Masonry. Some of these books have parts of the puzzle, and others have other parts, but here, for the first time on paper, you will learn about all of the parts that must be examined before you can know exactly what they believe in.

"THE SECRET" of Masonry has been discovered after thousands of years of their existence by someone who is not a member.

Because I have discovered their hidden agenda.

DEDICATION

I would like to dedicate this book to Rex Hutchens, an active member of the Masons and the author of the book entitled A BRIDGE TO LIGHT. His book has been officially published by the Masonic Lodge, so he is no doubt one of their leading writers. I am certain that he is not expecting me to afford him this rather dubious honor, and I will presume that once he discovers that I have taken this action, he will not approve of it.

Mr. Hutchens did not prod me into doing the research for this book, because I had started discovering the secret of Masonry some three or four years before we met for the first time. And after we met, I certainly had no idea that I would write it. But he indirectly convinced me that it was needed. And I am confident that he does not know that our visit several years ago had that kind of effect on me, but it did.

It might be helpful to you, the reader, to know how we came to meet in late 1988 or early 1989. (I am uncertain exactly when we had the first phone conversation that led to our meeting, but I remember having many over the course of several months that culminated in his personal visit to my home. The details of those conversations are more familiar, but I made no notes of the details, nor did I record them. So, I will recall their content as best I can, because they laid an enormous foundation for the base of this book.)

As I said, I was first introduced to Mr. Hutchens when he called me around the end of 1988. Mr. Hutchens was at the time a 32nd Degree Mason, and sometime after he completed his book entitled A BRIDGE TO LIGHT for the Masonic Lodge, he went on to become a 33rd Degree Mason. (These terms will be defined later.) So, I can understand why he had become concerned enough about me to place his first phone call.

After Mr. Hutchens confirmed that I was the Ralph Epperson he was looking for, the conversation went something like this:

Hutchens: "I just had a phone call from a friend of mine in Denver who called me to mention that he had heard you speaking out against Masonry in his city about two weeks ago. Is that true?"

I responded: "I was not in Denver two weeks ago, nor any-time in the recent past, so I must conclude that your friend was in error."

Hutchens: "Well, my friend indicated that he had just heard you a few weeks ago speaking out against Masonry."

I said: "Mr. Hutchens, I can assure you that I was not in Denver a couple of weeks ago, but I will tell you that I do speak out against Masonry."

There was more discussion about whether or not I was in Denver a few weeks or months prior to his phone call, and I repeated my denial. I said something to the effect that I had been in Denver several years ago to deliver a speech that dealt, in part, with Masonry, and that some people in attendance had video taped it. I conceded that it was possible that his friend had seen a copy of one of these videos "about two weeks" before he called him, but I reassured him that I had not been in that city at the time his friend claimed.

Mr. Hutchens finally conceded the point that the allegation that I was in Denver a few weeks ago was not the main reason for his call. He was in fact concerned about why I was "speaking out against Masonry."

Mr. Hutchens then asked something like: "Why are you saying anything at all about Masonry?"

I asked him if he would mind answering a few of my questions and he responded that he would not. I asked him whether he was a 32nd Degree Mason from the Scottish Rite, Southern Jurisdiction, and he replied that he was. In addition, he stated that he was the Master of one of the local Masonic lodges here in Tucson. I then briefly told him why I was delivering speeches about Masonry all over the country. I said something like: "I have done some research into the Masonic Lodge and I am concerned about what they believe in."

Hutchens: "Why are you concerned?"

"I won't tell you."

Hutchens: "Why not?"

"Because no matter what I say, you will deny it."

Hutchens: "What do you mean?"

"I won't tell you."

Hutchens: "I don't understand."

"I am saying something about the Masons that I can prove, and I know that when you hear my explanation of what that is, you will deny that I am correct."

Hutchens: "What are you saying?"

"Okay, I will tell you, and your response will prove my point. I am saying that there are two layers inside the Masonic Lodge."

16

Hutchens: "You are wrong."

"You just proved my point."

Hutchens: "What do you mean? There are not two layers inside the Lodge."

"You might remember, Rex, that I said that I can prove it. If I am right that there are two layers inside the Lodge, one for the average Mason, and another for what I call 'the illuminated Mason,' or 'the Adept Mason,' you would deny its existence whether you knew about it or not.

In other words, this second layer is protected by an oath of secrecy, which means that if you knew about its existence, you would be obligated by an oath not to tell anyone. So, if I discuss it's existence with you and you know that it is real, you are obligated as a Mason to deny it.

Secondly, if you do not know that it exists, you would deny it as well.

So, you would deny the existence of this second layer whether you knew about it or not. So I can learn nothing from you when you deny that it exists and I can now prove that this second layer is real."

As I remember, that ended the discussion on the subject of the second layer.

However, before I continue my recollections of that conversation, I would like to provide the reader with just one of many quotations from key Masonic writers that prove the existence of this "second layer" inside the fraternity. This quotation comes from page 433 of a book written by Manly P. Hall, the author that I quoted to open this book and another 33rd

Degree Mason, and also one of the most prolific writers in the world about the secrets of the Masonic Lodge. That book is entitled LECTURES ON ANCIENT PHILOSOPHY.

There is no doubt that he is one of the key Masonic writers of all time. In fact, on July 7, 1985, when he was presented with "a 25-year Masonic pin," THE NEW AGE magazine, the official journal of the Scottish Rite 33rd Degree Council, called him "one of America's foremost authorities on esoteric philosophy." [3] Later, after he died on August 7, 1990, the same Journal, now called THE SCOTTISH RITE JOURNAL, called him the "Illustrious Manly P. Hall," and said that he was "often called 'Masonry's Greatest Philosopher.'" Their notice ended with the comment that:

> "The world is a far better place because of Manly Palmer Hall, and we are better persons for having known him and his work." [4]

So it can be fairly said that this man's opinions about Masonry are accepted as being valid by the Masons.

This is what he wrote:

> "Freemasonry is a fraternity within a fraternity -- an outer organization concealing an inner brotherhood of the elect.
>   . . . it is necessary to establish the existence of these two separate yet interdependent orders, the one visible and the other invisible.
>   The visible society is a splendid camaraderie of 'free and accepted' men enjoined to devote themselves to ethical, educational, fraternal, patriotic, and humanitarian concerns [meaning that he is acknowledging that these patriotic and humanitarian concerns that the public sees are a front for something else.]

18

The invisible society is a secret and most August [defined as: "of majestic dignity, grandeur"] fraternity whose members are dedicated to the service of a mytedious *arcanum arcandrum* [defined as: "a secret, a mystery."]" [5]

I will let the reader decide which of these two 33rd Degree Masons is telling the truth, especially after we review additional evidence that Manly P. Hall is correct.

There was a point of time, maybe some months later, when we arranged for a meeting in my home, and a short time after his arrival, we exchanged copies of our two books: I gave him a copy of my book entitled THE UNSEEN HAND, and he provided me with a copy of the book that he had written entitled A BRIDGE TO LIGHT. I knew that he was not going to be concerned about what I had written about Masonry in my book because I had made only a very brief mention of the organization inside its pages, and was in the midst of researching my second book, the one entitled THE NEW WORLD ORDER, that exposes this second layer inside Masonry for all to see. And in addition, I show in this book why the Masons feel there is a real need for the second layer inside the Lodge.

We both autographed our respective books, and this is what he wrote in the book that he gave to me:

"To Ralph Epperson. May we both continue to seek the Light of Truth. (Signed) Rex R. Hutchens."

As I remember it, Mr. Hutchens called me a short time later and invited me to be a guest speaker at one of his lodge meetings. I can only presume that the reason he invited me to speak was because he felt that I knew very little about Masonry, and would not expose much about them to his members. In that conversation, he explained why he was making the invitation.

He informed me that he had been scheduling a second lodge meeting night wherein he or outside speakers discussed various topics about Masonry, and he felt that he would like to invite me to share my views with his lodge members. I might add that during our visit in my home, I provided him with a copy of my video entitled SECRET SOCIETIES AND THE NEW WORLD ORDER, [6] basically the lecture that I delivered in Denver and some 90 other cities during the years of 1985 to 1988. This is quite possibly a video of the speech that his friend heard and/or saw that prompted his call to Mr. Hutchens.

I declined his offer to address his lodge because I was then continuing my research for my second book. I told him that I wasn't ready yet to speak to his lodge because I hadn't finished reading all of the Masonic material that I had hoped to. I then asked him to call me back about a month later because I was hopeful that I would have completed those readings by then, and he did. During his second call, I once again turned him down because I was still reading for my second book. So I invited him to call again and I informed him that I was hoping that I would have completed my task by then. He made several phone calls to my home, but I informed him each time he called that my reading was not as yet complete and that he should call again.

As I remember, he made a total of five or six calls, and after a while, he stopped calling. And he has made no further attempt to contact me since I published my second book in 1990.

I know that he still believes that I live in Tucson, because he told a mutual friend of mine who happens to be a member of the Masons, just a few months ago, that he "knew Ralph Epperson" when my friend mentioned that I still lived here. Yet he has made no other attempt to contact me about speaking to his lodge. So it would be fair to conclude that he has decided that he is not going to invite me to speak to his members.

I want him to know that I have accepted the challenge he offered me in the statement that accompanied his signature in his book. (Actually, as he recommended, I have "continued to seek the Light," a search that started many years before he asked me to "continue." I started my search about four years before we met.)

But the reason Mr. Hutchens' book was important to me was because it informed me that Albert Pike, perhaps the greatest Masonic writer of all time, had written additional books besides MORALS AND DOGMA, the only one that I was aware of. In fact, on pages 330 and 331 of A BRIDGE TO LIGHT, Mr. Hutchens lists many of Mr. Albert Pike's books in a section entitled SELECTED REFERENCES, including these two that I knew nothing about:

The Magnum Opus, and
Legenda. [7]

His urging for me to continue reading the other works by Mr. Pike has opened an immense area of research to me. Because these are amongst the books that one needs to "read and study," as Mr. Hall has put it, "to know or appreciate the mystic meaning concealed within these [Masonic] rituals." [8]

The book that you are about to read has, to the best of my knowledge, never been written by anyone in the 200 plus years existence of the Masonic Lodge (nor for that matter, in the previous 6,000 years of recorded history.) I not only "continued" my search for the "Light," but I have indeed found the source of "this Light" inside the Masonic Lodge. This book will be, as far as I am able to determine, the first thorough exposure of the true purpose of the Masonic Lodge by someone who is neither a member of the Lodge nor supportive of its beliefs, that I can find in over thirty-four years of research.

As you have recommended, Mr. Hutchens, I continued to "seek the Light." And I want you to know that I have found it!

And, Mr. Hutchens, I am exposing it to be, not the "Light," as you call it, but the "darkness!"

I am now ready to speak to your Lodge.

PURPOSE OF THE AUTHOR

It shall be my purpose to examine the Masonic fraternity as thoroughly as is humanly possible for someone who is not a member. This has been a difficult task since the Masons are a "secret" organization. Another friend of mine also knows Mr. Hutchens and he says that he, Mr. Hutchens, made the statement during one of their discussions about Masonry that they "were not secret." If this report is true, I am hereby asking Mr. Hutchens to arrange for me to attend one of their "non-secret" 33rd Degree Rituals in Washington D.C. Tell me when you have scheduled that invitation, and I will be there!

However, I must state that there will be no invitation.

Because their 33rd Degree Rituals are "secret." And to confirm that, one must only open the pages of a dictionary, for it is in there that one learns that Masonry is indeed a "secret society." The word "secret" is defined as: "kept from public knowledge."

They do not allow non-members inside to see their rituals being performed for the benefit of the initiate. As far as I can determine, even the wives of members cannot attend the ritual that initiates their husbands.

The dictionary further defines the word "secret" as: "hidden from others. Revealed to none or a few."

The Masons are "secret."

However, that does not mean that their publications are "secret." It means that those who want to know what they believe in can discover their motives by a dedicated effort into locating and then reading as much as they have made available for that purpose. As far as I can discover, they have not published their true secrets in any single book, but they are available to the researcher in a variety of sources if one cares enough to locate them.

In other words, the researcher will have to read a number of Mr. Pike's books to find all of the pieces of this enormous puzzle, some parts of which are in one of his books, and some parts are in another. In addition, some pieces are in the works of other Masonic writers. But the answer has been made available to anyone who wants to find it.

Quite simply, my search for the "Light" that Mr. Hutchens wrote about is over.

I have found the source of this "Light." And I have discovered that this knowledge of what it is and what they are going to do with it is the single secret inside the Masonic Lodge. So, quite simply, both the non-Mason and the Mason who does not know, can now know for certain what the Masons stand for. The search for "the secret" of Masonry involves finding out where this "Light" comes from, and what they plan on doing with it.

I have found this truth by reading their own literature, written by their official and semi-official writers. I have found it by reading enough of their materials to know just what that secret is. And I am attempting to make it available to you, the reading public, as simply as I know how.

Because their secret is something that all thinking Americans should be concerned about.

This might be the appropriate time to explain that I am not a member of the Masons, nor have I ever been. But I have read much of their written material, the books that I can locate through Masonic sources, catalogs, used bookstores or from friends.

What you are about to read consists of three parts: I will start this study with a review of the book entitled MORALS AND DOGMA in Part 1, and then, in Part 2, continue with the study of the secret inside the Masonic Lodge. Then, I will attempt to summarize what we have learned in Part 3.

So, may I suggest that you read on.

EXPLANATION

I would like to explain a little about the techniques that I used in writing this book.

1. First of all, the quotations taken from all of the sources utilized in this book will all be indented on each side on the pages that follow. I have done this in all sections of this book except in the INTRODUCTION chapter, and in the introduction to the two DEMIT letters towards the end of the book. The reason I did this here was to save a little space.

Whenever I have added one of my own thoughts into one of these quotations, I will separate my words from theirs by the use of these brackets:

[   ]

So that the reader can verify that the quote is accurate, I have always attempted to properly identify the writer, the title of the book, and the page number from the book that I found the quote in.

However, I must be honest. Attempting to properly record each quotation accurately and then document it with the precise location of the quote is difficult because of the great number of them that I used. I want the reader to understand that if I did not record the words exactly, nor cite the precise location of the quotation, it was not an intentional act. I do all of my research by myself, meaning that I have no staff to assist me, but I do try to be as accurate as is possible. But I am human, and can make mistakes, although I have dedicated all of my writing and speaking efforts to being as accurate as I can. All of the other thoughts in this book are mine.

2. Whenever I define a word in this book, I have taken it from one or both of the following dictionaries:

1. Webster's Collegiate Dictionary, fifth edition, published in 1947, or
2. Webster's New World Dictionary, second college edition, published in 1984

3. All scriptural references used in my book come from the King James version of the Bible.

4. This book was originally a 90 page booklet entitled A RE-VIEW OF MORALS AND DOGMA. [9] After I learned that Albert Pike wrote additional books, I decided to expand this booklet and write a far more complete book on the subject. So I added the remaining material to the previously existing booklet.

That means that there might be some duplication between the first two parts of this book, but I thought I would leave the completed book in this format because it seems to be the way to write it: first a review of Mr. Pike's book and then a review of the newer material I found from his and other key writings. I am sorry if this causes the reader any inconvenience.

5. I have taken the liberty to define certain words throughout this book to assist the reader in understanding the material. Obviously, this might be unnecessary for some of the readers since they are already familiar with the defined word. Once again, I am sorry if this causes some of the readers any inconvenience, but I was motivated only by a desire to make this book as easy to understand as possible because of the complex nature of the information.

6. All the italicized words in this book were recorded exactly like I found them in the original work.

ABOUT THE AUTHOR

I have been researching the evidence that there is a massive conspiracy at work in the world for over thirty years. I have written two books, produced eleven videos, and written nine booklets, to prove that charge.

I have appeared as a guest on about 100 radio "talk shows," and about 30 nationwide, regional and local television programs. I have been interviewed for about 15 or so local "news programs," and maybe six or seven half-hour interview programs on television. I have been blessed by having our local newspaper feature two of my half-page "editorials" in their editorial sections. I once hosted my own radio "talk program" in Portland, Oregon, for three years and I was the only "conservative" voice on the airwaves in that city during that time.

I have lectured in about 100 cities, sometimes more than once during a series of lectures over the course of several days. I have spoken in about 35 states of the United States. In addition, I have spoken on college campuses all over this country. Even a few Christian churches in America have allowed me access to their pulpit to share what I have learned with their members.

I have received literally thousands of phone calls from people all over this country who wanted to discuss my material with me or to ask questions that they thought I might be able to answer.

My two books have gone on to become national "best-sellers." These books have been sold in English-speaking nations all over the globe, primarily in England, South Africa, and Australia. And in fact, my second book has been translated into their native language and sold in both Rumania and what used to be called Czechoslovakia.

The June 7, 1993 issue of the New Yorker magazine[10] mentioned my book entitled THE UNSEEN HAND twice in one of their articles, but those who read the article did not beat a path to my door. And, like the response to nearly all of my educational efforts, I sold no massive numbers of my book to those curious readers who saw the article.

The reason that I bring all of this to your attention is because I have not been successful in informing enough people that there is something happening in America, even though I have done all that I can think of to accomplish that task.

I am sorry that I did not reach a larger audience, but it appears as if the American people, in the main, simply do not care whether I am right or wrong, and are going to have to discover that my material has been correct all along when the horrific events scheduled to happen in this nation occur.

Because the overwhelming majority of the American people are simply not listening to my warnings. And one of the reasons that my warnings are being ignored is that I never received national coverage from the major "talk" programs in America. Phil Donahue, Geraldo Rivera, Oprah Winfrey, Sally Jessie Rafael, or Larry King: none of these programs invited me to present the evidence that there is a Conspiracy at work in the world.

And it is not that I have not tried. I mailed flyers to these programs describing me and my two "best-selling" books, and encouraged them to afford me an opportunity to present my evidence to a national audience as a guest on their programs.

Each of these hosts did nothing.

I even met Mr. Rivera in Tucson a few years ago at a University of Arizona homecoming event. He apparently is a fellow-graduate of that school, and as such he was invited to sit on the back seat of some new convertible that drove him along the route of the university's homecoming parade.

I decided to catch up with him at the end of the parade, and when I did, I introduced myself. We talked for about five minutes, and I told him that I had learned about the existence of a conspiracy in America and that I needed his help in exposing it. I gave him flyers on my two books and I am sad to report that he did absolutely nothing with them. I received no invitation from him nor his producers to appear on his television program. One can reasonably conclude that he knows that I am right and is afraid to tell his listeners. And that is a real pity, because what I have to say needs national attention.

I once met a famous Christian tele-evangelist in the Reno, Nevada airport. We were both on the same plane by coincidence, and after we embarked, I caught up with him as we both were on our way to pick up our luggage. We talked for about 10 minutes, and I asked him to help me promote my concerns by putting me on his national television program to inform his viewers of the dangers that this conspiracy presents to all Christians. I gave him flyers on my two books, and he used the address on them to put me on his mailing list! He made no move to put me on his television program.

I once appeared on a local half-hour "Donahue" type interview program in Tampa, Florida, hosted by the "obligatory blonde" from the six-o'clock news program, to debate a gentleman on the subject of Masonry. This debate had been scheduled about six months after I appeared by myself as a guest on her program. I was called a few weeks after my first appearance by the program's producer and informed that my appearance had stirred up more controversy than any other guest they had ever interviewed on one of their programs. And the reason I had stirred up so much interest was because I was talking about the Masons.

She asked me if I would like to come back and debate a member of the Masonic Lodge if she could arrange the meeting, and I encouraged her to try, because I would truly welcome the opportunity.

Several months later, she called me and reported that she had been unable to locate any member of the Masonic Lodge willing to debate me. However, she told me that she had been called by a local lodge member who had brought someone to Tampa who was not one of their members to speak to them and they would be happy to make this gentleman, named John Robinson, available to appear on their television program. She apparently asked the Mason if he would mind if she arranged a "debate" between their guest and me and he reported that he would have no problem with that.

The producer then called me, provided me with the details, and I consented. I then made arrangements to fly to Tampa for our joint appearance.

I met Mr. Robinson, the man I was to debate, prior to our interview, and he informed me that he was not a member of the Lodge, but that he was an historian who had found their involvement in the events of the past. He claimed that he did not know anything about me nor why I was concerned about Masonry's intentions. He informed me that he believed that they had been a beneficial force in the world. I urged him to read my book entitled THE NEW WORLD ORDER, [11] to find out just exactly what they believed in. I continued to make an attempt to convince him in the few minutes that we had together that it was imperative that he find out what their true goals were.

When we walked into the studio together, we were probably the only non-Masons (with the exception of possibly the 5 or 6 station employees who were inside the studio) in a room with about 100 members of various Masonic organizations, both male and female. Needless to say, the audience did not appreciate what I was saying when I discussed what I had learned about the Freemasons, even though I had the material that I was discussing in my possession and showed it to them and the viewers on the program.

After my appearance had concluded, not one of the Masons in attendance asked for permission to see the two Masonic books that I had showed on the program. And I find that hard to understand.

If I had been a member of the Lodge in attendance that day and heard someone say what I had said, I would certainly ask to see the materials that this person had brought with him to prove his point. But not one member of the Lodge made an attempt to do that after the program concluded. And I find that to be absolutely incredible! Because I made some incredible accusations, based upon their own material!

It would be no stretch of the imagination to say that I hold controversial views because I believe that the conspiracy behind the major events of the past is real, and that the Masons are directly involved because they are a major part of it. Many people, if not most people, simply do not agree with me.

And often, the dissenters show their displeasure at what I am saying by becoming angry.

Sometimes the opposition to what I am saying takes the form of verbal condemnation and angry abuse. But I can honestly say that none of the Masons have ever called me on the telephone to debate me with specific concerns.

For instance, my critics, including the Masons, have tried to belittle my name and reputation rather than offer whatever "proofs" they claim to have to prove that I am wrong.

The January, 1993 issue of THE NORTHERN LIGHT magazine, published by the 33rd Degree Council of the Northern Jurisdiction of the Scottish Rite of Freemasonry, wrote this about me in its review of television host Pat Robertson's book entitled THE NEW WORLD ORDER:

> "If Freemasonry historically was composed of the re-tarded, the illiterates and the misfits of society, I might be able to comprehend the attitude of men like [tele-evangelist Pat] Robertson, [Dr. Larry] Holly, [television host] John Ankerberg, [Ralph] Epperson and others in their fanatical devotion to attacks against Freemasonry and Freemasons." [12]

Only the Masons have ever said that my writings on their fraternity were "fanatical" or that they were even "attacks." The author of this article is typical of the Masonic response to me and my work because he did not dispute one single statement that I had ever made about them: he called whatever I had written a series of "fanatical attacks." Secondly, all I have ever done in my lectures and writings about Masonry is to quote their own writers from their own literature. And yet the Masons are charging that my writings are "fanatical." And thirdly, it is interesting to note that the writer of this article did not include my first name when he mentioned me, although he did with one of the other individuals he cited. Am I to assume that this meant that the author of these words knew that his Masonic readers would automatically know our first names? I know most people could identify the first names of famous people like Columbus, Einstein, and Ruth. So, I guess that I should be flattered that he presumed that his readers would know who "Epperson" was!

Another writer spoke about me when he addressed the Southeast Masonic Conference in August of 1993. He said that I was, along with other researchers in this field, like Gary Kah, and William Still, one of those "other well-known conspiracists [that was a compliment. He admitted that I was "well-known"] who see Freemasonry as a part of a worldwide conspiracy." He referred to me by my full name, Ralph Epperson, so I guess this author didn't believe that I was as well known as Columbus, Einstein or Ruth, because he included my first name!

Someone once wrote, "I don't care what they say about me, as long as they spell my name right!" So, I guess I shouldn't complain. At least they spelled my name correctly!

But others have not been as kind as these two. Often, when I am a guest on a "talk-program," I get phone calls from angry listeners, and because some of these do not agree with what I am saying, they show their frustration by calling me many names, some of which I would not put in writing. I have been told that I am "paranoid," and "delusionary." My motives for writing my two books have been questioned, and several of these callers have said that I was "doing this for the money."

My favorite story about this charge occurred when I appeared on a radio talk program in Tampa, Florida, hosted by Mark Larson. One caller decided that he did not want to talk to me directly about his concerns about what I was saying, so he decided to attack my motives. He told Mr. Larson that "I was doing this for the money." After I heard the man make this claim, I told the host, on the air, that I would like to get this man's name and phone number, and talk to him off the air, since he was saying that I could do this AND make money! I had to admit that I didn't know that, and that I certainly wanted to "make money" if I was going to expend all of this energy!

But perhaps the most flagrant example of the intolerance of my critics occurred the week after I delivered a speech on the subject of the Masons to a club that I belong to here in Tucson. They allow me to speak about once or twice a year to my fellow members. This gentleman stepped to the podium and announced that he was "a Mason," and he was "offended" that I had made a series of "false premises and misrepresentations" about the Masons during my speech. That was a strange statement for him to make, since I had provided each attendee, including him, with a copy of the exact wording of all of the quotations that I had used during that speech, so that all could read along with me as I read the words from my prepared speech. In addition, I knew that this individual had not approached me after my speech and compared the exact quotations that I had used against the printed words in the books that I had brought with me and held up to document my case during the speech. In other words, I had brought the actual source of the quotations that I had read during my speech with me as documentation of my statements, and he had chosen not to compare it to the actual words I read during my speech.

In other words, he had not compared the actual quotation I used with the quotation in the book that I had brought with me for that purpose. And yet when he addressed the group the next weekend, he claimed that I had "misrepresented" the information that I had taken from the Masonic literature.

I decided that I would not give my fellow members a response after he had spoken but chose to discuss his incredible statement with him after the meeting had concluded. I approached the gentleman and asked him if he had read any of the dozen or so books that I had brought with me and physically displayed during my speech, and he admitted that he had read "some" of them. But when I asked him to be more specific, he said that he could not. I then asked him if he had made any attempt to compare the quotation in my handout against the actual words from inside the book, and he admitted that he had not. And he had no answer when I asked him why he could make that statement that I had "misrepresented" the material, without checking the two quotations against each other. I then invited him to visit my home at his convenience so that he could personally compare the two from the actual source in my library, and to this day, about ten months after the two incidents, he has made no such attempt.

The behavior of this Mason simply defies explanation. How can anyone accuse a speaker of "misrepresenting" the information he was providing the listeners when the detractor has not compared the quotations that the speaker had used with the actual quotes in the material that the speaker brought with him for that purpose?

But the reason I bring this story to your attention is because this appears to be the standard way of dealing with me and what I have discovered.

Notice that this Mason did not wish to learn the truth about his own organization, from their own material! I brought my documentation with me; it was available to him or anyone else who wanted to challenge it.

Yet he did not!

And that does not make sense.

But this experience is typical of the response from the Masons no matter where I go nor what I say about their organization.

Others of my detractors have called me "a Nazi," and "a Ku Klux Klan member," a "wacko," a "kook," a "paranoid, right-wing fascist," whatever that means, and, as just reported, someone who "misrepresents" material that I use during a speech.

So, I think it is fair to admit that most people simply do not wish to learn the truth, because they have chosen to believe that I say things that I cannot prove. And yet the exact opposite is true. I can honestly report that I meticulously try to document my every charge with the exact quotation from the very source I am using in my speech or in one of my books.

And all of what I have been saying for these thirty-four years is true.

The conspiracy that I have spent most of my adult life exposing is real. All of the abuse that I have taken as I exposed it has been worth it, because I know that I am correct.

However, most people have chosen not to believe me, in spite of every effort that I can think of to accurately expose the truth.

But, in the main, this type of reaction to my information is not unusual. In fact, it is in accordance with Masonic instruction.

Adam Weishaupt, the founder of the Illuminati, (this organization will be discussed more in detail in later parts of this book,) a group directly connected to Masonry, allowed the writer of the rituals to include the following instruction to his initiates:

> "If a writer publishes any thing that attracts notice and is in itself just, but does not accord with our plan, we must endeavor to win him over, or decry him."[13]

The word "decry" is defined as: "to denounce, to depreciate officially or publicly, to censure freely, to clamor against, to speak out against strongly." Notice that the word Mr. Weishaupt chose to explain what the official response was to be with critics, does not say anything about proving the critic's research wrong, by showing the critic where he misinterpreted the information, misquoted it, or where he took it out of context.

So, if they cannot "win" the critic over, they are simply to "decry" him.

I think it is fair to conclude that exposing the Masonic Lodge for what it truly believes in "does not accord with [their] plan," so I can expect to be "decried" for revealing the truth, since I will not "be won over." And I have been "decried" whenever I have presented my research. And not one Mason, anywhere in these United States that I have been, has agreed to debate me on these matters.

And I will make that challenge once again because I have made it all over America:

I will debate any Mason, anywhere and anytime one would agree to do so!

PART ONE

A REVIEW OF MORALS
AND DOGMA

Baphomet

chapter 1
INTRODUCTION

As I have said, I have attempted to utilize the key Masonic writers in my attempts to expose Masonry. The following are quotations taken from the writings of these men, all of whom will be discussed in more detail later in this book.

ALBERT PIKE: "It is in your hands to unlock the Secrets of Masonry. The rest depends on yourself." [14]

ALBERT PIKE: "It is for you to discover this Law and this Secret [notice that there is but one "Secret"] for yourself. The Initiate learns by reflection, and not, like the children, by committing words and definitions to memory." [15]

MANLY P. HALL: "The initiated brother [in Masonry] realizes that his so-called symbols and rituals are merely blinds fabricated by the wise [the second layer of Masonry] to perpetuate ideas incomprehensible to the average individual [the first layer of Masonry.] He also realizes that few Masons of today [the first layer] know or appreciate the mystic meaning concealed within these rituals [by the second layer.]" [16]

ALBERT PIKE: "These degrees are also intended to teach *more* than morals. The symbols and ceremonies of Masonry have more than one meaning. They rather *conceal* than *disclose* the Truth. They *hint* it only, at least; and their varied meanings are only to be discovered by reflection and study." [He is encouraging the members in the first layer to reflect and study so that they can join the second layer.] [17]

ALBERT PIKE: "You have now made the first three of the seven symbolic Circuits or journeys. To call them symbolic is

41

to announce that they have a mystic meaning. You must discover this for yourself." [Notice that Mr. Pike admonishes the members of the first layer to try and figure it out so that they can become members of the second layer.] [18]

ALBERT PIKE: "To many of these symbols there are other meanings which it should be your study to discover for yourself. Often they are indicated to the initiate by a hint or a suggestion only . . . . it is more incumbent on you, by reflection and study, to learn the true meaning for yourself." [19]

ALBERT PIKE: "Whether these degrees have for you a real value depends upon your capacity to understand them, and upon the amount of study and the degree of reflection you have bestowed upon them. No man can understand them fully, without close and long study, and profound thought." (Another appeal to the second layer to "study and reflect.") [20]

JAMES L. GOULD: "The Mason who does not look beyond the mere forms and ceremonies of the institution fails, utterly fails to realize the import of its teachings. Its sublime truths are indeed mysteries to him . . . . [The Mason in the first layer is to reflect and study since the Masons in the second layer do not reveal their true meaning to them.]
No matter in what direction he may turn, the lessons of truth are set before him on every side, and it only remains for him to study their deep and hidden meaning." [21]

W. L. WILMSHURST: "The method in question [of instruction] is that of Initiation; the usage and practice is that of allegory and symbol, which it is the Freemason's duty, if he wishes to understand his system, to labour [his spelling of the word] to interpret and put to personal application. If he fails to do so, he still remains -- and the system deliberately intends that he should -- in the dark about the Order's real meaning and secrets, although formally a member of it." [22]

ALBERT PIKE: "It is for each individual Mason to discover the secret of Masonry, by reflecting on its emblems, and upon what is said and done in the work. Seek and ye shall find." [23]

ALBERT PIKE: "It is for each individual Mason to discover the secret of Masonry [notice again that there is only one secret] . . . . Masonry does not *inculcate* [defined as:"to teach by frequent repetitions"] her truths. She *states* them, once and briefly; or hints them, perhaps darkly; or interposes a cloud between them and eyes that would be dazzled by them." [24]

ALBERT PIKE: ". . . the principal purpose of the Mysteries was to teach the Initiates '*the Secret of Holy Doctrine,*' the Theology and Philosophy, which the Priests concealed from the vulgar [defined as: "the common," meaning the average person,] as beyond and above their comprehension." [Here Mr. Pike states that some of the public will be unable to understand the true meanings of the symbols.] [25]

ALBERT PIKE: "Masonry permits the utterance of false interpretations which serve the double purpose of misleading the ignorant, the idle and indolent, whom it is desirable to lead astray [meaning the Mason in the first layer,] and of indirectly indicating to the wise and studious [meaning the second layer] the true way leading toward the Light." [26]

ALBERT PIKE: "Masonry also has its ancient Symbols, inherited from the Mysteries . . ., and intended to veil and conceal the truth from all except the Adepts [meaning the secret second layer.] Masonry gives false interpretations to its Symbols. [Mr. Pike is reporting that only a small percentage of the first layer" will be able to discover the true meanings of the symbols.]" [27]

ALBERT PIKE: "All of its symbols, . . . have a concealed meaning, . . . these containing only hints cautiously given, and ideas easily misunderstood (and so intended to be) by all but the Adepts [meaning the second layer.] . . . . But he is misled by a *Substitute* that has for him no meaning, although it indeed contains his reward if he but knew it." [28]

ALBERT PIKE: "Whether these degrees have for you a real value depends upon your capacity to understand them, and upon the amount of study and the degree of reflection you have bestowed upon them . . . .
No man can understand them fully, without close and long study, and profound thought." [29]

ALBERT PIKE: "The Lectures of the Lodge of Perfection are contained in its Liturgy and Legenda and in the MORALS and DOGMA. By reading and study, you should make yourself familiar with them." [He is urging the members in the first layer to read and study so that they may become a part of the second layer.] [30]

ALBERT PIKE: "It long since became very evident to us . . . that the true secrets . . . of Masonry are unknown to *itself*, having been concealed under so many veils as to have become in part undiscoverable; and that the ordinary explanations of its symbols have merely been adopted to mislead the multitude of the initiates [meaning the first layer,] the knowledge of the esoteric meaning having been confined to a few [the second layer] . . . .
There are perhaps few *thinking* Masons to whom it has not seemed strange that the TRUE WORD, promised to every

Master Mason, is not given to every one, but only a substitute, of no particular sanctity or significance; not an approximation to the lost Word, but a mere trivial ordinary Pass Word, not even alluding to the Deity." [31]

ARTHUR EDWARD WAITE: "On his entrance into Freemasonry the newly received Brother has come into a world of emblems or symbolism and whatsoever takes place therein has a meaning behind it, being one which is not always indicated on the surface." [32]

These words by Albert Pike, perhaps the greatest Mason of all time, and other key Masonic writers, set the tone of this book: the person seeking the truth about Masonry must extend his research beyond the rituals that the initiate goes through. He must read the works of the Masonic writers, because as Mr. Pike has written, it is here that one finds the complete truth about their beliefs. The initiate will not learn it by proceeding through the rituals of the various degrees, and the researcher will not find it by reading the words of the ritual. The ultimate secret is found in the works of the Masonic writers.

The key to the entire puzzle is, I believe, found in the writings of Albert Pike himself. And a good place to start is in his book entitled MORALS AND DOGMA. So I would like to basically review pertinent quotations from this book. I will intersperse quotations from other Masonic writers when it is appropriate to add clarification or additional support for the ideas expressed by Mr. Pike.

The book entitled MORALS AND DOGMA was written in 1871 by Mr. Pike, the Sovereign Grand Commander, (the Masonic equivalent of a President) of the Scottish Rite of Freemasonry from 1859 to 1891. The full title of the book is

"MORALS AND DOGMA of the Ancient and Accepted Scottish Rite of Freemasonry Prepared for the Supreme Council of the Thirty-Third Degree for the Southern Jurisdiction of the United States and Published by its Authority." That means that this is official Masonic literature, written by probably the number one Mason of all time, and published by the Council as official information.

Mr. Pike was born in 1809 and died while in office in 1891. He became a 32nd Degree Mason in 1853, and achieved the highest degree, the 33rd Degree, in 1857 (the meaning of these degrees will be discussed later.) Between the years of 1855 and 1857, he was the prime author of all of the rituals for the 33 degrees inside the Lodge.

It might be helpful for the reader to know one particular fact about Mr. Pike's activities during the time he was their Sovereign Grand Commander. Henry Wilson Coil, another 33rd Degree Mason, with the assistance of three other 33rd Degree Masons, wrote COIL'S MASONIC ENCYCLOPEDIA in 1961. He added this biographical insight into Mr. Pike's past on page 620 of his book:

> "In May, 1866, [Mr. Pike was Sovereign Grand Commander from 1859 to 1891] a group of returned veterans [from the Civil War which ended in 1865] and other young men of Pulaski County, Tennessee, undertook to organize a social or recreational society, the name *kuklos* (Greek for band or circle) being suggested, which was promptly converted into *Ku Klux,* and *Klan* [the K.K.K.] naturally followed.
>
> About that time, a body of bad Negroes and worse Whites had begun a career of outrage against southern Whites, [these outrages were being orchestrated by a

group called the Knights of the Golden Circle, the parent organization to the K.K.K. They created the problem, and then solved it by creating the K.K.K.] and the unusual social conditions prevailing caused Ku Klux Klans to be organized in adjoining states, and the development went into its second stage in which it revenged some wrongs and committed others of its own

. . . .

> Albert Pike was the Chief Judicial Officer of the K.K.K." [33]

Mr. Coil is not telling his readers the entire truth, because the purpose of the Ku Klux Klan was not to be a "social or recreational society," but was to be the organizer of an effort to create a second Civil War after the first one had failed to achieve the goal of the bankers who had planned the war in the first place. It was these bankers who had created the parent organization of the K.K.K. known as the Knights of the Golden Circle. It was these bankers who had planned the Civil War itself, and they created the Knights to stir up the issue of the Civil War, meaning slavery. Their purpose was to make it the single issue of the war, and it was not. The bankers wanted a "central bank," but the Knights were created to stir up bitterness between the North and the South over slavery. It was this group that later created the K.K.K.

For those wishing to know more about the involvement of men like Albert Pike and Jesse James, the famous outlaw and, by the way, another 33rd Degree Mason, in this plan to create a second Civil War, additional details about this period are included in my video entitled SECRET SOCIETIES AND THE NEW WORLD ORDER, in my book entitled THE UNSEEN HAND, and in my booklet entitled JESSE JAMES, UNITED STATES SENATOR. [34]

So Mr. Pike had an interesting and controversial past.

His book entitled MORALS AND DOGMA is 861 pages long, and appears to have had an index of 218 pages added in its 1927 edition.

I have two copies of this book, one being the original 1871 edition, and the other the 1871 edition with the 1927 index added, and the two books appear to be identical, except for inclusion of the index in the second.

The book consists of 32 chapters, each one of which was written to explain one of the 32 degrees of the Masonic Order. There are drawings included, but they generally seem to have been added only as a filler, rather than for assisting the reader in understanding the contents of the book.

It is this reviewer's opinion that the book is boring and difficult to read. And it is my opinion that this is intentional. The second layer of the Masons believe that the boring nature of the book will cause many of the Masons inside the first layer to not complete the book, and that only those diligent enough, those that they want to join the second layer, will read it in its entirety.

But the student of the Mason Lodge must read it because there are enough meaningful quotations inside of it to show the reader just why the Masons consider it to be a valuable work. Because the book is difficult to obtain, I have decided to include what I consider to be the most important of the quotations inside of it in this book.

I would like to add at this point that should any reader wish to discuss this book, or any matter pertinent to the study of the

Masonic Lodge, he or she may contact me at the phone numbe or address shown elsewhere.

Before I start this review, it might be helpful to the student to examine a little information about the Masonic Lodge, the number of the "degrees" and some of the various organizations inside the Masonic fraternity.

There are three basic fraternal lodges inside the male only Masonic Lodge system: the Blue Lodge, the Scottish Rite and the York Rite.

The base on which both the York Rite and the Scottish Rite stand is the Blue Lodge of Masonry. This organization requires the new member to go through three separate initiation ceremonies, called Rituals, and once the Mason has completed all three ceremonies, he can stop there should he choose to do so. He can remain in the Blue Lodge and call himself a Master Mason, meaning that he will have completed three rituals inside the Blue Lodge. He can call himself a Third Degree Master Mason, a member of the Blue Lodge.

Should he choose to go further, he may do so, but he has two options: he can go into either, or both, of the two Rites: either the York Rite or the Scottish Rite. The York Rite has ten more degrees for a total of 13, and the Scottish Rite has 29 more for a total of 32.

The 13 and 32 degrees inside the Masonic organization are earned by the initiate, meaning that he decides himself to go through their rituals, and there is one more degree on the top of both organizations, called the 33rd Degree. This degree is honorary, and the Mason must be invited to become a 33rd Degree Mason. He cannot ask to become a member of that

49

degree. (Mr. Hutchens, Mr. Pike, Mr. Coil, Mr. James and Mr. Hall are, or were, all 33rd Degree Masons.)

It might be interesting at this point to interject my opinion as to why there are 32 and 33 degrees inside the Scottish Rite of Freemasonry, because I believe these are symbolic numbers concealing an important truth.

The human backbone has 32 vertebrae in it, and "the vertebra" that sits on top of it, the skull, would be the 33rd. The skull houses the brain, the "seat of man's ability to reason." This fact will become significant later in this book, but this is why I believe the numbers 32 and 33 are symbols of a far more important truth.

The Council, meaning the ruling body, of the 33rd Degree Masonic organization claims to be the parent organization that controls both of these two other Rites. They call themselves "the Supreme Council of the 33rd Degree," and their literature says that they are "The Mother Jurisdiction of the World," or the "Mother Council of the World." In fact, in the pamphlet written by Henry C. Clausen, the Sovereign Grand Commander of the Masons, entitled "What Is the Scottish Rite," he states:

> "Our Supreme Council was organized at Charleston, South Carolina in 1801 as the Mother Supreme Council of the World, and hence all regular and recognized Supreme Councils throughout the world in some 33 nations must trace their pedigree to us." [35]

It is interesting to note that the city of Charleston is underneath the 33rd Degree Northern Latitude (an imaginary line around the earth parallel to the equator.) Perhaps this is the symbolic reason that the Masons selected this city as their home back in 1801. It is also thought provoking to remember that it was in Charleston that the first shots of the Civil War were fired at Ft. Sumter. It is also interesting to mention that Jesse James, a 33rd Degree Mason, made the claim that it was his father, Captain George James, who fired the first shot at Ft. Sumter. Maybe the Masons did "shape the destinies of the (Civil War) world."

One more item of interest occurred under the 33rd Degree Northern Latitude. President John Kennedy was assassinated in Dallas, Texas on November 22, 1963. Dallas is underneath the 33rd Degree as well, and the day he was assassinated, the 22nd, when added to eleven, the number of the month of November, equals 33. The site of the assassination, a park called Dealey Plaza, has an obelisk in it with a plaque commemorating the park as being the site of the "first fraternal Lodge in Texas." Texas was created by the Masons, and their flag was designed by a member of the Masonic Lodge. Should anyone wish additional information about why President Kennedy was assassinated, may I suggest that you obtain my videos entitled VIETNAM, AMERICA'S BETRAYAL AND TREASON, and THE KENNEDY ASSASSINATION. The Masonic involvement in his assassination is covered in my video entitled THE NEW WORLD ORDER. [36]

The quotation by Manly P. Hall that I cited to begin this work says that the Masons "ordain kings." The assassination of John Kennedy appears to teach that they also "un-ordain" kings. (I must be fair to the Masons. They were only one of six organizations responsible for the death of our President.)

So this organization of honorary Masons invited into the degree claims to be the controller of all of world-wide Masonry.

Further support of the position that the 33rd Degree Council controls all of Masonry is found on a plaque at the base of the statue of Albert Pike in Washington D.C., the home of the Council of the 33rd Degree after it was moved there from Charleston. This plaque, and the statue, were put there by the 33rd Degree Council, and it reads:

> "Dedicated 1977 under auspices of Henry C. Clausen, Sovereign Grand Commander of the Scottish Rite Mother Jurisdiction. To the loving memory of Albert Pike, leader of the world wide Masonic movement."

So the 33rd Degree Masons acknowledge that Mr. Pike was the leader of the entire Masonic movement.

Henry Wilson Coil, one of the key Masonic writers, confirmed this in his encyclopedia:

> "The institution known as a *Supreme Council* was first authorized by the Constitutions of 1786 . . . .
> 'The First Degree will be subordinated to the Second, and that to the Third, and so in order to the Sublime, Thirty-third or last, which will watch over the others, will correct their errors, and will govern them . . . . " [37]

I have in my files a petition that a 3rd Degree Blue Lodge Mason completes to receive the 4th through 32nd degrees from the Ancient and Accepted Scottish Rite of Freemasonry. The member is asked to complete this application that asks him to supply personal information, such as his name, date of birth, wife's name, etc.

The introductory paragraph of the form states:

"I do hereby respectfully petition for the degrees, from the 4th to 32nd, inclusive, and I promise always to bear true faith and allegiance to the Supreme Council of the Thirty-third Degree for the Southern Jurisdiction of the United States."

So it is obvious that the 33rd Degree of the Southern Jurisdiction runs all of Freemasonry, worldwide, as they claim. And Albert Pike was a 33rd Degree Mason, and since he was the Sovereign Grand Commander of their Council, he was the leader of the entire worldwide Masonic movement.

As I mentioned earlier, the title page of the book entitled MORALS AND DOGMA says that it was:

"prepared for the Supreme Council of the Thirty-Third Degree for the Southern Jurisdiction of the United States and published by its authority."

So it can be inferred from these claims that what this book teaches the Mason can be considered to be the official position of all of Freemasonry. In fact, Henry C. Clausen, the official spokesman for all of Freemasonry, praised it with these words of commendation :

". . . an inspired and classical compilation of Pike's own research and the writings of others . . . ." [38]

So now the reader can see just how important this book is to all of the members of the world-wide Masonic movement.

Mr. Pike revealed that the 33rd Degree Masonic Council is the controller of all of Freemasonry with this oath taken by the initiate during the 18th Degree of the Scottish Rite:

> "I [the initiate cites his name] . . . promise and swear
> that I will observe and obey all the rules and laws of
> this order of Knights of the Rose Croix [the title of the
> 18th Degree] and the decrees and mandates that may
> be transmitted to me by the Sov∴ [Sovereign] Inspec-
> tor Gen∴ [General. The three dots in the form of a
> pyramid appear to mean that the word just preceding
> the dots is an abbreviation of a Masonic word or title]
> in Sup∴ [Supreme] Council of the 33rd Degree in
> whose jurisdiction I may reside." [39]

Both the 32nd and 33rd Degree Scottish Rite Mason and the
13th Degree York Rite Mason can join a Masonic organization called the Shriners. This organization is the one that spon-
sors the East-West Football game, the circus that comes to
your town and other charitable activities like children's burn
hospitals. I have been told by some Masons that the reason
they joined the Masons is so that they could become Shriners,
because "that was where all of the fun was." And I believe that
they are the cover for the "second layer" of the Masons.

But returning to the discussion of Mr. Pike, let me add that
many historians, both inside and outside of the Order, consider
Mr. Pike to be one of the greatest Masonic writers of all time.
One of these writers was Albert G. Mackey, another 33rd De-
green Mason, and the author of the authoritative two volume
encyclopedia entitled AN ENCYCLOPEDIA OF FREEMA-
SONRY. The writer of the information on the inside cover of
the first volume describes Mr. Mackey with words of praise,
inferring that the student can rely on the material contained inside. This is what he wrote:

> "His writings are universally esteemed for their sincer-
> ity, honest records and common sense.

A leader, . . . he was a pioneer of that increasing number of the Fraternity who value accuracy." [40]

So the student of Masonry can believe his words.

And these are his words of praise for Albert Pike, being somewhat typical of those made by Mr. Pike's fellow Masons:

"His standing as a Masonic author and historian, and withal as a poet, was most distinguished, and his untiring zeal was without a parallel." [41]

Arthur Edward Waite, another 33rd Degree Mason and the author of another authoritative encyclopedia on Masonry, wrote that Mr. Pike was:

" . . . characterized as 'a master-genius of Masonry . . . .'" [42]

Carl Claudy, also one of the key Masonic writers, and another 33rd Degree Mason, called Mr. Pike:

"One of the greatest geniuses Freemasonry has ever known . . . . He was a mystic [the word mystic is defined as: "of or pertaining to the ancient mysteries," a connection that Masonry makes back to the distant past and an ancient religion still being practiced today,] a symbolist, a teacher of the hidden truths of Freemasonry." [43]

It might be pertinent to mention here that the Mason who addressed the club in Tucson after I spoke said that he considered Mr. Pike to be a "renegade Mason" and not a reliable source of information on the Lodge. I have since shown him

the words of praise that I just quoted, but he has chosen not
to make a comment. I will let you be the judge of which of
these positions on Mr. Pike is correct.

There is some disagreement inside the Masonic Order as to
whether or not MORALS AND DOGMA is to be read by all
of the Scottish Rite Masons of the advanced degrees. I once
had been told by a Mason that their libraries inside their temple buildings are open to the public, so I visited the Masonic
Lodge building in Tucson in 1985 to do some research in
Mackey's ENCYCLOPAEDIA for my speech entitled SE-
CRET SOCIETIES AND THE NEW WORLD ORDER.
(You might recall that I am not a Mason.) I was told by the
two Masons inside the Lodge who allowed me to come in that
this book was given to all Masons upon completion of the
14th degree. In fact, they actually showed me a copy of the
book that was on the other side of a counter near the front
door of the Temple. However, my guest Rex Hutchens denies
that this statement is true. He has written the following on
pages vii and 2 of his book:

> "The apex of our teachings has been the rituals of our
> degrees and *Morals and Dogma*, written by our be-
> loved Sovereign Grand Commander Albert Pike.
> [This book] was traditionally given [notice he has
> chosen to use the past tense of the word, meaning that
> they no longer give it] to the candidate as a gift upon
> his receipt of the 14th Degree." [44]

Mr. Hutchens offers his reader another clue in this passage
from his Introduction:

> "Thus after 1974 it was no longer given to the candi-
> dates." [45]

Then Mr. Hutchens tells his readers why the book is no longer being read by the Masons of today. He informs the reader that:

"The latter, once widely read, has become less so today." [46]

Mr. Hutchens explains that the reason that the book is no longer being read as much today as it was in the past is because:

"the changes in educational emphasis in America made the lectures in MORALS AND DOGMA almost incomprehensible to many." [47]

This statement, by the way, is an interesting one. Mr. Hutchens is admitting that the reason today's initiates into the Masonic Lodge cannot understand Mr. Pike's book is because the public schools of the United States have not been teaching reading skills to their students. This is a strange statement for him to make, because the Masons have issued position papers to their members stressing that the Masons should strongly support public education! A good example of this is a little pamphlet written in 1983 by Henry C. Clausen, 33rd Degree, at that time the Sovereign Grand Commander of the Supreme Council of the 33rd Degree, entitled "Devilish Danger." [48] He ends his discussion of public education with this warning to those concerned about the subject: "Hands off our public schools!"

Yet here they admit that public education is not teaching the public to read and comprehend what they are reading! But, if you object to that fact, you are told by the Masons to keep your "hands off our public schools!"

So Mr. Hutchens has written his book to bridge that gap between education and the Mason of today. He explained on page vii of his book:

> "A Bridge to Light seeks to overcome this difficulty by presenting passages from Morals and Dogma which best reinforce the teachings of the rituals of the degrees." [49]

However, Mr. Hutchens admits that the book is still extremely important to all of Masonry. He writes:

> "Contained within its pages are some of the most profound teachings of the Rite." [50]

So, MORALS AND DOGMA is still an important book whether it is being offered to the Scottish Rite 14th Degree Mason or not. Even today the Masons themselves admit that the book continues to provide their brothers inside the Lodge with parts of the true knowledge of their Order.

As previously mentioned, this reviewer is not a member of the Masons, but considers himself to be a student of the worldwide Lodge, having spent the past twelve years reading a large variety of material on the Order from at least twelve of the top Masonic writers. Because of this, I too consider this book (MORALS AND DOGMA) to be one of the most important books ever written by any Mason.

It is urged by the reviewer that anyone reading any quotation from MORALS AND DOGMA that I utilize in this section of my book should actually do so alongside a copy of the book itself so that they can make certain that the quotations contained herein have been accurately recorded. Should the reader not have a copy of the book nor be a member of the Masons able to obtain a copy, copies of the book can often be found in used book stores or in libraries. Also, it is possible that a non-member of the Masons might be able to obtain a copy of the book from a friend or relative who is a member. However, it must be presumed that Masons will be reluctant to share their copy of the book with non-Masons, since the book is not to be read by "the world at large," so the student must be forewarned that their friends or relatives who are members of the Lodge are not a probable source of the book.

So I cannot stress enough how important it is for anyone to read the book itself. The quotations I am citing are only a small percentage of the material in the book, so there is certainly more to read and understand. The quotations I have utilized in this review are the ones that I thought were important.

This might be the appropriate place to mention just how important Mr. Pike was to the Masonic Lodge.

Henry Wilson Coil, as previously pointed out, was another 33rd Degree Mason, and he wrote the following about Mr. Pike on page 472 of his book MASONIC ENCYCLOPEDIA:

> ". . . he [meaning Albert Pike] rewrote the lectures, rituals and laws of 33 degrees of the Ancient and Accepted Scottish Rite." [51]

A further evidence that Mr. Pike wrote all of the rituals comes from the introduction to one of Mr. Pike's key books, entitled MAGNUM OPUS. The following quotation appears on an unnumbered page at the beginning of the book, and quite possibly was written by Roger Kessinger, the reprinter of this and other "scarce Masonic and related books." Mr. Kessinger declares himself to be a "32nd Degree" Mason, and has made available to his "Brother Masons," an expanding list of the key books inside the entire spectrum of the field known as "esoteric wisdom." (By the way, I have purchased books from this source and have never been asked if I was a member, so it appears as if his reprints are available to both Masons and non-Masons alike.)

This is what that page says:

> "One of the rarest and most important books ever published on the Ancient and Accepted (Scottish) Rite of Freemasons is now available as a first ever facsimile reprint.
>
> In 1855 the Supreme Council 33°, Ancient and Accepted (Scottish) Rite, Southern Masonic Jurisdiction, U.S.A. appointed a committee to revise the fragmentary rituals in their possession.
>
> This task was completed two years later when, in 1857, Albert Pike single-handedly published the so-called *Magnum Opus* or *'Great Work,'* being his first revision of the complete rituals of the Scottish Rite.
>
> Pike's ritualistic revisions were so impressive he was made an active member of the Supreme Council and became the most revered Sovereign Grand Commander of the history of the Rite.
>
> . . . this special reprint makes available to the serious student the complete authentic rituals . . . ." [52]

So both the student of Freemasonry and the Mason himself can now read the entire rituals of the 4th through 32nd Degree. However, the author of this quotation was quick to point out on the next page:

". . . Kessinger Publishing Company wishes to make known the following:

1. The rituals in the Magnum Opus are not those currently used by the Supreme Council 33°. . . .
4. We, as Masons, are bound by obligation to spread true Masonic Light and knowledge to the less informed." [53]

But, before the critic rushes in to say that no one can rely on the rituals published in this book because they are "not those currently [being] used," let me provide you with three good reasons why the rituals written by Mr. Pike are probably still the ones being utilized in the Lodges today:

1. Notice that Mr. Kessinger points out that the Mason is "bound by obligation to spread true knowledge to the less informed." Yet he admits that he has published a set of rituals that are not "true," because they are not "currently used." It seems to me that these two statements are contradictory. How can he expect us to believe that he would violate his promise to the Masons to "spread true Masonic Light" by publishing something that is no longer "true Masonic Light?" The only thing that makes sense to me about these two statements is that his first one must not be true, because if it were, he would not be "spreading true knowledge" by reprinting Mr. Pike's rituals. So, I believe these rituals are still being utilized by the Masons in the Scottish Rite today because he is duty bound to "spread true knowledge."

2. The Masons would have to change only one word of Mr. Pikes rituals so that they could claim that they were not those "currently used" anymore. So, the claim that Pike's rituals are not the ones being used today means little, especially after re-

viewing the words of praise that the Masons have written about their former Sovereign Grand Commander many years after he wrote the Rituals. My research has not revealed one critical comment made about Mr. Pike since he wrote the rituals over one hundred years ago. So, the Masons have not repudiated him, nor his rituals.

Secondly, I can find no literature inside the Masonic material that I have read that claims that new rituals were written to replace those written by Mr. Pike.

And the statue of him in Washington D.C. continues to stand. One would presume that if he had been discredited, because they believed his rituals were inappropriate, or that they no longer felt his rituals expressed the true intent of the Masons, they would have removed his statue, and Mr. Kessinger would not be reprinting his books.

It certainly was the intent of the Masons to use these rituals as the official ones and after they were written, Mr. Pike became "the most revered Sovereign Commander of the history of the Rite." So, it does not sound as if they "repudiated" these rituals with a complete, or even a partial, rewrite. It does seem unlikely that they would change the rituals written by such a man.

3. One can read other works by other Masons, including A BRIDGE TO LIGHT written by Mr. Hutchens, completed after Mr. Pike's rewrite of the rituals, and they confirm that little, if anything, has been changed.

So it is my opinion that the basic secret concealed inside the rituals and the writings of Mr. Pike, and the other authors cited, remains unchanged.

But, for the purpose of exposing a secret inside the Lodge, it doesn't matter whether or not Pike's rituals have been replaced. The information that I am using to reveal the secret is consistent from many sources, including the other writings of Mr. Pike and the more recent book by Rex Hutchens. In addition, I will be later be examining the writings of two 18th Century critics of the Masons and, as you will see, both of these scholars were saying the same thing that Mr. Pike's rituals are saying. And they wrote their books about 68 years before Mr. Pike released his rituals. In other words, the material I am using is official: this is what the Masons are teaching, because it is in their writings from the books written by the two critics in 1798, from Mr. Pike's rewriting of the rituals in 1857 and from the more modern date of 1988 and Mr. Hutchens' book.

It is fair to conclude that, even if this Mason is correct and Mr. Pike's rituals are not the ones being used today, the Masons have not changed their basic goal. They still have the same message and the same pur-pose. And I shall examine both in this book.

So, it shall be my purpose to use these writings by Pike and others, as being still legitimate and authoritative.

So the Masons acknowledge that Mr. Pike wrote the rituals for all of their degrees. But now let me return to the main issue of this part of my book, a reading of the pertinent quotations in his book, MORALS AND DOGMA.

It is hoped that these quotations from this book, and from other official and semi-official writers of the Masonic Lodge will be of assistance to those who will be unable to obtain copies of the books quoted herein.

Because the contents of these books must be read by both the Mason and the non-Mason alike.

Our future as a people demand it.

chapter 2
THE MIND OF
ALBERT PIKE

Before I start quoting from Mr. Pikes book, I thought it would be important to discuss several miscellaneous quotations from his writings to show the reader a little about the character and wisdom of the writer.

Mr. Pike had some strange views, and the following quotations should help the reader in understanding the man who wrote them. For instance, he wrote this on page 293 of MORALS AND DOGMA:

> "The horse, the dog, the elephant, are as conscious of their identity as we are.
> They think, dream, remember, argue with themselves, devise, plan, and *reason*.
> What is the intellect and intelligence of the man but the intellect of the animal in a higher degree or larger quantity?" [54]

This is a curious statement for Mr. Pike to make because it is commonly held today that this view was not scientifically correct when he wrote the book (animals do not make conscious efforts to "plan" nor do they "reason." "Plans" demand "reason," and animals do not "reason.") And it does not seem to have much place in a book about the Masons by a Masonic writer, but it does provide the reader with a little insight into the mind of Mr. Pike.

Another of Mr. Pike's strange views is this one, taken from page 297 of his book:

"Everywhere in the world labor is . . . the slave of capital . . . ." [55]

This is also the view of Karl Marx, the so called "father of Communism," and has been frequently stated by other Socialists and Communists.

This is not the place to challenge both this statement by Mr. Pike and the similar one by Mr. Marx at any great length, but very simply, this belief is not true. But should the reader wish to examine this fallacy of both of these men, they may refer to the chapters on Communism and Socialism in my book entitled THE UNSEEN HAND. Because it is there that I prove that this assertion is a gross distortion of the truth.

Mr. Pike also wrote about one of the public claims of the Masonic Lodge. (This will be examined later in my book as well.) It is their position that they are not involved in politics, but that they are a charitable group, out to further the best interests of mankind.

However, Mr. Pike in his book takes the contrary position. He clearly states that they are involved in fomenting revolutions all over the world. He states this on page 330:

Masonry ". . . hatches no PREMATURE revolutions." [I added the emphasis] [56]

Notice that the Masons "HATCH" no "PREMATURE" revolutions. That means that they wait until it is the proper time to "hatch" a revolution. Yet the Masons officially are quick to point out that they are not involved in politics. But here Mr. Pike points out that they are indeed a political organization, "hatching revolutions" when the time is ripe.

In fact, Mr. Pike says on page 24 of MORALS AND DOG-MA that Masonry:

". . . aided in bringing about the French Revolution . .
. ." [57]

So, apparently the "hatching" of this Revolution was deemed not to be "premature;" in other words, the Masons felt it had to occur and they "hatched" it.

And the reason that the world does not notice that they are actively "hatching" revolutions was stated by Kenneth MacKenzie:

". . . Freemasonry works in secrecy, but its benignant [defined as: "kindly (to inferiors)"] fruits are visible in all lands." [58]

Notice that Mr. MacKenzie considers the works of the Masons as being beneficial to us "inferiors," and that we would be thankful if we only knew that they were the ones dispensing these "fruits," such as a "hatched" revolution.

Because, as W.L. Wilmshurst put it:

"The world little suspects what it owes to its hidden Initiates." [59]

And the second layer of the Masons number themselves as being amongst the "hidden initiates."

And to show you that Mr. Pike's statement about their involvement in world affairs is true, the reader is urged to remember the quotations from Manly P. Hall, another 33rd De-green Mason, cited in the beginning of this book, who wrote the following about Masonry on page 451 of his book entitled LECTURES ON ANCIENT PHILOSOPHY:

It is ". . . the most powerful organization in the land." [60]

And to show you just how powerful they are, he wrote this on page 100 of another of his books, this one entitled THE LOST KEYS OF FREEMASONRY:

"Masonry is an ordainer of kings. Its hand has shaped the destinies of worlds . . . ." [61]

Mr. Hall knows that the Masons that "hatch no premature revolutions" "shape the destinies of worlds," and that the average person in the world simply has not heard this. And to show the reader that he considers the public to be too ignorant to discover this truth, he contemptuously wrote about us, the people on this earth, on page 58 in another of his works, entitled WHAT THE ANCIENT WISDOM EXPECTS OF ITS DISCIPLES:

". . . the ancient initiates [whom the Masons link themselves to] . . . are the invisible powers behind the thrones of earth, and men are but marionettes, dancing while the invisible ones pull the strings.
We see the dancer, but the master mind that does the work remains concealed by the cloak of silence."[62]

So, fellow "marionettes," I am hopeful that you can see just how important it is that we learn all that we can about the Masonic Lodge. Because, even if we do not know that the Masons are behind the scenes ruling the rulers of our governments, they are, and the Masons are telling us that fact. In fact, it appears as if Albert Pike pointed out in his book that we will soon demand that we be led by them.

On pages 814 through 821 of MORALS AND DOGMA, Mr. Pike wrote about the "Anti-Masons" and others who had become concerned in 1826 about the Masonic Lodge in America. He went on to say that:

"It will be easy, as we read, to separate the false from the true, the audacious [defined as being: "bold in wickedness, insolent"] conjectures [defined as: "from the simple facts.]" [63]

Then Mr. Pike has several pages of comments he believes the "Anti-Masons" would make. And on page 817, he says the "Anti-Masons" would contend that the Masons would claim that:

". . . the World will soon come to us [apparently meaning the Masons] for its Sovereigns [apparently meaning its governmental leaders] and Pontiffs [apparently meaning its religious leaders.]

We [the Masons] shall constitute the equilibrium of the Universe, and be rulers over the Masters of the World." [64]

Mr. Pike addresses several of the other claims made by the "Anti-Masons" directly in the many pages in his book addressed to the issue, but he makes no specific comment to refute this statement by these anonymous "Anti-Masons." So one can fairly conclude that "the Anti-Masons" are correct when they assert that the Masons are out to rule the world, and that the Masons believe they will "soon" assume these positions in the world of the future.

So, we the people of the world, according to both of these Masons, will soon be asking the Masons to rule our churches and our governments. But, it would seem that the process has already started, but we the people are blissfully unaware of that fact.

Because, in the 32nd Degree, according to Mr. Pike:

> "The true Initiate is both King and Priest over the people." [65]

We the people simply do not understand, because they are not telling us the entire story.

We are being "intentionally misled" as we shall see.

chapter 3
MORALS AND DOGMA:
AN "ESOTERIC BOOK"

A good place to start a study of the Masonic part of Mr. Pike's book entitled MORALS AND DOGMA would be on page iv. The unnamed author of the Preface on the next two pages states that the book is "not intended for the world at large." And that statement was further amplified on the first page of one of the MORALS AND DOGMA books that I found in a used bookstore. That page had a statement printed by a black-inked rubber stamp that stated:

> "Esoteric book, for Scottish Rite use only; to be returned upon withdrawal or death of recipient."

The word "esoteric" is defined by a dictionary as being:

> "intended for or understood by only a chosen few, as an inner group of disciples or initiates."

So it appears that the reason the public is not to read this book is because it contains hidden meanings concealed inside words and symbols that are not to be understood by the average citizen, and, as will be proven from the contents inside the book, by even a percentage of the Masons themselves. The book conceals many ideas and thoughts inside words that have two meanings: one for those who understand the symbolism, and one for the rest of the world.

But those who read the book can know what it says, even though Mr. Pike attempted to conceal the truth from the average reader.

chapter 4
CONSPIRACY DEFINITION

It becomes important at this time to define the word Conspiracy, because the reader is going to be asked to begin looking at Masonry as being the very embodiment of the word.

Webster's Dictionary defines the word:

> "CONSPIRACY: A planning and acting together secret, especially for an evil or unlawful purpose."

With that definition in mind, the reader will no doubt find the evidence that Masonry is a Conspiracy as their own material is reviewed in the pages that follow.

Because:

1. The Masons are secret;
2. The Masons have an evil purpose;
3. The Masons are planning and acting towards their goal.

chapter 5
REVIEW OF
MORALS AND DOGMA

So the book entitled MORALS AND DOGMA was written for only certain people to read. The Masons are keeping the truths in the book from us, the non-Masonic public, by first stating that we are not to read it, and then by telling us that if we do, we will probably not understand it because even some of the Masons who read the book will not discover its truths.

That means that even if a non-member did purchase the book from a used bookstore or was given one by a Mason, Mr. Pike is saying that he could not understand what the book was say-in because the writer had used a concealed language inside of the book, and that this language was used to keep the truth from the reader as well as from even some of the Masons.

In fact, only certain individuals are capable of breaking the coded language so that they can learn the real truth behind the symbols. And the book calls these certain individuals "Adepts."

Mr. Pike wrote this on page 849:

> "It is for the Adepts to understand the meaning of the Symbols." [66]

So only "the Adepts" understand the true meaning of the symbols inside the lodge.

But Mr. Pike has opened the door to the true meaning, but only a little. This is from page 772:

"If you desire to find and to gain admission to the Sanctuary, we have said enough to show you the way. If you do not, it is useless for us to say more, as it has been useless to say so much." [67]

But notice that Mr. Pike said that there are many secrets inside his book. I believe that this statement is only partially true, because all of the secrets in the book concern themselves with only ONE SECRET. I believe that I have discovered that the book does indeed contain only ONE secret and I will attempt to make that secret known to the reader as I progress through this review of his book.

So, if the new brother in the Masons wants to know the secrets, he has to think about the words because the secret meaning will not be explained to him directly. This quotation comes from page 781:

"If you reflect my Brother, . . . you will no doubt suspect that some secret meaning was concealed in these words." [68]

He repeats the thought on page 370 and then on page 218:

"You [the Mason who is proceeding through the rituals] have received only hints of the true objects and purposes of the Mysteries . . . .

Be content, therefore, . . . and await patiently the advent of the greater light." [69]

"It is for each individual Mason to discover the secret of Masonry . . . .

Masonry does not *inculcate* her truths [meaning she does not repeat them often.] She *states* them, once

74

and briefly; or hints them, perhaps, darkly; or interposes a cloud between them and eyes that would be dazzled by them." [70]

Notice that there appears to be only ONE secret inside the words of the book (Pike mentions "THE secret.") Once again, I believe that he reveals what that "ONE SECRET" is elsewhere in his book.

The following quotation is from page 219 of his book:

"That Rite [apparently the Scottish Rite] raises a corner of the veil, even in the Degree of Apprentice [once again, the first of the three degrees in the Blue Lodge of Freemasonry;] for it there declares that Masonry is a *worship*." [71]

And Mr. Pike explained why certain men will not be able to understand the hidden and concealed words inside his book. He wrote on page 224 that the Mason:

". . . believes that God has made men with different intellectual capacities; and enabled some, by superior intellectual power, to see and originate truths which are hidden from the mass of men." [72]

So the book was written for only those with "superior intellectual power," because the rest of the world would not be smart enough to "see the truth." Mr. Pike was confirming his understanding that only certain men would be able to understand the hidden meaning behind the words inside his book.

But, as will be shown, he has revealed enough of the hidden language so that all who read his book can know exactly what he has concealed inside his words. In other words, if the average Mason reading Mr. Pike's book is not bright enough to discover "the secret" by himself, the Masons who know the secret will not, and cannot, assist him. They have attempted to tell him, but if he did not see it himself, they cannot help him by saying more.

So, here the Mason learns that some men are better able to understand the secrets than others.

It follows, therefore, that they would have the right to keep this knowledge from "the less intelligent" by the use of concealed secrets. And, as will be shown in other quotes from Mr. Pike's book, there are other Masons who are not able to understand the Masonic secrets. That is what the Adept Masons have done: keep the secrets from those they deem to be the "less intelligent" Masons.

Pike explained on page 225 that these men with the "superior intellectual power" have a "mission:"

> "The Mason believes that God [I believe that he is not referring to the God of the Bible, but is writing about the Masonic god, whom they call "the Great Architect of the Universe"] has arranged this glorious but perplexing world with a purpose, and on a plan. He holds that every man sent upon this earth, and especially every man of superior capacity, has a duty to perform, a mission to fulfill, a baptism to be baptized with [here he is referring to "the secret," that certain men are to figure out and then act upon;]
>
> that every great and good man possesses some portion of God's truth, which he must proclaim to the world, and which must bear fruit in his own bosom."[73]

But Mr. Pike is saying that only other men of "superior intellectual power" will be able to understand his "proclamation" of their purpose. The average man on the earth will not be able to comprehend the hidden meanings of the words that conceal this "mission."

So the Adepts are concealing the truth from the world by using false explanations of the words. He wrote on page 104:

> "Masonry . . . *conceals* its secrets from all except the Adepts and Sages, or the Elect, and uses false explanations and misinterpretations of its symbols to mislead those who deserve only to be misled; to conceal the Truth, which it calls Light, from them and to draw them away from it." [74]

This thought that the secrets of the Masons are concealed from even the majority of the Masons is consistent throughout this book, as the reader is hopefully beginning to discover.

But the most startling discovery as to how they conceal the true meaning from their fellow Masons is the fact that Mr. Pike writes that the Adept Masons simply lie to them! He actually admits that the "Adept" Masons are intentionally lying to their fellow Masons! Mr. Pike wrote this on page 819:

> "The Blue Degrees [once again, the first three degrees, called the Blue Lodge] are but the outer court or portico [defined as: "a covered porch" meaning the outer portion of the temple, not quite inside of it] of the Temple [meaning the Masonic temple.]
>
> Part of the symbols are displayed there to the Initiate, but he is intentionally misled by false interpretations.

It is not intended that he shall understand them; but it is intended that he shall imagine he understands them.

Their true explication is reserved for the Adepts, the Princes of Masonry [meaning the Masons in the second layer.]" [75]

Mr. Pike repeated that thought in his book entitled LEGEN-DA, which will be analyzed more in detail a little later in this book. This is what he wrote:

"It was never intended that the mass of Masons should know the meaning of the Blue degrees . . . . They [apparently he is referring to the Adepts, the second layer] deceive and delude those who read their works [the first layer] . . . .

Masonry . . . permits the utterance of false interpretations, which serve the double purpose of *mis*leading the ignorant, the idle and the indolent [defined as: "disliking or avoiding work, lazy,"] whom it is desirable to lead astray, and of *indirectly* indicating to the wise and the studious the true way leading toward the Light." [76]

So Mr. Pike refers to those of us who do not understand the symbols as "ignorant, idle and indolent."

Thank you very much for these very kind words, Mr. Pike.

And he stated his case very simply in his book entitled LE-GENDA when he wrote that it was in:

". . . the Blue degrees, where no symbol receives its true explanation . . . ." [77]

So Mr. Pike is admitting that the Adept Masons actually lie to their fellow Masons. They intentionally conceal the true explanation of the symbols that they are explaining to their brothers in the Order.

It will assist the reader to remember that it was Mr. Pike himself who wrote the rituals to all of their 33 degrees, so if anyone knows that the Adept Masons lie to their fellow Masons, it is Mr. Pike.

So, the Mason who wants to know the true meaning of the secrets cannot understand them by directly hearing the explanation of the symbols being offered to him during the initiation ceremony. He has to learn that the Adept Mason is lying to him, and that all of the explanations of the symbols that he is being offered are not true. So, he must truly "reflect" upon the meanings of the words, because his fellow Masons WILL NOT tell him the truth during the rituals.

And this practice of intentionally lying to the initiate has been in keeping with the history of the Masons since even before 1717, their traditional founding date.

Mr. Pike wrote that the Knights Templars, commonly referred to as the Templars, the parent organization of the Masons, reportedly founded in the 1100's, had two doctrines as well: one for the Templars and one for the "Masters."

Mr. Pike wrote on page 817:

> "The Templars, like all other Secret Orders and Associations, had two doctrines, one concealed and reserved for the Masters [the second layer,] . . . the other public . . . ." [78]

So, keeping the truth from their fellow Masons is not new. It has been practiced by their parent organization for nearly 900 years.

The reader should now be asking the question:

What do the symbols really mean?

And the "first layer" Mason and non-Mason alike can now know exactly what they mean.

chapter 6
BELOW IS ABOVE

Even though Mr. Pike considered most of his readers to be "ignorant, idle and indolent," he did provide us with enough clues to enable us to know the truth about the Masonic Lodge. And the first clue that this is true comes from this thought on page 324:

> *"What is Superior is as that which is Inferior, and what is Below is as that which is Above . . . ."* [79]

The Mason is taught by these words that often the actual meaning of the symbol is exactly the opposite of the explanation offered. Since Mr. Pike is the author of this statement, one can be certain that it refers to works inside his book. This would obviously be the case in an "esoteric" (meaning secret, hidden) work such as MORALS AND DOGMA.

Now, if the reader "reflects" on the words, armed with the knowledge that certain of the words have a meaning that is the exact opposite of the supposed meaning, he can understand some of the concealed, secret meanings of some of the writings of Albert Pike.

Please keep this in mind as we read the words of Mr. Pike, because it will assist the reader in understanding THE secret inside the Lodge.

chapter 7
MASONRY IS A RELIGION

But first, the reader of Mr. Pike's book needs to know more about Masonry.

Mr. Pike stated the official position of the Masonic Lodge in his book entitled MAGNUM OPUS about whether or not the Masons are a religion. He said simply:

"Masonry is not a religion." [80]

Yet in another part of the same book, in the "Reception" of the 18th Degree, he has one of the Masonic leaders ask the initiate the following question:

"My Brother, there are several questions that you must answer sincerely and truly . . . .

1st: What is your religious belief?" [81]

The obvious question one must ask is why would a "non-religious" organization care what the initiate's "religious belief" was if they were truly "not a religion?" It would seem that only a "religious organization" would care to inquire about these personal beliefs before the member joined it. But the reason the Masons ask this question is simple: they want to make certain that the initiate shares their views before he is allowed to join.

In addition, the reader must remember that one of the qualifications of the Masonic Lodge is that each initiate has to believe in a supreme being.

Secondly, if the Mason truly believes the following statement of Mr. Pike's, they would have no right to ask the question about what the initiate's religious beliefs were.

Mr. Pike wrote this on page 13 of the 29th Degree in his book entitled MAGNUM OPUS:

> "The Mason's creed goes further than that. No man, it holds, has any right in any way to interfere with the religious belief of another.
> It holds that each man is absolutely sovereign as to his own belief, and that belief is a matter absolutely foreign to all who do not entertain the same belief . . . ." [82]

So, that denial of Mr. Pike in his book that they are not a "religion," is incorrect for the following reasons:

1. In other writings of Mr. Pike, the most respected writer of all of the Masonic writers, he says that his claim that they are not a religion is not true. He wrote on page 213 of MORALS AND DOGMA:

> "Every Masonic Lodge is a temple of religion; and its teachings are instructions in religion." [83]

Apparently the student of the Masons is not to see the contradiction between these two statements that they are "not a religion" because they are a "temple of religion" with "instructions in religion." He further compounds the problem when he makes a similar statement in his book entitled LEGENDA:

> "So Masonry teaches the people . . . that Masonry is the pure and primitive Religion." [84]

So now Mr. Pike says that Masonry "is not a religion," but that they are "the pure and primitive Religion."

Apparently these contradictions are not to be pointed out to the Mason who believes that Masonry is "not a religion."

And in a quotation already cited previously in these pages, Mr. Pike further compounds the question with this thought, taken from MAGNUM OPUS:

> ". . . the Ancient and Accepted Rite . . . raises a corner
> of the veil even in the degree of Apprentice; for in that
> it declares that Masonry is a worship." [85]

So here we have Mr. Pike admitting that "Masonry is not a religion," it is "a worship" in "a temple of religion" with "instructions in religion."

The student of the Masonic Lodge could really get confused with these obviously contradictory statements. But fortunately, another of the key 33rd Degree Masons has totally cleared up the mystery.

Manly P. Hall took it one step further and finally ended the debate once and for all. He truly wrote the obvious when he categorically stated that Masonry WAS a religion.

He wrote this in his book entitled THE SECRET TEACHINGS OF ALL AGES:

> "Despite statements to the contrary, Masonry is a re-
> ligion seeking to unite God and man by elevating its
> initiates to that level of consciousness whereon they
> can behold with clarified vision the workings of the

84

Great Architect of the Universe [the god of the Masons.]" [86]

To confirm that Mr. Hall is correct in his assertion that Masonry is a religion, one must only go to a common dictionary to define the word.

The word Religion is defined as:

"1. A belief in a divine or superhuman power or powers to be obeyed and worshiped as the creator(s) and ruler(s) of the universe;

or

2. Any specific system of belief, worship, conduct, etc., often involving a code of ethics and a philosophy."

Any fair observer would have to conclude after examining the various statements by Mr. Pike, the final deciding quotation from Mr. Hall, and the dictionary definition of a "religion," that Masonry is "a religion" by any fair evaluation.

And it appears that Mr. Pike was attempting to explain just what the "Morals and Dogma" of the Masonic religion were by writing his book by that name. Yet, even today, the Masons claim that "Masonry is NOT a religion."

To further confirm the obvious, Mr. Pike explained on page 7 of MORALS AND DOGMA that:

"Every [Masonic] Lodge is a Temple . . . ."[87]

He made a similar statement on page 16 of the 13th Degree in his book entitled MAGNUM OPUS:

"So every Masonic Lodge is a Temple of Religion; its officers, ministers of religion; its teachings, instruction in religion." [88]

Webster's New World Dictionary defines a Temple as:

"a building for the worship of a god or gods."

So Mr. Pike has written that every Masonic Lodge is "a Temple," a building used for the purpose of worshiping a god. And, by definition, people who meet in a religious building to worship a god are members of a religion. Yet, he claims that "Masonry is not a religion."

If Masonry is a religion, it must have a god that is to be worshiped. And the Masons do.

They call their god "The Great Architect [sometimes Masons call him "The Grand Architect"] Architect of the Universe."

This observation by Mr. Pike is typical of those proclaiming the name of their God:

"We conclude this Lecture with that which has always been, and we believe always will be the Masonic idea of the Supreme Being:
We call Him the Grand Architect of the Universe, considering that Universe as His most significant temple and perfect work of architecture." [89]

Notice first of all, that Mr. Pike states that the "universe" was a "perfect work of architecture." This is a very revealing statement, and should be examined in more detail at this juncture, because the student must know who this god is.

As I said, it is a requirement of the Masons that each person desiring membership into the Lodge must believe in a supreme being. This prospective new member can believe in any god, because the Masons do not specify that they must be God-fearing Christians, Jews, Buddhists, or Muslims, or a member of any other faith, to join. The Masonic requirement is simply that they must believe in a supreme being, and who that supreme being is does not concern the Masons.

However, as the reader will discover, Mr. Pike is going to explain that the Masons believe that the supreme being that they call "The Great Architect of the Universe" is not the god that the initiate himself believes in, but is another god. As the evidence will show, it is definitely not the god or God that the Mason himself believes in.

It will be helpful if I add this thought that the Masons believe that there are two gods in the universe. The confirmation of this statement comes from page 494 of Henry Wilson Coil's ENCYCLOPEDIA, as he discusses the several "Qualifications of Petitioners," meaning the qualifications that the prospective initiate must possess to join. One of those qualifications is "religious" and this is how he states what those "religious" requirements are:

"RELIGIOUS: Belief in God or T.G.A.O.T.U." [90]

So the Mason can believe in "God", traditionally considered to be the "God of the Bible" OR the Masonic god referred to as "The Great Architect Of The Universe," abbreviated T.G. A.O.T.U. So the initiate can believe in EITHER of these two Gods. Which god the initiate believes in does not concern the Adept Masons.

chapter 8
TWO WORSHIPS

Mr. Pike also explained that it was not just the Knights Templars, and now the Masons, that have two truths inside their religion. This is how he provided the reader with this truth, taken from page 352:

> "Among most of the [religions of the] Ancient Nations there was, in addition to their public worship [of a particular god,] a private one styled the Mysteries; to which those only were admitted who had been prepared by certain ceremonies called initiations." [91]

Manly P. Hall confirmed the view that the Masons were the ancestors of a secret, ancient religion. He wrote:

> "The leading Masonic scholars of all times have agreed that the symbols of the Fraternity are susceptible of the most profound interpretation and thus reveal to the truly initiated certain secrets concerning the spiritual realities of life.
>
> Freemasonry is therefore more than a mere social organization a few centuries old, and can be regarded as a perpetuation of the philosophical mysteries and initiations of the ancients." [92]

The Masons are aware that many of the religions of the past had a false worship: some knew that the identity of the god being worshiped was different from the one that the worshiper thought he was worshiping. This thought is covered by other Masonic writers, so the thought is not unique to Mr. Pike. These are the thoughts of Manly P. Hall:

"The arcana [defined as: "a secret of hidden knowledge"] of the ancient Mysteries were never revealed to the profane [defined as: "those not initiated into the inner mysteries"] except through the media of symbols." [93]

Mr. Hall dedicated his book that contained these words to:

". . . the proposition that concealed within the emblematic figures, allegories and rituals of the ancients is a secret doctrine concerning the inner mysteries of life, which doctrine has been preserved *in toto* [meaning in the whole] among a small band of initiated minds since the beginning of the world." [94]

In other words, the early gods were worshiped by two classes of worshipers: those who knew the secret identity of the god, and those who did not. And to show that it is not just the ancient societies that believed this way, Mr. Pike repeatedly states that the Masons conceal the true identity of their god from the majority of the brothers in the Lodge.

In fact, Mr. Pike also connected Masonry with the ancient religions that had two worships. He wrote this on page 483:

". . . and our Lodges [called temples, where they worship their god] are full of the ancient symbols." [95]

So Masonry can trace their history back to the ancient religions: they have a god that they worship that is not revealed in its true identity to their fellow Masons.

So the Masons admit that they can trace their ancestry back to the ancient mystery religion which is close to 6,000 years old.

In fact, Mr. Pike even goes further on page 624 and says that the two are the same:

> ". . . Masonry is identical with the Ancient Mysteries
> . . . ." [96]

In fact, another Mason wrote that Webb's Monitor claims that:

> "from the commencement of the world we may trace the foundation of Masonry." [97]

The reader will remember that Mr. Hall stated that the ancient doctrine:

> ". . . has been preserved *in toto* [meaning in the whole] among a small band of initiated minds since the beginning of the world." [98]

These comments about how long Masonry has been in existence are an admission that the Masons are a part of an ancient worship on this earth, one that goes back to the beginnings of the world.

And Mr. Pike wrote that in the ancient mysteries they used symbols with more than one explanation. He wrote this on page 205:

> "The ancient symbols and allegories always had more than one interpretation. They always had a *double* meaning, and sometimes *more* than two, one serving as the envelope of the other." [99]

And we have seen that what he says is true.

So Masonry connects itself with an ancient religion on the earth. And the fact that this ancient religion has kept itself secret from the world is perhaps the greatest secret in the world.

And Masonry is part of it.

chapter 9
MASONRY'S MORALITY

If Masonry is a religion, it must have a code of morality: it must teach a moral set of values. Mr. Pike said on page 35 that it was required:

"... the sole purpose of Religion is an Ethic." [100]

A dictionary defines the word Ethic as:

"having to do with a standard of morality."

And Masonry, like all of the other religions, has a "standard of morality."

Their code of morality is called "Situation Ethics."

Mr. Pike wrote on page 37:

"... all truths are *Truths of Period*, and not truths for eternity ...." [101]

It might be helpful to remind the reader that Mr. Pike's book is entitled <u>MORALS</u> and Dogma. So one of the major purposes of his book is to teach the morality of the worldwide Masonic Lodge to the reader.

And this book does teach the Mason how the Masonic Lodge views the subject of Morality.

In the quotation just cited, and in others as well, Mr. Pike starts by instructing the Mason that there are no "moral absolutes" because there are no "truths."

The moral teaching that holds that there are no "truths" in morality is called "Situation Ethics." A dictionary defines the term:

"SITUATION ETHICS: a system of ethics according to which moral rules are not absolutely binding but may be modified in the light of specific situations."

Therefore, the Mason is taught in their book called MORALS AND DOGMA that there are no truths in any morality, and if that is true, the Mason is free to determine his particular morality for himself depending upon the situation. This moral code of the Masons is called "Situation Ethics."

And the place where the Mason learns that truth is in their book entitled MORALS and Dogma.

Mr. Pike amplified that thought on page 52:

". . . what is untrue today may become true in another generation . . . ." [102]

This is an odd statement by Mr. Pike. The dictionary defines the word "TRUE" as being:

"in accordance with fact; that agrees with reality; not false."

If something is "unTRUE" today, and becomes "TRUE" tomorrow, it had to be "TRUE" from the beginning.

If it changes to a "truth" with the passage of time, it could not have been "unTRUE" in the beginning. It had to be "TRUE" then as well.

93

Yet Mr. Pike said that TRUTH can change in time. Obviously, according to Mr. Pike, that which is "unTRUE" today can change to become "TRUE" tomorrow. That, in turn, can become "unTRUE" sometime in the future.

One can only conclude that Mr. Pike believed that there were no permanent TRUTHS, such as Moral Absolutes, in a constantly changing universe!

Mr. Pike even went further and stated that no one knows "the truth." He wrote this on page 160:

> ". . . no human being can with certainty say . . . what is truth, or that *he* is *surely* in possession of it, so every one should feel that it is quite possible that another equally honest and sincere with himself, and yet holding the contrary opinion, may himself be in possession of the truth . . . ." [103]

This quotation should be of concern to the Christians and Jews, who believe that the Bible is inspired by God, who they contend is the author of all truth. So, according to Mr. Pike, those believers are wrong because "no human being can with certainty say . . . what is truth."

Mr. Pike further defined their position with these four quotations, taken from pages 163, 165, and 166. He states that the Mason:

> ". . . is not confined to set forms of thought, of action or of feeling. He accepts what his mind regards as true, what his conscience decides is right . . . all else [meaning a belief that there are moral absolutes] he puts far from him . . . .

His mind acts after the universal law of the intellect, his conscience according to the . . . universal law of each . . . ." [104]

"No man is entitled positively to assert that *he* is right, where other men, equally intelligent and equally well-informed, hold directly the opposite opinion." [105]

"When men entertain opinions diametrically opposed to each other, and each is honest, who shall decide which hath the Truth . . . ." [106]

These quotations show just how convoluted Mr. Pike's think-in about morality is. He wrote on page 167 that:

"No man, . . . has any right in any way to interfere with the religious belief of another." [107]

I can show with a little example that it is nearly impossible for Mr. Pike to believe that.

Let's say, for example, that Mr. Pike was out in public, and was approached by another man who was a member of "the Squashers" religion. This religion holds two basic tenets: that their god demands that each member has to kill one man each day, and that "no man has any right in any way to interfere with the religious belief of another." This second tenet would be, of course, in agreement with what Mr. Pike himself has stated that he believes.

He approaches Mr. Pike with a gun in his hand, and says:

"My religion teaches me that I have to kill one man each day and I have selected you as today's victim."

Mr. Pike would be obligated to say, of course, "It is also a tenet of my religion that no man has the right to interfere with the religious beliefs of another. And, since there are no moral absolutes like 'thou shalt not murder,' I cannot interfere with your right to kill me. So please proceed as your religion mandates."

It does not take a genius to conclude that in all likelihood, Mr. Pike would not say that. He could reasonably be expected to do all within his power to subdue this "Squasher" and remove the threat to his life. He would not practice what his religion inside the Masonic Temple teaches. He would act on a real belief that the moral absolute "thou shalt not murder" is correct, and that no man has the right to take his life, even if that man's religion demands it. It can also be presumed that he would correctly make a determination that he has a God-given, unalienable right to self-defense, because he would know that the fact that no man has the right to take another's life was a "moral absolute," and he would attempt to subdue this religious fanatic, even though he has stated that he does not believe that he as a Mason would have that right.

Hypocrisy, thy name is Pike!

But Mr. Pike is not alone with this line of thinking. Others have made similar outlandish statements.

John Dewey, the American educator and so-called "father of progressive education," was one of those who believed in "situation ethics." He held to a similar morality. He has been quoted as saying:

> "There is no God and there is no soul. Hence there are no needs for the props of traditional religion.

96

With dogma and creed excluded, then IMMUTA-
BLE TRUTH IS ALSO DEAD AND BURIED. [I added the emphasis]
There is no room for fixed, natural law or permanent absolutes."

I do not know whether Mr. Dewey was a member of the Masons, but he certainly wrote like one. He certainly believed in
the same Situation Ethics that Mr. Pike believed in. But, just
like Mr. Pike's statement that a fact that "is untrue today" may
become true tomorrow, the words of Mr. Dewey also contain
an "absolute moral absurdity."

Notice that Mr. Dewey wrote that a "immutable truth is also
dead and buried." A dictionary defined the word IMMUTA-
BLE as:

"Never changing or varying."

Mr. Dewey said those truths which are immutable can be
changed: he said that "an immutable truth IS ALSO DEAD
AND BURIED." That means that Mr. Dewey believed that
"truth" could be killed, meaning that he believed that it could
be changed from a living condition to a dead condition. Yet,
by definition, something that is immutable cannot change.

Once again, one does not have to be a genius to understand
that something that is unchangeable, is, by definition, unchangeable. So something that is unchangeable cannot change.
Yet Mr. Dewey said that something that is unchangeable can
change.

Another historic figure who said something similar to these
statements by Pike and Dewey was Nikolai Lenin, the father

of Russian Communism, the man who murdered as many as 40,000,000 Russians to provide that nation with the economic and political system known as Communism. He has been quoted as saying:

"Communism abolishes eternal truths. It abolishes all religion and morality."

And just like Dewey and Pike, Mr. Lenin believed in the unbelievable. He wrote that "an eternal truth" could be "abolished." The word ETERNAL is defined as:

"Without beginning or end. Forever the same. Always true or valid."

That which is ETERNAL cannot change; it is always true. That which is eternal, cannot be abolished because it is, by definition, unchangeable. Yet Lenin, the Communist, said that "Communism abolishes ETERNAL truths."

Once again, it doesn't take a genius to understand that his statement was a monstrous absurdity, because THAT WHICH IS ETERNAL CANNOT, by definition, CHANGE. But Pike, Lenin, and Dewey all thought that those things that cannot change are changeable. These are the thoughts of men who are not capable of clear thought, men out of touch with reality.

Anyone out of touch with reality is called "insane."

It doesn't take a genius to understand that simple absolute.

Pike wrote that he shared the views of Marx, Dewey and Lenin when he confirmed that he also did not believe in moral absolutes. He wrote on page 833:

"It is not true to say that 'one man, however little, must not be sacrificed to another, however great, to a majority, or to all men.'

That is not only a fallacy, but a most dangerous one. Often one man and many men must be sacrificed, in the ordinary sense of the term, to the interest of the many." [108]

And then Mr. Pike repeated the thought on page 834 so that no one could question what he meant. He wrote:

". . . the interest and even the life of one man must often be sacrificed to the interest and welfare on his country." [109]

Just to make certain that all can know exactly what Mr. Pike is saying, I went to my dictionary to define the word:

"SACRIFICE: the act of offering the life of a person or animal in homage to a deity; or the destruction or surrender of some desirable thing in behalf of a higher object"

So it appears that Mr. Pike was saying that one man's life meant nothing if it had to be sacrificed to "a higher object." And this implies that the act must be performed without the permission of the individual being "sacrificed."

The Biblical teaching is that every human has an absolute, God-given, unalienable (meaning that the right cannot be taken away except by God) right to life, and therefore the "sacrificing" of one man's life for any cause is called murder. That would include the sacrificing of the life of one man for the benefit of another. Here Mr. Pike stated that "often one man must be sacrificed" if it benefits the many. This is called "murder" by the God of the Bible, who specifically forbade man from committing this act (He taught man "Thou shalt not murder.") And this teaching is called a "moral absolute," one that God wanted man to obey at all times.

And to show that at least one member of the Masonic Lodge believed in the literal translation of Mr. Pike's permission to a member of the Lodge that he could sacrifice one man for the cause of the many, it is only necessary to examine the involvement of President Franklin Roosevelt in the Japanese attack at Pearl Harbor in Hawaii. That attack which occurred on December 7, 1941 was called "A Day of Infamy" the next day by the President when he asked the Congress of the United States for a Declaration of War against the attackers.

President Roosevelt was a member of the Masons at the time and for those who would enjoy seeing a picture of our President in his Masonic apron, all you must do is look up the article on the Masons in the March 28, 1949 issue of Life Magazine, and on pages 54 and 55 you will see various pictures of Masons in America. One of those picture shows Franklin Roosevelt "photographed in 1935 at [a] Masonic meeting with sons James and F.D. Jr.," wearing his apron as a symbol of his membership in the Order.

The student of history will remember the President's supposed anger when he called the attack "unprovoked" that day. He was in essence admitting that he had no prior knowledge of the Japanese attack on the facilities of America's armed forces at Pearl Harbor.

Historians even today teach that the President did not know before the attack that they were going to, so he was therefore powerless to prevent it. And to make the American people believe that he did not know, he appeared to be angered.

However, all he had to do to know that the Japanese were planning the attack on that Sunday, December 7, 1941, was to read the Hilo, Hawaii Tribune Herald of the Sunday before. It is now history that the writer of that article knew in advance, because the headline for the Sunday, November 30, 1941 edition reads:

"JAPAN MAY STRIKE OVER WEEKEND." [meaning the weekend of December 6th and 7th, 1941.]

One can only wonder how it was that the Hilo newspaper was able to figure this out and know in advance, but the intelligence departments of the government of the United States were not.

So all the President had to do was read one newspaper.

Yet we are being taught that he did not know.

But the terrifying question is not being answered because it is not being asked. How could President Roosevelt, if he knew about the impending attack before it happened, allow it to happen?

And the answer is that he knew and did nothing because he must have read and believed Albert Pike's teaching about the "sacrifice of one man for the many."

It certainly appears as is The President must have read and understood the teachings inside the book entitled MORALS AND DOGMA after he received the 14th Degree:

"It is not true to say that 'one man, however little, must not be sacrificed to another, however great, to a majority, or to all men.'

That is not only a fallacy, but a most dangerous one. Often one man and many men must be sacrificed, in the ordinary sense of the term" [110]

And:

". . . the interest and even the life of one man must often be sacrificed to the interest and welfare on his country.[that means that the President understood that he could sacrifice the life of one human, or many humans] to the interest of the many." [111]

If you believed Mr. Pike's teaching of the MORALS of the Masonic Lodge, and President Roosevelt, as a 32nd Degree Mason, should have read Pike's book entitled MORALS AND DOGMA after receiving the 14th Degree, then it would not be a stretch of the imagination to believe that the President could have "sacrificed" those men at Pearl Harbor for what he perceived to be a greater good.

And there is ample evidence to believe that the President had been offered what he considered to be a "greater good," the biggest prize ever offered to any individual in the history of the world: the Presidency of a world government, to be called the United Nations, that would be created after the end of World War II.

If you believed, as apparently President Roosevelt did, that a world government was of great benefit to mankind, and if you believed that "one man may be sacrificed to the cause of the many," it is no stretch of the imagination to deduce that the

President believing that what happened at Pearl Harbor was acceptable for the greater good of mankind.

And for those who want to know that this evidence in the Hilo, Hawaii newspaper that he knew about the attack on Pearl Harbor in advance is only one of an incredible accumulation of evidence on the subject, may I suggest that you read my book entitled THE UNSEEN HAND. Because it is in the chapters on World War II that I discuss the evidence that these statements are true, beyond a shadow of a doubt.

The last piece of the evidence that the President knew in advance about the attack comes from the last few pages of the book entitled CLAUSEN'S COMMENTARIES ON MORALS AND DOGMA written by Henry C. Clausen, a 33rd Degree Mason.

At the time the book was written, meaning in 1974, Mr. Clausen was the Sovereign Grand Commander of the Scottish Rite, meaning he held the same position as did Albert Pike himself years before.

The short biography of his life in these pages reveals that:

> "Brother Clausen was a member of the Army Pearl Harbor Board and conducted also further investigations into the Pearl Harbor disaster." [112]

If Mr. Clausen felt that the truth about Roosevelt's foreknowledge about the Japanese attack would bring discredit to the Masonic Lodge if it ever became public, it would be in keeping with several of the oaths he took in the Masonic Lodge to make certain that the American people did not find out. In other words, if Mr. Clausen was asked to sit on a government

board to determine if President Roosevelt could have prevented this "disaster," and if he found out that he could have,
Brother Clausen had taken oaths inside the Lodge to protect
his brother Mason.

Some of those oaths that Mr. Clausen took as he progressed
through the 4th through 32nd Degrees are as follows, beginning with the 15th Degree as quoted from Albert Pike's book
of the rituals he wrote, entitled THE MAGNUM OPUS:

> "I furthermore promise and swear that I will assist,
> protect and defend my brethren of this degree [Frank-
> lin Roosevelt also went through the 15th Degree] by
> all lawful means consistent with the character of a true
> Mason . . . ." [113]

> The obligation of a 16th Degree Mason: "I further-
> more promise and swear that I will never abandon a
> Brother, in whatever adversity he may be, in combat,
> or in sickness, or in prison; but will aid him with my
> counsel, my friends, my sword and my purse." [114]

> The obligation of a 17th Degree Mason: "I further-
> more promise and swear . . . that I will, at all times,
> when he has justice on his side, be ready to aid and
> support him against any who seek his life, or to de-
> stroy his honour [the spelling in the book,] reputation,
> peace of mind or estate . . . ." [115]

> The obligation of a 28th Degree Mason: "I, [name] .
> . . hereby now and forever solemnly pledge my word
> and troth, and most sacredly promise, as a man and
> Mason, that . . . should I fail to aid a Brother Knight
> in his necessities, to defend his character when unjustly

assailed . . . I pray that I may be denounced everywhere as one disloyal, . . . and that the punishment of Judas Iscariot [the betrayer of Jesus Christ in the Bible] may be visited upon my head!" [116]

The obligation of a 29th Degree Mason: "I furthermore promise and swear . . . that I will aid and assist, cherish, and protect a worthy Brother Knight, and see that no wrong be done him, if it be in my power to prevent it." [117]

So it can reasonably be inferred from these solemn oaths that Mr. Clausen repeatedly pledged to assist a Brother Mason in trouble. These oaths that he took as a Mason told him that he would be required to do all within his power to assist President Franklin Roosevelt, his fellow Mason, in protecting his reputation and character in the investigation into the "Pearl Harbor disaster." That means that he would do all within his power, including serving on a board investigating the attack, to keep the fact that he knew about the impending attack in advance away from the American people, because the President was his Masonic brother. He had taken several oaths to do so that he was obligated to keep as he progressed through the rituals of Masonry.

So, now we know why the American people believe today that President Roosevelt did not know of the impending attack of Pearl Harbor. At least one Mason, "brother" Henry C. Clausen, took oaths as a Mason to protect him and his reputation. And no one in the Roosevelt administration, apparently including the President himself read the Hilo paper that Sunday morning.

But back to the issue at hand.

Remember that Mr. Pike has said that what "is untrue today may become true in another generation."

The opposite of that position, also true by Mr. Pike's statement, is "what is true today may become untrue in another generation."

So yesterday's absolutes do not have to be tomorrow's absolutes.

Because there are no such things. And even if there are "absolutes," they can change with time. But then they weren't absolutes then either.

This statement by Pike is complimentary to the ones in which he expresses the Morality of the Masons, called Situation Ethics, and the belief that there are no moral absolutes.

And to show you that he understood that his book was to teach the morality of the Masonic Lodge, he entitled his book MORALS and Dogma.

Let there be no doubt about it: the Masons do not believe in Moral Absolutes!

They teach that each man is free to find his own morality.

And this teaching is called "Situation Ethics!"

And if you believe this, and are President of the United States, you can sit by and watch thousands of your countrymen die during an attack that you could have prevented.

Your religion allows it.

chapter 10
MASONRY'S MORALITY, CONTINUED

Since the Masons teach that there are no "moral absolutes" in the Masonic Lodge, each man is to decide for himself what is moral or immoral. And Mr. Pike is telling the Mason that he is to determine these things for himself. He wrote on page 169:

> "The true use of knowledge is to distinguish good from evil." [118]

So, the Mason seeks "knowledge" so that he can decide for himself what is right and wrong.

The Bible teaches that man is not to decide for himself what is "good" and what is "evil." This ability to know for himself was called "the fruit of the Tree of the Knowledge of Good and Evil" in the garden of Eden into which God placed the first man and woman. And Man was instructed by God not to "eat" of this knowledge. Man was to learn "good and evil" from the "moral absolutes" taught to him by God.

In fact, it is an interesting exercise to check the number of times that the word "evil" is used in the Bible. My personal computer has a program of the King James Version of the Bible in it, and I did "a word search" on the word "evil." It is used 568 times in both the Old and New Testaments.

If you add in the number of times that the word "good" is used, and that number is 655 times, the total number of times that the two words are used is 1,223, exceeding the 942 times that the word Jesus is used. That means that the Bible is not only about Jesus, it is about "good" and "evil," and how man is to learn the difference between the two.

But, as was just explained, the "first layer" Mason is taught that there are no "Moral Absolutes." They have been, and are being, taught that each man is to make his own decisions as to what is right and wrong. And that is the reason that the Masons used to ask him to read the Masonic book entitled MORALS AND DOGMA.

It was so that he could learn the MORALS of the Masonic Lodge.

And that their morality was that there was no morality.

chapter 11
"SUN" WORSHIP

If Masonry is a religion, it must not only have a code of morality, as it does, but it must also have a god to worship. And Masons do.

But the second layer inside the lodge does not want their fellow Masons to know that they worship a different god than does the first layer Mason. So they keep this knowledge from their fellow Masons by concealing that truth behind a symbol that they "intentionally mislead" their brothers about when they explain it to the initiate during the rituals.

And the symbol used for this purpose is a "Sun."

Mr. Pike wrote on page 366:

> "Our Lodges are said to be due East and West, because the Master represents the rising Sun . . . ." [119]

Notice that Mr. Pike identified the fact that their "Master," the equivalent of the "President" of the Lodge, is a symbol of the "rising Sun."

Here he is not talking about the "sun," the brilliant orb that lights the day and disappears during the night. He is talking about the "Sun," a concealed god for whom the "sun" is a symbol. He explained that the "Sun" is only a symbol of something else on page 12:

> "The three lesser, of the Sublime, Lights . . . are the Sun, the Moon, and the Master of the Lodge . . . .

But the Sun and Moon do in no sense light the Lodge, unless it be symbolically, and then the lights are not they, but those things of which they are the symbols." [120]

Notice that Mr. Pike has deified the "sun" so that it becomes the "Sun." He wrote on page 13:

"The Sun [notice the word is capitalized as you would do for the name of a deity] is the ancient symbol of the life-giving and generative power of the Deity." [121]

So the Sun is a symbol of a deity. Mr. Pike will identify that deity in other parts of his book.

One of the ways he does so is through comments like this one from page 15:

". . . Osiris, himself symbolized by the Sun . . . ." [122]

Mr. Pike later disclosed that Osiris, the Egyptian Sun god, has a rival God. This quote is taken from page 697:

"Long known as . . . Adonai [one of the names of God in the Bible;] . . . the Rival of Bal and Osiris . . . ." [123]

Here Mr. Pike admits that the God of the Bible was the rival of Osiris, previously identified as being a god representing the god of the Masons. (This is a strange statement for Mr. Pike to make. He will later make a statement that he does not believe in the God of the Bible.

So one can only presume that he is leading the initiate through a series of steps: this one teaches him to think that there are

110

two gods in the universe. Later he will teach him that there is in truth only one god, "the Great Architect of the Universe.)

So the Mason learns that the Sun inside their Lodge was a symbol of Osiris, an early god of the Egyptians. This quotation comes from page 776:

"The Sun is the hieroglyphical sign of Truth, because it is the source of Light . . .;" [124]

Once again, Mr. Pike reveals the fact that the explanations of the symbols offered in his book are not the correct ones. This is what Mr. Pike wrote on page 32:

"Masonry is a march and a struggle toward the Light."[125]

And the Mason is told that he is to seek the "Light:"

"In every Degree in Freemasonry, the Candidate [this is the initiate] seeks to attain Light." [126]

And, in fact, he is told to seek the "Light" in secret:

". . . while scientific and social objects can be easily pursued in the broad light of day, it is still necessary to combat the influence of darkness and night by less open means." [127]

And Henry Wilson Coil provides the Mason with a little clue about the real nature of the "Light" he is seeking:

"Light is everywhere the symbol of intelligence, information, knowledge [Mr. Pike has written that "the true use of knowledge is to distinguish good from evil,"] and truth, and is opposed to darkness which symbolizes ignorance and evil." [128]

Albert Mackey repeats the theme in one of his books:

"*Light*, therefore, became synonymous with truth and knowledge, and *darkness* with falsehood and ignorance." [129]

And he expands the thought in this quotation:

"When the candidate makes a demand for light, it is not merely for that material light which is to remove a physical darkness;
    that is only the outward form, which conceals the inward symbolism.
    He craves an intellectual illumination which will dispel the darkness of mental and moral ignorance, and bring to his view, as an eyewitness, the sublime truths of religion, philosophy, and science, which it is the greater design of Freemasonry to teach." [130]

So the Mason is a "Light-seeker." And the source of this "Light" is "THE SECRET," or at least one part of "THE SECRET," inside the book entitled MORALS AND DOGMA.

Mr. Pike later connects the "Light" to a God in what appears to be a prayer, because during the 24th Degree ritual, he has the Mason say the following:

"Have mercy upon us . . . . Thou art the Light . . . .
    Guide our footsteps, and direct us in the right path, O LORD our GOD . . . .

Be merciful unto us, and with thy great Light drive back the Powers of Darkness!" [131]

He confirms this thought that the "Light" comes from a God with this quotation:

"Truth is the Light that emanates from God . . . ." [132]

Then Mr. Pike expanded the worship of the "Light" from their god when he connected it to the worship of the "sun" or the "Sun." He wrote these comments on pages 77 and then 593:

". . . thousands of years ago, men worshiped the Sun . . . . Originally they looked beyond the orb [the "sun"] to the invisible God [the "Sun"]. . . ." [133]

"The worship of the Sun became the basis of all of the religions of antiquity." [134]

Notice that Mr. Pike once again capitalized the word "Sun." He is making a distinction: he states that the object being worshiped was not the "sun," the star that lights the earth during the daylight hours. He states that they worshiped the "Sun."

The "Sun" is not an object to be worshiped, it is a symbol of an invisible god, because the identity of this god is being kept secret from the overwhelming majority of mankind.

The identity of this "invisible God" was known only to a small percentage of the men on the earth. And he is connecting the Masons to this "worship of the Sun," because he and other Masonic writers, as I shall show later in this book, have connected their religion to the "Ancient Pagan Mysteries," which involved a worship of the "Sun" as well.

113

Manly P. Hall, as identified earlier, is another 33rd Degree Mason, and perhaps the most prolific writer on the subject of "occult" practices. He wrote this in his book entitled THE SECRET TEACHINGS OF ALL AGES:

> "Sun worship played an important part in nearly all the early pagan Mysteries. The Solar Deity . . . was slain by wicked ruffians, who personified the evil principle of the universe. By means of certain rituals and ceremonies, symbolic of purification and regeneration, this wonderful God of Good was brought back to life and became the Savior of His people [this ritualistic slaying is also practiced by the Masons and will be examined later in this book.]
>   . . . in Masonry, the ancient religious and philosophical principles still survive." [135]

I believe that the reader can see that the Christians who read these words, without knowing the concealed meaning behind them, could reasonably expect that Mr. Hall is talking about Jesus Christ. But, as we shall see, that is the conclusion they want the Christians to draw, and is not the true explanation. There is an "invisible" meaning reserved for the "adepts."

So Masonry connects itself with an older and far more extensive worship of a "Sun God." I will not attempt to take the time to detail the evidences of this religion in this book; however, for the student of "the ancient mystery religion", as it is called, you might refer to my book entitled THE NEW WORLD ORDER, and the 14 hour lecture video [136] by the same name that extends the research beyond the book. I'll only attach the Masons to this ancient worship by quoting their own words. But the worship of this "Sun God" is 6,000 years old, in every culture, and on every continent, and it needs to be examined and understood. Mr. Pike even connected the Sun to another symbol inside the Lodge. He wrote this on page 477:

"The Sun . . . his is the All-Seeing Eye in our [Masonic] Lodges." [137]

Here Mr. Pike connects the Sun with the "All-Seeing Eye" that is apparently displayed in their Lodges. Others have connected the Masonic "All-Seeing Eye" to the "All-Seeing Eye" on the back of the American dollar bill in what has been called The Great Seal of the United States. (It is the eye on the back of the dollar bill just above the pyramid on the left side.) Both Masonic and non-Masonic writers have concluded that members of the Masons designed both sides of the Great Seal of America. (This subject is covered in the reviewer's book entitled THE NEW WORLD ORDER, [138] and in AMERICA'S SECRET DESTINY. [139])

Mr. Pike states that many of the symbols inside the Lodge are identical with the symbols of the early sun worshipers. He wrote on page 495 that to the Egyptians:

"The horned serpent was the hieroglyphic for a God" [the God the ancient mysteries worshipped.] [140]

Notice that the word "God" is capitalized. The serpent is identified in the Bible as being connected to Lucifer, the devil. The significance of this statement will become apparent a little later in this review. Mr. Pike wrote this on page 506:

". . . the Blazing Star has been regarded as an emblem of Omniscience, or the All-Seeing Eye, which to the Ancients was the Sun." [141]

This "Blazing Star" has been described on page 106 of Albert Mackey's ENCYCLOPEDIA, under that heading, as "one of the most important symbols of Freemasonry," and as a "symbol of God."

So, here the reader can see that Mr. Pike is connecting the "Sun," a "serpent" and the "All Seeing Eye." This connection is extremely significant as the reader shall soon see.

Mr. Pike identified this "Sun" god as being a deity other than the God of the Bible with this quotation taken from page 254 (this quote is repeated by Mr. Pike on page 15 of the "History" section of the 17th Degree, in his book entitled MAGNUM OPUS:)

    ". . . the Sun God . . . created nothing." [142]

This is an incredible revelation! This thought acknowledges that the Masons believe that there are two Gods in the universe, a Creator God, and this other "deity," a "Sun God," who has "created nothing."

The Masons call their deity "The Great Architect of the Universe." (For confirmation of that truth, see Mackey's ENCYCLOPEDIA, page 310. [143] Mr. Mackey says, under the heading of "Great Architect of the Universe: "The title applied in the technical language of Freemasonry to the Deity.") It is important to note that the Masons call their Deity an "architect" god rather than a "Creator" God. Human architects do not create anything. They design buildings for the contractor who will take already existing materials to build their structures.

A creator would actually create the building materials out of nothing, but, by calling their deity an "architect," the Masons are admitting that their deity has not created anything, just like Mr. Pike's "Sun God."

Mr. Pike amplified this thought on page 42 of the "Lecture" section of the 28th Degree in MAGNUM OPUS:

> "We conclude this Lecture with that which has always been, and we believe always will be the Masonic idea of the Supreme Being: We call Him the Grand Architect of the Universe, considering that Universe as His most significant temple and perfect work of architecture." [144]

So, the Great Architect of the Universe, the Masonic deity worshiped in the Masonic Temples, connected to the "Sun," a "serpent," and the "all-seeing eye," is NOT the God of the Bible, because that God is a "creator God," who created the universe out of nothing.

The Masons have said it in their own literature.

So the Masons can believe in "God or T.G.A.O.T.U." ["the Great Architect of the Universe,"]" as Henry Wilson Coil stated.

But the Masons say that they believe in only one of these two Gods: The Great Architect of the Universe.

chapter 12
"LIGHT" SEEKERS

Albert Pike has written that they distinguish between the "sun" and the "Sun," and between "light" and the "Light."

And the difference between these words is important.

As already discussed, when the initiate Mason joins the Lodge, he goes through three separate initiation rituals.

It might be appropriate at this juncture to interrupt my review to make this comment.

I must be fair to the Masons. These initiation ceremonies are "secret," and the investigative reporter who is not a member of the Lodge is not allowed to view any of their ceremonies. So, no one outside of the Lodge knows for certain just what the exact nature of the initiation ceremony is.

However, there have been at least two copies of the old initiation ceremony published, one of which is in a book entitled DUNCAN'S RITUAL OF FREEMASONRY published by the David McKay Company of New York. The book purports to:

> ". . . furnish a guide for the neophytes of the Order [presumably the initiates of the Masons,] by means of which their progress from grade to grade may be facilitated." [145]

The preface of the book contains this statement as well:

> "Every statement in the book is authentic." [146]

A second source of the actual words of the Masonic ritual is contained in a book entitled FREEMASONRY EXPOSED. [147] It was published in 1826 by Captain William Morgan, who claimed to be a Mason for 30 years, and its publication exposing the ritual of the Masons caused a national scandal after the Captain was murdered by them on September 11, 1826.

Most of the observers of the day believed that the Captain was murdered by the Masons because he had published the rituals of the Lodge in violation of an oath he had taken as a member not to reveal their secrets. Some of the American people were so outraged by this murder that they formed the "Anti-Mason Party," the first of this nation's third political parties, and they ran candidates for the Presidency and Vice-Presidency of the United States in the election of 1832. They received about 7% of the national vote, and actually received the majority of the votes in the state of Vermont.

It is true that both of these books were written before Albert Pike rewrote the rituals in 1857. However, a comparison of these two rituals with the ones written by Mr. Pike himself reveal that basically the same information is contained in all three. I will refer to all three of these rituals to show the reader just how consistent the three rituals are.

And all three of these books report basically the same thing: that during each of the first three rituals that the initiates goes through inside the Blue Lodge, the initiate is asked by the Worshipful Master, the equivalent of the President of the Lodge, the same or similar question:

"What do you most desire."

And the initiate responds:

In the First Degree: "Light." (found on page 35 of DUNCANS. Page 36 of Morgan's book says he responds with the same word. Pike's answer follows.)

And in the Second Degree he responds with the words: "More light in Masonry." (found on page 66 of DUNCANS. Morgan's book, on page 53, says that his response is simply "More light.")

And in the Third Degree: "Further light in Masonry." (found on page 96 of DUNCANS. Morgan's book, on page 92, says that his response is, once again, "More light.")

These thoughts that the initiate Mason asks for "Light" during the ritual is confirmed by Albert Pike in his book THE PORCH AND THE MIDDLE CHAMBER. It is during what he calls "THE OBLIGATION" of the First Degree, the ritual for the Entered Apprentice Mason. Mr. Pike writes that the Worshipful Master, the "President" of the Lodge, asks his fellow Mason, the Brother Orator, another officer in the Lodge:

"Brother Orator, what dost thou ask for this Candidate [meaning the initiate]?"

And the orator answers:

"Light!"

And then he asks his fellow Mason, the Senior Warden, another officer of the Lodge:

"Brother Senior Warden, what dost thou ask for this Candidate?"

And he answers:

"THE GREAT LIGHT!!" [148]

Albert Mackey helped the Mason to understand the "Light" that he is seeking concealed a mystery.

He wrote this in Volume 1 of his Encyclopedia, on page 446:

"Light is an important word in the Masonic system. It conveys a far more recondite [defined by Webster's as: "hidden from sight, concealed"] meaning that it is believed to possess by the generality of readers." [149]

Then he confirms my readings of DUNCAN'S RITUALS, FREEMASONRY EXPOSED and Pike's books entitled MAGNUM OPUS, and THE PORCH, by adding this comment:

"It is in fact the first of all the symbols presented to the neophyte, [Mr. Mackey is confirming that the word is partially examined in the first three degrees as explained by Duncan and Morgan and later by Pike himself] and continues to be presented to him in various modifications throughout all his future progress in his Masonic career.
    It does not simply mean, as might be supposed, *truth* or *wisdom*, but it contains within itself a far more abstruse [defined by Websters as: "concealed, difficult to understand"] allusion to the very essence of Speculative Masonry, and embraces within its capacious [defined as: "large, roomy, spacious, able to contain much"] signification all the other symbols of the order.
    Freemasons are emphatically called the 'sons of

light' because they are, or at least are entitled to be, in possession of the true meaning of the symbol." [150]

But what this "light," or "Light," is, and from whence it comes, is not answered, as far as I can determine, by any of the three versions of the rituals inside the Blue Lodge.

But the answer to those questions can be found in Mr. Pike's book entitled MORALS AND DOGMA.

The Mason can know exactly where this "light" or "Light" comes from, by reading his book. It is to be remembered that the Mason did not get this book until he had passed the 14th Degree. So, he did not have the answer as to where this "Light" came from until he read this book.

That also means that the Blue Lodge Mason was not officially told what this "Light" was. He had to voluntarily ask to be included in the initiation ceremonies from the 4th through the 32nd Degree before he found out.

He was not to know unless he read the book, because Mr. Pike gives him the answer in MORALS AND DOGMA after he reached the 14th Degree.

Pike identifies the source of the "Light," as coming from a "Light-bearer!"

He wrote this on page 321 of MORALS AND DOGMA:

> "LUCIFER, the *Light-bearer!* Strange and mysterious name to give to the spirit of Darkness! Lucifer, the Son of the Morning! Is it *he* who bears the *Light* . . . ? Doubt it not!" [151]

And he repeats the thought on page 324 when he discusses:

"a Devil, the fallen *Lucifer*, or *Light-bearer* . . . ." [152]

It is true!

The Masons acknowledge that the "Light" that they are asking for comes from Lucifer the light-bearer, also known as Satan, or the devil! The Masons seek "Light" and Pike identifies the "bearer" of that "Light" as Lucifer! In fact, the Mason is told to "doubt it not!"

Webster's defines the name Lucifer as meaning: "L, for Latin, bringing light. From *lucis,* light + *ferre* to bring." The dictionary then says: "Satan as identified with the rebel archangel before his fall." So, LUCIFER is Latin for "light-bringer" or "light-bearer," the name of "Satan before his fall."

So the 14th Degree Mason has just been taught that he is askin for "Light" from the "Light-bearer," who according to the Bible was a being who fell to the earth at the beginning of time. If the ancients believed that this "fallen" being was a "god," they would have constructed a religion around his worship. They would have decided to keep this worship secret from their fellow believers, so it could have been called "the ancient mystery religion."

Remember that the Masons have connected themselves to "an ancient mystery religion," which means that they have connected themselves to the ancient worship of Lucifer.

Let there be no doubt about it: the "Light" that the initiate Mason asks for comes from Lucifer, because he is the "Light-bearer!" In fact, he is told "to doubt it not!" And as we shall see a little later in this review, he is told that the "Light" is "Good."

Because the "Adept" Mason already believes that the "Light" is "Good." He knows that the "true knowledge of Deity" is that Lucifer is God!

And to show the reader that it is not Mr. Pike alone as a Mason who knows that Lucifer is the Light bearer, let me provide a quotation from Manly P. Hall's book entitled THE LOST KEYS OF FREEMASONRY. This quote by this 33rd Degree Mason is another source for this belief, because he wrote:

> "When the Mason learns the key to the warrior on the block is the proper application of the dynamo of living power, he has learned the mystery of his Craft. [What this seems to be saying is that the key to understanding the Masons is to know that the "mystery of the craft" is knowing that the Mason has a "warrior" on his side.]
>
> The seething energies of Lucifer are in his hands and before he may step onward and upward, he must prove his ability to properly apply energy. [So, Lucifer is the "warrior" that the Mason must learn to control before he moves upward through the degrees inside the Masonic Lodge.]" [153]

There is one more way that the Mason can know that Lucifer is the god of their worldwide organization, and that is by studying the symbol of the Eastern Star, an auxiliary group primarily for women, separate from the male only Masonic Lodge. This group may be joined by "the wives, daughters, sisters, mothers and widows of third degree Masons." However, not only women may join this group. A male Master Mason, meaning a Third Degree Mason (or higher,) must preside at all of the meetings where degrees are conferred on their initiates.

The symbol of the Eastern Star is a star with one point down and two points up. That means that the star is the reverse of the star that we traditionally see, the five pointed star with two points down and one point up. The star on the American flag is the traditional one, with the star resting on two of its points. However, when you rotate it so that it rests on one point, you have the symbol of the Eastern Star.

The meaning behind the symbology of the Eastern Star was discussed in a book entitled HISTORY OF FREEMASONRY AND CONCORDANT ORDERS, written by "a board of editors," in 1890. This book was published by The Fraternity Publishing Company of London, England, but the articles inside the book were written by a total of 80 Masons: an Editor, a European Editor, 19 men on a "Board of Editors," and 59 men called "Additional Contributors." The book listed their names with a brief description of their Masonic affiliation, and most of them came from the United States. However, ten of them came from Canada, and two from England. Nine of the "Board of Directors" and seventeen of the "Additional Contributors" were 33rd Degree Masons. So it is fair to conclude that this book contains valid Masonic thought.

There are at least two discussions of the star with "one point down" in these pages. (See page 166 for drawings of the two stars.) The first comes from page 49 and it reads:

"This star [meaning a five pointed star] represents GOD, all that is *pure, virtuous,* and *good*, when represented with one point upward [this is, of course, the way we traditionally draw the star:] but when turned

> down it represents EVIL, all that is opposed to the
> *good, pure,* and *virtuous;* in fine, it represents the
> GOAT of MENDES." [154]

And to show the reader what these two stars look like, they are both shown on the page, at the sides of paragraph that has been indented to allow for this. The star with "one point down" has been drawn with a goat's head inside of it, with his chin and chin whiskers in the bottom point, his right and left ears inside the two side points, and the two horns inside the two points that point upward.

The second quotation comes from page 101 under the heading of THE HOLY AND MYSTERIOUS PENTAGRAM. This is what this section reports:

> "It is the star of the Magi [the Magi are defined as: "A priestly caste of order of ancient Media and Persia." Many Bible scholars believe that the Magi who came to see the infant Jesus were not "kings," but were in truth astrologers and/or believers in the ancient mystery religion;] . . . and according to the direction of its rays this absolute symbol represents Good or Evil, Order or Disorder, the blessed Lamb of Ormuzd (Ahuro-Mazdao), and Saint John, or the accursed Goat of Mendes (see page 49.) [This is, of course, a request by the Masons that the reader should refer to the first quotation about the star.]
>
> It is initiation or profanation [the word is not defined by either of my two dictionaries. However, the word profane is defined as: "not connected with religion," so it might mean that Masonry is secular, and stands by itself, not choosing to associate itself with religion;]

it is Lucifer or Vesper, the morning or the evening star . . . .

When the Pentagram elevates two of its points [meaning when it has one point down] it represents Satan, or the goat of the Mysteries; and when it elevates one of its points only [meaning like the star on the American flag,] it represents the Saviour, goodness, virtue." [155]

So the star of the Eastern Star, according to 80 top Masonic leaders, "represents Satan."

And the proof of this statement lies in the fact that the Church of Satan run by Anton LaVey uses both the pentagram with one point down, and the goat of Mendes, the drawing of the goat inside a star with one point down, in its rituals and in its written materials.

I have one story that might illustrate that all that I have just written about this star is accurate.

I once appeared on a television program in Tampa, Florida, called ACTION 60's. The program was hosted by Herman and Sharron Bailey, two Christians who did this daily show that was ultimately sent out on cable television all across America. They invited me to visit with them for three consecutive programs and discuss my second book entitled THE NEW WORLD ORDER, and I did.

They allow a small live audience into their studios each day and after the second of the three programs, while I was talking to several of these people, a man stepped forward and asked me if I wanted a Masonic Bible. He told me that he was a Christian and that he received it as a Christmas gift from someone who thought he might find it useful. When he said that he opened the cardboard box it came in, he felt "an evil presence" around it and put it back into the box. A short time later, he decided to re-examine the Bible and pulled it out of the box once again. He said that he felt the same presence and decided that he would close up the box and never look at it again. When I accepted his most gracious offer, he handed me the Bible, still in its cardboard box.

I opened the box and pulled the book out. I opened it and noticed that it was a King James Version of the Bible. However, the first few pages showed that it was a Masonic Bible because these pages had Masonic symbols and writing printed on them. I must admit that I felt no "evil presence" as I handled the Bible, so I continued to examine it, looking to see if I could identify the cause of his feelings.

Then I noticed that the Bible had about 70 additional pages added to explain certain information inside the Bible that the Masons believe supports their religion.

On the cover of this Bible are two things of interest: one is a rather well done painting of a young man, apparently Jesus Christ at 12 years of age, meeting with a group of aged men. This painting appears to be illustrating the story contained in Luke chapter 2, verses 45-48, when Jesus disappeared from his parents for three days, only to be found later "in the midst of the doctors," in the temple, where they were "astonished at his understanding and answers."

The second is a star with one point down, about 1 3/4" high.

There is no explanation by the Masons of either the drawing or the star in the pages of this Bible.

But as soon as I saw the Eastern Star on the lower right hand corner of the Bible, I knew why the gentleman felt "an evil presence" when he brought the book out from inside the box.

It is because the Masons have put the star that "represents Satan" on the cover of the Holy Bible. It is there for all to see, but not for all to understand.

These two books were the two books that I had with me on that television program in Tampa that none of the Masons in the room wanted to see.

It might be helpful for me to interrupt my review of MORALS AND DOGMA to explain a little about this Lucifer, also known as the devil, from the words of the Bible.

The Bible student knows that "Lucifer" is not "Good," but evil. He knows, as does the reader of the dictionary definition, that "Lucifer" is another name for Satan, the devil.

The Bible reveals that Satan was once an angel who fell from God's presence. The prophet Ezekiel wrote this in chapter 28 verses 14-15:

"Thou are the anointed cherub that covereth; and I have set thee so: thou wast upon the holy mountain of God . . . ;
Thou wast perfect in thy ways from the day that thou was created, till iniquity was found in thee.

So here we learn that Satan is a created being, who was appointed by God as the "cherub that covereth." Some believe that this means that Lucifer protected the very throne of God itself.

But, Lucifer fell. The Bible continued in verses 16-17:

> ". . . thou has sinned: therefore I will cast thee as pro-
> fane [defined as: "not connected with religion or relig-
> ious matters"] out of the mountain of God . . . .
>   . . . thou hast corrupted thy wisdom by reason of
> thy brightness . . . ."

The prophet Isaiah, who wrote around 740 B.C., included
some additional information about why Lucifer fell. He wrote
in Isaiah chapter 14, in the following verses, that the story
continued:

> 12: "How art thou fallen from heaven, O Lucifer,
> son of the morning! how are thou cut down to the
> ground which didst weaken the nations!
>   13: For thou has said in thine heart, I will ascend
> into heaven, I will exalt my throne above the stars of
> God: I will sit also upon the mount of the congrega-
> tion, in the sides of the NORTH:" [I added the empha-
> sis]
>   14: I will ascend above the heights of the clouds;
> I will be like the most High."

So Lucifer attempted to replace God in heaven. This is what
this "battle" was all about: Lucifer wanted to replace the God
of the Bible on the throne of the universe. And that is still his
task on earth.

It is important at this point to break with this explanation and
add one more piece to the puzzle.

Isaiah wrote that "the throne" of God was "on the farthest
sides of the north." It appears that it would be fair to conclude

that the Bible teaches that this must be where God reigns over the universe. Yet, the Masons teach that this is a "place of darkness." Albert Pike wrote on page 592:

> "To all Masons, the North has immemorially been the place of darkness; and of the great lights of the Lodge, none is in the North." [156]

The word "immemorially" is defined as "extending beyond the reach of memory, record, or tradition, indefinitely ancient." So the Masons are saying that the North has been the "place of darkness" forever.

So it does not appear as if the failure to find any northern locations inside of the Masonic lodges and temples all over this world is by "coincidence." It is apparent that they know why they do not utilize the North as a direction in their rituals.

And the student of the Masons can now understand what they believe "the darkness" is a symbol of

Quite simply, it is because they believe that "the darkness" is a symbol concealing the God of the Bible. And to understand that, it is necessary to study the Devil a little more in detail.

The Book of Revelation Chapter 12, verses 7-9, adds this about the being known as the Devil:

> "And there was war in heaven: Michael and his angels fought against the dragon; [shown later in these verses to be Satan, the devil] and the dragon fought and his angels,
> And prevailed not; neither was their place found any more in heaven.

> And the great dragon was cast out, that old ser-
> pent, called the Devil, and Satan . . . and his angels
> were cast out with him."

And God proscribed the punishment for the Devil's act of rebellion in Ezekiel Chapter 28, verse 17:

> "I will cast thee to the ground, I will lay thee before
> kings, that they may behold thee."

When he fell, he brought one third of all of the angels with
him. This quote comes from Revelation chapter 12, verse 4:

> "And his tail drew the third part of the stars of heaven,
> and did cast them to the earth . . . ."

So, Lucifer fell from heaven to earth with one third of the angels. This fact will become important a little later. (But, now
let me say that the "third part" of anything would be a little
more than 33 percent. This might be at least one of the reasons why the number 33 is symbolic to the Masons.)

Satan came to the earth, and it was there that he continued his
work. He appeared to Eve, the first female, in the Garden of
Eden.

God's garden had at least one restriction in it to Adam and
Eve. It is described in the book of Genesis, chapter 2, verses
16-17:

> "And the LORD God commanded the man, saying, Of
> every tree of the garden thou mayest freely eat:
>   But of the tree of the knowledge of good and evil,
> thou shalt not eat of it . . . ."

It might be important at this point to remember that the Masons have said that: "the true use of knowledge is to distinguish good from evil."

And Satan took advantage of that teaching, and tried to convince Eve to violate God's law. The Bible continues in Genesis chapter 3, verses 4 and 5:

"And the serpent said unto the woman: Ye shall not surely die: For God doth know that in the day ye eat thereof, then your eyes shall be opened, and ye shall be as gods, knowing good and evil."

And Eve listened, and broke God's law, and tasted of "the knowledge of good and evil." What this means is that she decided that she, and later Adam, could "be as gods," deciding for themselves what was right and wrong. She fell for the lie that men and women should decide these matters for themselves, and that they should not listen to the moral teachings of God. The first man and woman decided that they were going to make their own morality. In modern times, as was discussed previously, this is called "situation ethics." And that teaches that each man is to decide for himself what is right or wrong in each situation.

All of these bits of information will have relevance in the following sections of this book.

So, it is possible to summarize what the Bible teaches the reader:

1. God created Lucifer.
2. Lucifer wanted man to replace God in the scheme of things; in other words, he wanted mankind to

"be as gods," by teaching them that they did not need God's absolutes to live their lives. He knew that God was the father of all morality and if he could convince Adam and Eve that they should decide these things for themselves, he would have succeeded in his goal of replacing God.

3. He tempted Eve, and she succumbed to that temptation. She later convinced Adam, and ever since, certain men, including some of the key writers inside the Masonic Lodge, have been convincing the world that all men should decide for themselves what is right and wrong, and that they should disregard the moral teachings of the God of the Bible.

All of this is important for reasons that will follow.

Because the Masons believe these verses in the Bible as well.

chapter 13
LIGHT AND DARKNESS

Mr. Pike has just stated that the "Light" that the Mason asks for comes from "Lucifer, the light bearer." He then continued to explain that this "Light" is "good" on page 287:

"You see, my brother, what is the meaning of Masonic 'Light.' You see why the East of the Lodge . . . is the place of Light.

Light, as contradistinguished [defined as: "a contrast of opposite qualities," meaning one is the opposite of the other] from darkness, is Good, as contradistinguished from Evil: and it is that Light, the true knowledge of Deity, the Eternal Good, for which Masons in all ages have sought. [I believe that the Christian would contend that all men are striving for the "true knowledge" of God, but that this "light" comes from the Bible and not from the Masonic Lodge. In fact, the Bible teaches in John chapter 8, verse 12 that Jesus, the one revealed in the scriptures, claimed to be the source of the light when he said:

"I am the light of the world . . . ."

So there are two claimants in the world to being the bearer of Light: Satan, and Jesus.]

Still Masonry marches steadily onward toward that Light that shines in the great distance, the Light of that day when Evil, overcome and vanquished, shall fade away and disappear forever, and Life and Light be the one law of the Universe, and its eternal Harmony." [It is important at this juncture to remember that Pike is alluding to the day when "Light" conquers "Evil," meaning the day that Lucifer replaces God in the Universe. This statement will be proven later in the words of Mr. Pike and other Masonic writers.] [157]

Mr. Pike equated "Light" with "Good," and "Darkness" with "Evil." He continued on page 660:

". . . thus the words 'Light' and 'Good' became synonymous, and the words 'Darkness' and 'Evil.'" [158]

And to further convince the skeptic that Mr. Pike believed that Lucifer was good and that the God of the Bible was evil, he wrote this on page 567:

"To prevent the light from escaping at once, the Demons forbade Adam to eat the fruit of 'knowledge of good and evil' by which he would have known of the Empire of Light and that of Darkness. He obeyed; an Angel of Light induced him to transgress . . . ." [159]

As was just pointed out from the words of the Bible, "the demons" who forbade Adam to eat the fruit of the tree was the Triune God of the Bible, meaning the God who consists of three beings: the Father, the Son, and the Holy Spirit. And that the "Angel of Light" who induced Adam to do so was Lucifer, also called Satan, the devil. Mr. Pike has everything backwards. (Or, one could say that the Masons claim to have it right, and that the Bible has it all backwards.)

The thought that the Christians have it backwards when they claim that the Devil is "evil" can be traced to sources other than Albert Pike. The quotation that will follow comes from a book entitled THE HISTORY OF MAGIC, written by Eliphas Levi. In an explanation of the book in a catalog, the writer explains that Mr. Levi has been described by Arthur Edward Waite as:

> ". . . undoubtedly one of the most distinguished of the Continental exponents of occult science which the nineteenth century produced, and his writings attain an important position in the estimation of modern schools of higher magic." [160]

So, once again, we can rely on the thoughts of another writer in the field. Therefore, when Mr. Levi writes, the world can know that his words are those of an expert. This is what he wrote about Lucifer in his book entitled THE MYSTERIES OF MAGIC, A DIGEST OF THE WRITINGS OF ELIPHAS LEVI:

> "XXXVIII: What is more absurd and more impious than to attribute the name of Lucifer to the devil, that is, to personified evil.
>   The intellectual Lucifer is the spirit of intelligence and love; it is the paraclete [defined as: "an advocate; one called to aid or support,"] it is the Holy Spirit, while the physical Lucifer is the great agent of universal magnetism." [161]

And, in fact, the reader can know that Albert Pike also believed the writings of Mr. Levi. The following quotation also comes from Mr. Waite, who wrote:

> ". . . Eliphas Levi, to whom Albert Pike was more indebted than he let us know." [162]

This thought by Mr. Waite is similar to another confirmation of the mutual admiration between Mr. Pike and Mr. Levi. It comes from Henry Wilson Coil's Encyclopedia, under the heading of LEVI, ELIPHAS:

> "The pen name of Louis Alphonse Constance, French occultist, [defined as: "one who believes in occult forces and powers"] born in 1810, died in 1875. [It will be remembered that Mr. Pike lived from 1809 to 1891.] He was a prolific but not very reliable writer on magism [defined as: "a belief in a priestly caste in ancient Media and Persia, supposedly having occult powers"] and occultism, especially as they related to Freemasonry . . . .
>
> It will be observed that the most productive period of Levi was almost coincident with that in which Albert Pike rewrote the rituals of the Scottish Rite, beginning about 1854, and also *Morals and Dogma*, which was completed in 1871.
>
> Pike . . . had recourse to numerous sources, but it is said that he leaned most heavily on Levi . . . . Pike seems never to have entertained any other idea from first to last than that Freemasonry was the direct descendant of the Ancient Pagan Mysteries." [163]

Albert Pike learned at the feet of Eliphas Levi, and he learned his lessons well. But the reason why he would choose to connect with "a prolific but not very reliable writer on magism and occultism" was not explained by either of these writers. But we know that he did.

Other key Masonic writers knew Mr. Levi as well. Kenneth MacKenzie wrote that Mr. Levi was:

> ". . . an eminent author of works on philosophical magic . . . .

The editor of this book [meaning himself, Kenneth] knew him personally . . . ." [164]

Other words of praise for Mr. Levi, the friend of several key Masons, come from Doreen Valiente, the self-professed witch who wrote these comments about him in her book entitled THE ABC OF WITCHCRAFT:

"Eliphas Levi, another great nineteenth-century magus . . . . [plural of magi, defined previously as: "a priestly caste or order of ancient Media and Persia."] [165]

and elsewhere in her book, she wrote:

"The distinguished nineteenth-century French occultist, Eliphas Levi, declared Baphomet [see page 40 for a drawing of this god] of the Templars to be identical with the god of the Witches' Sabbat . . . .
    This explanation may sound somewhat far-fetched; but Eliphas Levi was in touch with secret occult fraternities [that is true, he was in touch with certain important members of at least one of the "secret occult fraternities" known as the Masons and, apparently, many other secret societies as well] which preserved traditional knowledge . . . ." [166]

So there is a connection between Albert Pike, the Masons, the Knights Templar and witchcraft: a belief in Baphomet, although there is not a general agreement amongst the Masons that Baphomet was the "god" of the Templars.

This quotation taken from Albert Mackey's ENCYCLOPEDIA, for instance, teaches that the "god" known as Baphomet was imaginary:

> "BAPHOMET: the imaginary idol, or rather, the symbol, which the Knights Templars were accused of employing in their mystic rights [presumably this is Mackey's spelling of the word "rites."] [167]

So the question remains unanswered, because the Templars are not around to deny the charges, and the current Masonic writers claim that this "god" was not worshiped by them.

However, Mr. Levi did include a drawing of the "god" known as Baphomet in his book entitled TRANSCENDENTAL MAGIC. This drawing shows a being that appears to be both goat and human. His arms and body appear to be human, but the head and cloven feet are from a goat. The animal has two horns, and appears to be bi-sexual (it has female breasts.) It also has wings and appears to be seated on the top of a globe. This is also the same drawing that Doreen Valiente, the witch, used on the cover of her book.

So, at least the "god," also known as the Goat of Mendes, was real to a witch, and Eliphas Levi, the friend of several important Masons, including Albert Pike.

But returning to the point being discussed, the reader of these words can know that the Mason, and the other writers on the occult science believe that the Christians have it all backwards: Lucifer is the "good god," and the God of the Bible is "the evil one."

It might be important to mention here that Lucifer is not a god, and that he can never be a god. And the reason for that is because there is only one God.

The God of the Bible teaches in Isaiah chapter 45, verse 22:

". . . for I am God, and there is none else."

But the belief that Lucifer is a "good God" should not come as a shock to those who have read Albert Pike's book entitled MORALS AND DOGMA. The reader is urged to remember the following quotation by Albert Pike from page 324 of MORALS AND DOGMA as quoted earlier. Pike wrote:

"What is Superior is as that which is Inferior, and what is Below is as that which is Above . . . ." [168]

The Masons teach publicly that those Masons who believe that Jesus Christ is the Son of God may freely do so inside the Temple. They do not explain to the public that they consider Jesus to be the "darkness." In other words, the reader is instructed to reverse the thought.

But the reader of MORALS AND DOGMA may know that they do.

All they have to do is to read the book.

All they have to do is to read quotations like this one, taken from page 294:

". . . Christ, teaching the religion of Love . . . . The Religion of Love proved to be . . . the Religion of Hate and infinitely more the Religion of Persecution . . . ." [169]

So Mr. Pike believes that it is the Christians who preach "love," but practice "hate." They preach "toleration" and practice "persecution." According to Mr. Pike, they are truly the "force of darkness."

141

Remember, Albert Pike said it in his own words.

The reader might consider examining additional quotations from other Mason "adepts" that show that they also consider Christ to be the enemy by reading both THE UNSEEN HAND and THE NEW WORLD ORDER. These books have been described in my catalog, a copy of which may be obtained from the publisher of this book. Because what the Masons truly believe is worse than what we have seen thus far.

But now the coded language has been broken.

When the Masons say that they worship a God, they do!

They worship their god: Lucifer!

We can know it for certain, because they have said it in their own literature.

They have stated that secret in a coded language that has been broken so that all can understand!

chapter 14
LIGHT WILL
VANQUISH DARKNESS

The reader will remember that Mr. Pike stated on page 32 that Masonry:

> "is a march and a struggle toward the Light." [170]

Manly P. Hall discussed his understanding about this struggle this way:

> "The Mysteries were institutions of liberation and were naturally opposed by groups seeking to keep their people in bondage through ignorance. The struggle was, therefore, between religion as temporal authority and the Mystery faith -- the internal 'road of light.'" [171]

So both Mr. Pike and Mr. Hall believe that the forces of "Light" are in a "struggle" with the forces of "Darkness." And Mr. Hall took it one step further by claiming that the battle was between "religion" and "the Mystery faith -- the internal 'road to light.'"

And Mr. Pike is certain which side will win that struggle. He wrote on page 275 of MORALS AND DOGMA:

> ". . . Light will finally overcome Darkness . . . ." [172]

Now the reader can see just how important it is that Mr. Pike identified the God of the Bible as being the "force of darkness." It is here that he admits that the religious view of the

Masons, the "Light" seekers, and their "Light-bearer" god, will "finally overcome" the God they claim is of the "Darkness," the God of the Bible.

He repeats the thought several times elsewhere in his book. This quote comes from page 287:

> ". . . the East of the Lodge . . . is the place of Light. . . . Masons in all ages have sought . . . that Light . . . of that day when Evil, overcome and vanquished, shall fade away and disappear forever . . . ." [173]

Kenneth MacKenzie told his readers that one side in the struggle was having to conduct their warfare in secret. He wrote:

> ". . . while scientific and social objects can be safely pursued in the broad light of day, it is still necessary to combat the influence of darkness and night by less open means." [174]

And Mr. Pike is saying that the day when Lucifer conquers the God of the Bible "by less open means" is not far away. He wrote this on page 715 of MORALS AND DOGMA in the year 1871:

> ". . . we can look on all the evils of the world, and see that it is only the hour before sunrise, and that the light is coming . . . ." [Mr. Pike wrote that their day of victory is coming soon, and it should be pointed out that he wrote this in 1871. The day of this "victory" is known and I will reveal it later.] [175]

So, in this "struggle," Lucifer is going to conquer God in the near future.

We can know that because Albert Pike told us.

In his own words.

In his book entitled MORALS AND DOGMA.

But the people are not to know this.

Because his book is not intended to be read by the public.

And his fellow Masons are being "intentionally misled with false interpretations" so that they will not know the truth.

So it took a non-Mason to reveal the truth to the public.

chapter 15
FAITH AND REASON

The next area that should be examined is Mr. Pike's statement that their god represents man's ability to "Reason," meaning each man's ability, as he terms it, to use his mind without any barriers from anyone, including the God of the Bible, to determine right from wrong. He wrote this on page 718:

> "Masonry propagates no creed except its own most simple and Sublime One; that universal religion, taught by Nature and by Reason." [176]

And again on page 737-738 :

> "God . . . *can* exist only in virtue of a Supreme and inevitable REASON. That REASON, then, IS THE ABSOLUTE; for it is in IT we must believe . . . ." [emphasis in original.] [177]

Here Mr. Pike states that the Masons do not worship a god, but they worship "Reason," the use of the mind and logic. It is known that to be a Mason, one must believe in a supreme deity. He is now stating that the Mason's god is not the God of the Bible, nor any other god believed in by their members. He is identifying that supreme deity as being "Reason," the use of man's mind. The reader will remember that it was Lucifer who encouraged Adam and Eve to use their "Reason" for themselves and thereby decide what was right and wrong. The devil "reasoned" that man did not need God and taught that to Adam and Eve.

Mr. Pike then states that "Faith," defined by a dictionary as: "unquestioning belief that does not require proof or evidence,"

146

is the opposite of "Reason." The implication is that "Faith" cannot be proven by the mind. They believe that man's ability to "Reason" is superior to "Faith," because "Faith" in a god does not require a proof of his existence.

He made this comment in support of that position on page 296:

> "Faith and Reason are . . . antagonists and hostile to each other . . . ." [178]

And once again, his religion teaches that "Faith" is aligned with "darkness," while "Reason" is aligned with "Light."

So, Mr. Pike seems to be saying that a "Faith" in a God is something that the mind, called "Reason," cannot comprehend. So, man cannot know that God exists by using his mind, his ability to "Reason."

Yet I have written a pamphlet that uses the mind TO PROVE THE EXISTENCE of a Supreme Being, a God. That pamphlet is called GOD EXISTS! THERE IS NO OTHER OPTION, and details about its purchase are found in the catalog mentioned at the end of this book.

In other words, faith in God can be as absolute as man's ability to reason. "Faith" and "Reason" are not "contraries" as Mr. Pike contends: they are "allies," because man can use his reason to know with absolute certainty that God does indeed exist!

A faith in God need not be a faith anymore: it is the equivalent of a certainty, because man can prove it, using reason, logic and science.

Pike was wrong; "Faith" and "Reason" are not "antagonists," they are allies. Man can know, through the use of reason, that God exists! A belief in God does not have to be a "faith" any longer, it can be the result of man's ability to reason!

Pike repeated his thought on page 305, when he wrote about:

"... contraries, ... like Reason and Faith." [179]

Mr. Pike stated that man believes in a God as a matter of "faith," because God has not revealed Himself through man's ability to "Reason." Therefore, man cannot know for certain that He exists, so mankind believes in God as a matter of "Faith." So, according to this reasoning, man cannot use "Reason" to know that God exists.

Mr. Pike said that "faith" in a God is not "reason." In other words, he believes that man can know by the use of the mind, called reason, that God does not exist.

This statement by Pike is simply not true. "Reason" must conclude that a creator God does exist!

In fact, he wrote again about the victory of Lucifer, the releaser of man's "Reason," over the "Faith" of those who believe in a God. He wrote this on page 810:

"Human reason [freed by Lucifer] leaps into the throne of God and waves her torch over the ruins of the Universe." [180]

Here Pike states once again, that it is his belief that human reason, their god, will ultimately succeed in removing the God of the Bible from His rightful throne in the universe.

He is also saying that the God of the Bible has made a mess of the universe (he referred to "the ruins of the Universe") and that man's mind, released by Lucifer, will restore it to the perfection that mankind knew in the Garden of Eden.

Albert Mackey in his ENCYCLOPEDIA confirmed this fact, by writing this:

> "Ordo ab Chao. *Order out of Chaos.* A motto of the Thirty-third Degree . . . ." [181]

That means that the 33rd Degree Masons believe that they will bring "Order" out of the "Chaos," "the ruins," created by the God of the Bible.

The citation in Mackey's ENCYCLOPEDIA continues:

> "and having the same allusion as *lux e tenebris,* which see [this must mean that the reader is to look it up elsewhere in his encyclopedia.]" [182]

This is Mr. Mackey's explanation of what this second phrase means:

> "Lux e tenebris. *Light out of Darkness.*
> A motto very commonly used in the caption of Masonic documents as expressive of the object of Masonry and of what the true Mason supposes himself to have attained.
> It has a recondite [defined as: "concealed, or hidden from sight;"] meaning." [183]

Mr. Mackey went on to explain a little about the "hidden meaning:"

149

"So *lux* being truth of Masonry, and *tenebrae,* or darkness, the symbol of initiation, *Lux e tenebris* is Masonic truth proceeding out of initiation." [184]

But I prefer to believe that the "recondite" meaning is that the "Light" from Lucifer will overcome the "darkness" of God. The "order" of Lucifer will replace the "chaos" of God.

In fact, Mr. Pike states that Satan, the devil, also known as Lucifer, came to earth to benefit mankind. He came to free him from the tyranny of God, the God that they believe will not let man exercise his free will; the God who restricts man's freedom by providing him with a set of Moral Absolutes. Mr. Pike wrote on page 102:

". . . Satan . . . this is not a *Person,* but a *force,* created for good, but which *may* serve as evil. *It is the instrument of Liberty or Free Will* [meaning man's free choice without the moral restraints put on him by God.]" [185]

The Bible depicts Satan as a force of Evil, but here the Mason learns that he is a "force created for good." Satan is "an instrument of Free Will," meaning that Satan wants man to exercise his own free will, by deciding for himself what is right and wrong.

And to show the reader that Mr. Pike meant exactly that, he repeated the thought on page 94:

". . . the freedom of the man lies in his reason." [186]

So man is not totally free because God restricts man's freedom to think and to reason, by confining him with "Moral Absolutes." According to Pike, man is not totally free if he must obey the teachings of God.

This is the thinking of the Masonic Lodge.

We have seen that this is consistent with the other thoughts of Mr. Pike as recorded in his book entitled MORALS AND DOGMA.

So Mr. Pike is awaiting the day when Lucifer will free man from the alleged tyranny of God!

And the reader is asked to "doubt it not!"

And to conclude this section, all of what Mr. Pike said in his book may be summed up in this final quotation, taken from page 274:

> "Behold the object, the end, the results, of the great speculations and logomachies [defined as: "contention or strife in words only, or an argument about words"] of antiquity; the ultimate annihilation of evil, and restoration of Man to his first estate [meaning a return to the Garden of Eden where Man can live without the God of the Bible and His moral teachings] by a Redeemer, a Massayah, a Christos, the incarnate Word, Reason, or Power of Deity." [187]

Let the record show that Mr. Pike was not referring to the Biblically predicted return of Jesus Christ when he wrote about the return of a "Christos."

He was talking about the appearance of someone else who will free man by freeing his power to "Reason."

151

He was talking about a man-god who will lead the world away from "the tyranny of God." He will claim to be a man who will permit each man to decide for himself what is right and wrong.

Those who believe this man is needed argue that he is now on the earth (remember that I am writing this book in September of 1997) and that his name is Lord Maitreya.

And Mr. Pike believes that the day when he will make his presence known to all of the people on the earth is near!

You read it in his own book!

And if you want to know more about this man called Lord Maitreya and the future that he will bring with him, may I suggest that you read my book entitled THE NEW WORLD ORDER and watch my video by the same name.

This person is discussed there so that you will know that there are millions of people who believe that his claims about being this "Christos" are truthful and that he is on the earth now, awaiting his "day of announcement," the day he will disclose himself and his mission.

The Masons are waiting for that day as well.

So, if you want to see actual photographs of this man taken within the last several years, you can see them in my 14 hour lecture series, on video, entitled THE NEW WORLD ORDER. Details about it and all of my other materials are in the 14 page catalog that can be obtained from the publisher.

So, the Masons are expecting someone to lead them into a world where there will be no restrictions on the individual's right to "reason." In this world, man will be free to decide for himself in all things.

This position was confirmed with this quotation from Mr. Pike:

> "In these degrees you become pledged to the cause of true Freedom, of the PEOPLE as contradistinguished from the mob and populace; of Free Thought, Free Speech and Free Conscience [free from the restraints of God.] . . . ;" [188]

According to the Masons, man's desire is to be free of any restraints on his freedom. Religion is not to instruct him how to lead a "good" life. He must be free to choose his own course of action because he must be free to choose whatever action pleases him.

This is the vision of the future for the Mason. What Mr. Pike is saying is that the God of the Bible gave man free choice. Then that God restricted his free choice by teaching him to do or not to do certain things by stating: "Thou shalt . . . " and "Thou shalt not . . . ."

For man to be totally free to make all of his own decisions, he must remove God and his moral absolutes from the world. Then man will be completely free to exercise his "free choice." This is what Mr. Pike is saying. Additional proof comes from other quotations from Mr. Pike:

> "We must be well assured that you are sovereign over yourself and a king over your own passions [No government and no religion can tell you how to live your life.]" [189]

> "Masonry is of no Church, but it respects all, so far
> and so long as they only teach and persuade, and allow
> full freedom of thought and freedom of conscience,
> and the right of private judgment." [190]

This idea of Mr. Pike is a hard idea to fathom. If a Christian
goes to a Bible-believing church and that church tells him that
the God in the Bible has instructed him not to commit an act
of rape, for instance, Mr. Pike appears to be saying that the
Christian is to come out from that church, because "no
church" has a right to restrict your "right of private judg-
ment."

This is utter nonsense!

A Christian freely chooses to follow Christ, and when he does
so he will wish to obey His commandments or moral teachings. But Pike says that "no church" has the right to expect its
members to follow a righteous path.

Mr. Pike continues:

> "As Masons we deny the right of any Church or Pon-
> tiff or Council to prescribe to men what they shall be-
> lieve . . . ." [Here it is again. This is pure nonsense. I
> will further explain why I believe this way a little later
> in this book.] [191]

> "When the mob governs, man is ruled by ignorance;
> when the church governs, he is ruled by superstition;
> and when the state governs, he is ruled by fear. Before
> men can live together in harmony and understanding,
> ignorance must be transmuted into wisdom, supersti-
> tion into an illumined faith, and fear into love." [192]

"I furthermore promise and swear that I will ever maintain the cause of the oppressed against the oppressor; of every people that struggles against Tyranny . . .; of all who defend . . . Free Thought, Free Conscience and Free Speech . . . ." [193]

So there it is. In his own words.

No church can dictate man's conscience. He must be free to make these decisions for himself!

The battle lines are being drawn!

chapter 16
SUMMARY OF
MORALS AND DOGMA

I believe it is fair to make the following conclusions from these quotations taken primarily from Albert Pike's book entitled MORALS AND DOGMA:

1. There is a secret message inside the book.

2. That secret is not plainly stated, but it has been revealed and must be searched for.

3. Some Masons who will read Mr. Pike's book will not be able to figure it out.

4. The secret is kept from those Masons not able to locate it themselves, even to the point that the Masons who know the secret will lie to conceal it from some of the Initiate Masons.

5. But, simply stated, that secret is:

The god worshiped by some of the Masons inside their lodge buildings, called the Great Architect of the Universe, is in reality
LUCIFER!

And that is the secret kept from the majority of the Masons, called "the first layer," by the use of lies and deception by the remainder of the Masons, called "the second layer." It is the single secret of Mr. Pike's book entitled Morals and Dogma.

And that anyone can know this secret, because MR. PIKE, perhaps the greatest Mason of all time, HAS TOLD THE WORLD HIMSELF in a book published by the "Mother Council of the world!"

And Mr. Pike is dramatically wrong when he says on page 530:

> "And if men were all Masons . . . that world would be
> a paradise . . . ." [194]

Because Pike's world where only Masons live is so horrible that the moral mind cannot comprehend it. Picture this "paradise" as being a state where each man decides for himself what is right and wrong. Each man is "a law unto himself." That is called "Anarchy." And only the strong will survive.

So, if you want to know more about the Masonic future, where mankind will have asked the Masons to be their "sovereigns and pontiffs," you might consider reading my second book, entitled THE NEW WORLD ORDER.

Because it is the future of America, and ultimately the world. And it will come to pass unless you understand what it is and then inform others. And then prevent it!

The choice is yours!

But it is worse than this!

May I suggest that you read on!

chapter 17
A QUOTE FROM LEGENDA

Albert Pike wrote many other books, but one, entitled LE-GENDA OF THE ANCIENT AND ACCEPTED SCOTTISH RITE OF FREEMASONRY FOR THE SOUTHERN JURISDICTION OF THE UNITED STATES, has a quotation that is very revealing and should be examined before the reader proceeds with further study of the goal of the Masonic Lodge. Mr. Pike wrote the book in 1888, and it was published by the 33rd Degree Council when they had their headquarters in Charleston, South Carolina.

The book appears to be out-of-print, but has been reprinted by the Kessinger Publishing Company in Kila, Montana. They claim to "publish rare and out-of-print books on Alchemy, Ancient Wisdom, Astronomy, Esoteric Freemasonry, Occult, Spiritual, Symbolism, Tarot, plus many more!"

In a section of the book entitled PUBLISHER'S INTRODUCTION, the publisher says that LEGENDA is "a series of monographs intended to supplement the ritualistic instruction" of MORALS AND DOGMA, Pike's other great work.

But the key revelation of this book is the evidence that Albert Pike, perhaps the greatest Mason of all time, did not believe in a "CREATOR GOD." This quote, taken from page 109 of Pike's comments on the Twenty-eighth Degree, should clear up the question once and for all as to who the god of the Masons, called THE GREAT ARCHITECT OF THE UNIVERSE, really is. Because, it is not the God of the Bible, the God who created the universe! Because Albert Pike, the man who wrote the rituals for all of the Degrees, the man who has a statue erected to him by the 33rd Degree Council in Washington D.C., the man who was the "leader of the worldwide Masonic movement," stated that a belief in a Creator God was a "monstrous absurdity."

The first ten words of the Bible, Genesis 1:1, read:

> "In the beginning God created the heaven and the earth."

Notice that this creation had to be a creation out of nothing, since the word "beginning" implies that there was a time before the creation when there was nothing. There would have been no need for a "beginning" if God took existing materials to form the universe.

But Albert Pike renounced the first ten words of the Bible when he wrote this:

> ". . . nothing is produced from nothing, . . . because existence can no more cease to be than nothing can cease to be.
>
> To say that the world came forth from nothing is to propose a monstrous absurdity.
>
> Everything that Is proceeds from that which was, and consequently nothing of that which is can ever not be." [195]

Please take notice that the capitalization of the capital letter "I" in the word "Is" in the last sentence of this quotation was possibly done by Albert Pike, and may not be a typographical error. The rules of capitalization say that "Nouns and often also adjectives that refer to Deity" may be capitalized. Albert Pike capitalized the "I" and the implication is that he is acknowledging that matter is a deity. However, it must also be said that it could have been a typographical error in the original, so conclusions from the capitalization of the "I" cannot be fairly drawn.

However, there is no mistake about who the GREAT ARCHITECT OF THE UNIVERSE, the god of the Masons, is: he is NOT THE CREATOR GOD of the Bible!

Because to believe so is to believe in a "MONSTROUS ABSURDITY!"

Mr. Pike repeated this thought in his book entitled MAGNUM OPUS, on page 18 of his "closing instructions" of the 32nd Degree ritual. This is what he wrote:

> "As the world is unproduced and indestructible, as it had no beginning, and will have no end . . . ." [196]

If the world was "unproduced," there was no "producer." If it "had no beginning," it was not created out of nothing. If it was not created, there was no creator. If there is no creator, there is no God of the Bible, and to believe in one is to believe in a "monstrous absurdity."

So the Christians and the Jews who are Masons and who believe that the God of the Bible created the universe OUT OF NOTHING believe in a "MONSTROUS ABSURDITY."

Apparently in an effort to make certain that the Mason who read his books would not miss the point, Mr. Pike repeated the thought on page 66 of the 32nd Degree in his book entitled LEGENDA.

This is what he wrote:

"But it will certainly be difficult to prove, by any *direct* language of the Scriptures, that God *created* the Universe, and all Souls of men as well as worlds of matter, out of nothing." [197]

So the words in the Bible that read: "in the beginning, God created the heaven and the earth" are not "direct language" because, according to Mr. Pike, there are none in the Bible. Yet it can be proven that God *created* the universe out of nothing. (For the proof, please see my booklet entitled GOD EXISTS!) This is how Dr. Henry Morris phrased it in his book entitled THE DEFENDERS STUDY BIBLE:

"The laws of thermodynamics [this is the branch of physics that deals with the transformation of heat into other forms of energy] are the most universal and best-proved generalizations of science, applicable to every process and system of any kind, the First Law stating that no matter/energy is now being created or destroyed, and the Second Law stating that all existing matter/energy is proceeding irreversibly toward ultimate equilibrium and cessation of all processes. [Here he means that someday the universe will lose all of its heat, and there will be a heat equilibrium, because the universe will decay until all temperatures will be the same. All locations in the universe will be the same temperature. There will be no more "hot" and "cold."]

Since this eventual death of the universe has not yet occurred and since it will occur in time, if these processes [of decay] continue, the Second Law proves that time (and therefore, the space/matter/time universe) had a beginning.

The universe must have been created, but the First Law precludes the possibility of its self-creation. The only resolution of the dilemma posed by the First and Second Laws is that 'in the beginning God created the heaven and the earth.'" [198]

There is no confusion, because Albert Pike, perhaps the greatest Mason of all time, said it himself! At least three times! He is saying that THERE WAS NO CREATION!

And you may read it yourself on page 109, in Pike's comments on the Twenty-eighth Degree, in his book entitled LEGENDA, or on page 18 of "the closing instruction" of the 32nd Degree, or on page 66 of his explanation of the Thirty-second degree.

Perhaps we now know why Mr. Pike wrote this:

"The horse, the dog, the elephant, are as conscious of their identity as we are. THEY think, dream, remembe, argue with themselves, devise, plan, and _REASON_. What is the intellect and intelligence of the man but the intellect of the animal in a higher degree or larger quantity?" [199] (I added the emphasis)

Maybe the horse, the dog and the elephant have been able to "reason" it out that there was a creator God, but the "adepts," like Mr. Pike, haven't! But I am certain that the critics are saying that I have misunderstood these quotations by Mr. Pike. He certainly could not have said that to believe in a Creator God is to believe in a "monstrous absurdity."

I have in my possession a copy of a letter written by C. Fred Kleinknecht, the current Sovereign Grand Commander of the Supreme Council of the 33rd Degree. It was written on May 12, 1992 and was addressed to Rev. Pat Robertson, the author of the book by the same title as my second book, THE NEW WORLD ORDER.

Mr. Kleinknecht was writing to Rev. Robertson to let him know that he was taking exception to his utilization of a letter that Mr. Pike allegedly wrote some time before that Mr. Kleinknecht believes is bogus. I will discuss this letter allegedly written by Mr. Pike in a later chapter in this book. But the reason I mention Mr. Kleinknecht's letter now is because near the end of his two page letter, he says that:

"Albert Pike was a Trinitarian Christian [defined as: "one who believes in the doctrine of the Trinity of God." The Trinity of God is three beings in one God: Jesus, the Holy Spirit and the Father, all three constituting the Creator God!]"

So he was admitting that he is of the opinion that Mr. Pike believed in a Creator God!

But it is clear that Mr. Pike does not, because he wrote that to believe in the "Trinitarian" God as a Creator God is to "believe a monstrous absurdity."

But Mr. Kleinknecht wants us to believe that he was a "Trinitarian Christian."

Maybe the reader can make sense out of this apparent contradiction. Because I can't. You either believe in a creator God or you don't. Unless you're Albert Pike!

PART TWO

THE GOAL OF THE MASONS

This star represents GOD, all that is pure, virtuous, and good.

This star represents EVIL, all that is opposed to the good, pure and virtuous.

chapter 18
A STATEMENT

This has been a very difficult book to write, because most of the Masonic writers have not made their materials easy to understand. And it is hoped that the student of Masonry is beginning to understand why this is so. The Masons are obviously keeping "the Secret" from the rest of the world.

If there is a single secret inside Masonry, that the average person is not able to detect, and that even the overwhelming majority of the Masons is not to discover, those in possession of that secret must do all within their power to keep that mystery concealed, but still open to those whom they want to see it. This is a difficult, but not insurmountable, task.

Therefore, these Masons have constructed an elaborate maze in their writings, one that can be figured out only by those that they want to find their way through it. I believe that I have done that, even though I am not a member of the Masonic Lodge.

The problem then gets more difficult: if I have found the secret of Masonry, I must then reveal it in such a way that those who would not have seen it without my explanations must see it.

So, I have attempted to do that by locating the secret and then making it public. I have tried to make this information understandable.

But, as I have said many times before in my writings and lectures, I can only be accountable for the message, and not the response to the message.

All I can do is attempt to make the message as understandable as I can and then hope that those who read or hear it will be able to accept it.

I am earnest in my profession that I am hopeful that as you read this book you will see what the Masons believe in, because it is vital for all of those who love their freedom to do so.

I will presume that the Masons are hoping that I have failed in that task.

chapter 19
REFERENCES

I have often stated in my previous lectures and writings that I have built the case against Masonry by using their own materials. And that is true in this book as well.

As I remember, I started reading Masonic literature in 1984, when someone asked me to read MORALS AND DOGMA. I had completed a reading of that book when another friend of mine suggested that I read Manly P. Hall's book entitled THE SECRET TEACHINGS OF ALL AGES. These two books revealed to me just how much more there was to read in the field, so I eagerly continued my research.

I started reading the works of those writers, primarily Masons, who were writing about the "esoteric" mystery religion (once again, "esoteric" is defined by Webster's dictionary as being "intended for or understood by only a chosen few, as an inner group of disciples or initiates.") And I think it is important now to list the books that I have used in my book that prove my case against Masonry. These books are:

BOOKS BY ALBERT PIKE: a 33rd Degree Mason, and Past Sovereign Commander
LEGENDA OF THE ANCIENT AND ACCEPTED SCOTTISH RITE OF FREEMASONRY
THE PORCH AND THE MIDDLE CHAMBER, THE BOOK OF THE LODGE
LITURGY OF THE ANCIENT AND ACCEPTED SCOTTISH RITE OF FREEMASONRY
THE MAGNUM OPUS OR GREAT WORK
OLD CAHIER OF THE 33D DEGREE
BOOKS OF THE WORDS

BOOK BY HENRY C. CLAUSEN: 33rd Degree Mason, and
    Past Sovereign Grand Commander
  CLAUSEN'S COMMENTARIES ON MORALS AND
  DOGMA

BOOKS BY W. L. WILMSHURST: Past Provincial Grand
    Registrar (West Yorks)
  THE MEANING OF MASONRY
  MASONIC INITIATION

BOOK BY REX HUTCHENS: a 32nd Degree Mason but
    later elevated to the 33rd Degree
  A BRIDGE TO LIGHT

BOOKS BY JOHN J. ROBINSON: then not a member, but
    later became a 33rd Degree Mason
  BORN IN BLOOD, THE LOST SECRETS OF FREE-
  MASONRY
  A PILGRIMS PATH

BOOKS BY MANLY P. HALL: a 33rd Degree Mason
  THE LOST KEYS OF FREEMASONRY
  THE SECRET TEACHINGS OF ALL AGES
  WHAT THE ANCIENT WISDOM EXPECTS OF ITS
  DISCIPLES
  LECTURES ON ANCIENT PHILOSOPHY
  FREEMASONRY OF THE ANCIENT EGYPTIANS
  AMERICA'S ASSIGNMENT WITH DESTINY
  THE SECRET DESTINY OF AMERICA
  ORDERS OF THE QUEST

ENCYCLOPEDIA BY HENRY WILSON COIL: a 33rd
    Degree Mason
  COIL'S MASONIC ENCYCLOPEDIA

BOOKS BY ARTHUR EDWARD WAITE: Past Senior
    Grand Warden of Iowa
    A NEW ENCYCLOPAEDIA OF FREEMASONRY
    SOME DEEPER ASPECTS OF MASONIC SYMBOL-
    ISM
    THE SECRET TRADITION IN FREEMASONRY

BOOKS BY ALBERT MACKEY: a 33rd Degree Mason
    ENCYCLOPAEDIA OF FREEMASONRY, Volumes I
    and II
    SYMBOLISM OF FREEMASONRY

ENCYCLOPEDIA BY KENNETH MACKENZIE: 9th
    Degree Mason
    THE ROYAL MASONIC CYCLOPAEDIA

BOOK BY CARL H. CLAUDY: 33rd Degree Mason
    INTRODUCTION TO FREEMASONRY, Volumes I,
    II, and III

BOOK BY WILLIAM HUTCHISON: Master of the Ma-
    sonic Lodge of Concord at Barnard Castle
    THE SPIRIT OF MASONRY

I believe it is sufficient to say that if one cannot read the writings of the Masons themselves to know what they believe in, there is no way for anyone to know.

I believe that some of the books cited above are the writings of those Masons who know the secret.

I have read their books. And I have found the secret and I have exposed it here in this book.

chapter 20
THE LIGHT

As reported elsewhere in this book, the Masons are "seeking Light." This is confirmed in the books that I listed above. But, I will attempt to introduce the reader to additional material on why the Mason believes the search for "Light" is important.

Albert Pike wrote this on page 210 of his book entitled LITURGY:

> "In every Degree in Freemasonry, the Candidate seeks to attain Light." [200]

He explained that the Mason is encouraged to read some of his books in that search:

> "The Lectures of the Lodge of Perfection are contained in its Liturgy and Legenda and in the MORALS and DOGMA. By reading and study, you should make yourself familiar with them." [201]

So, the Mason is encouraged to read quotes like this one from Mr. Pike's book entitled LITURGY (previously cited in an earlier portion of my book):

> "It is for each individual Mason to discover the secret of Masonry [notice that here Mr. Pike repeats the claim that there is only ONE secret inside Masonry].
> . . . Masonry does not *inculcate* [defined as: "to teach by frequent repetitions"] her truths. She *states* them, once and briefly; or hints them, perhaps darkly; or interposes a cloud between them and eyes that would be dazzled by them." [202]

And this one from MAGNUM OPUS:

> "It is for each individual Mason to discover the secret
> of Masonry, by reflecting on its emblems, and upon
> what is said and done in the work. Seek and ye shall
> find [notice again that there is only "one secret."]" [203]

And then in another part of the same book, Mr. Pike says that
the secret is found through "reflection and study:"

> "To many of these symbols there are other meanings
> which it should be your study to discover for yourself.
> Often they are indicated to the initiate by a hint or a
> suggestion only . . . .
>   . . . it is the more incumbent on you, by reflection
> and study, to learn the true meaning for yourself." [204]

That thought is repeated in Mr. Pike's book entitled THE
PORCH AND THE MIDDLE CHAMBER. Here he has the
Worshipful Master tell the candidate in the Master Mason's
degree:

> "You have now made the first three of the seven sym-
> bolic Circuits or journeys [it is presumed that Mr. Pike
> is referring to the fact that during the initiation cer-
> emony, the Mason walks around the temple on a par-
> ticular route under the direction of one of the other
> members of the Lodge. This walk is called "circum-
> ambulation,"and represents, as Henry Wilson Coil puts
> it, "a rite of Sun-worship."] To call them symbolic is
> to announce that they have a mystic meaning. You
> must discover this for yourself." [205]

And this from Mr. Pike's book entitled LITURGY:

"These degrees are also intended to teach *more* than morals. The symbols and ceremonies of Masonry have more than one meaning. They rather *conceal* than *disclose* the Truth. They *hint* it only, at least; and their varied meanings are only to be discovered by reflection and study." [206]

But Mr. Pike teaches his reader that the secret begins with a study of the "Light" that the Mason is seeking. He has one of the Masonic officers ask the initiate in the Twelfth Degree of Masonry:

Q: "Of what art thou in search?"
Candidate: "Of wisdom."
Reply: "It is the true Masonic Light. He who obeys the Masonic law shall find it." [207]

Mr. Pike then explains that the Light involves "knowledge:"

"Knowledge is the most genuine and real of human treasures; for it is Light, as Ignorance is Darkness." [208]

And he brings this "knowledge" full circle when he traces it back to the "fruit of the tree of the knowledge of good and evil" in the Holy Bible. He wrote:

"The true use of knowledge is to distinguish good from evil." [209]

So the reader of Albert Pike learns that the "Light" that he is in search of involves "the knowledge of good and evil." And then that this knowledge comes from (a) god:

"Truth is the Light that emanates from God . . . ." [210]

Mr. Pike even has his Masons praying to this god, this time from the instructions on the 17th Degree, in his book entitled LITURGY:

"Hear us, our Father . . . .
    BE GRACIOUS UNTO US, OUR FATHER!
    We wander in the Desert in darkness, and turn anxiously to the East, and look longingly for the promised Light [presumably "the Christos."]
    SEND US THE DAWN OF DAY, OUR FATHER!
    Send us Thy Light, our Father . . . .
    THY LIGHT, TO BE THE LIFE OF MEN!" [211]

But Mr. Pike challenges the belief that this "god" that they pray to is the God of the Bible. He states that they worship the "true God" when he described the "Blazing Star"as a symbol:

"[it] represents the great Central Light, which so many nations have worshiped in the Sun, its representative; and the LETTER, surrounded by its splendors, is the Hebrew Initial of the name of the Great Archetype [defined as: "the model, the original pattern of which all beings are representations or copies"] of Light, the true God, whom all Masons revere." [212]

So Mr. Pike is teaching his fellow Masons that there is only one God, a "true God."

That must mean that he believes that this "true God" is not the God of the Bible because he is saying that only through Masonry can one learn who this "true God" is. What Mr. Pike is saying is that the Bible apparently does not reveal the identity of this "true God." Because if it did, there would not be a need for the Masons to create their organization.

And in this quote from MAGNUM OPUS, the reader further learns that only in Masonry can you learn the identity of this "true God:"

> ". . . man lost the perfect knowledge of the One True God, the Ancient Absolute Existence, the Infinite Mind and Supreme Intelligence . . . .
> We have returned again to the Primitive Truth; and that Truth is taught in Masonry." [213]

This "God" that the Masons pray to is the provider of "Light," the "light of Reason:"

> "The luminous pedestal, lighted by the perpetual and undying flame within, is a symbol of that light of Reason, given by God to man . . . . [what Mr. Pike is saying is that this god is the god of reason, because he will free man so that he can completely use his mind in determining for himself what is right and wrong.]" [214]

And this "God" is worthy of worship, according to this prayer in the 16th Degree:

> "O Lord our God! . . . Thou, Thou art the only God. [Here he offers the position that there is only one "God" in the universe, their god, the Great Architect of the Universe. Because, as we have seen, to believe in the other "God" is to believe in a "monstrous absurdity."]
> . . . the Armies of Light [apparently meaning the Masons and others] worship Thee!" [215]

And further proof is added by Mr. Pike that this "God" is revealed in Masonry:

". . . the Ancient and Accepted Rite . . . raises a corner
of the veil even in the degree of Apprentice; for in that
it declares that Masonry is a worship." [216]

And Manly P. Hall admits that most of the Masons will not
take, or have not taken, the necessary time to read the works
of their brothers that explain the true meaning of the symbols.
This is what he wrote in his book entitled THE LOST KEYS
OF FREEMASONRY:

> "The initiated brother realizes that his so-called sym-
> bols and rituals are merely blinds fabricated by the
> wise to perpetuate ideas incomprehensible to the aver-
> age individual. [Here he means, once again, that the
> average individual is not able to see the truth con-
> cealed in the symbols and rituals.] He also realizes that
> few Masons of today know or appreciate the mystic
> meaning concealed within these rituals. [So, only the
> Masons inside the second layer are intelligent enough
> to see the truth behind the symbols and rituals.]" [217]

So if you understand these things, you are further along your
walk than the average Mason who has simply not taken the
time to read the works of the Masons who are attempting to
let them know what "the secret" is behind their "blinds."

chapter 21
"MASONRY
IS NOT A RELIGION"

This is the official position of the Masonic Lodge: they deny that their fraternity is a religion. (We have already examined this thought earlier in this book. I am attempting now to explain it more thoroughly.) Their official position was stated in Albert Pike's book entitled MAGNUM OPUS, on page 10 of the 29th Ritual:

"Masonry is not a religion." [218]

But some of the Masons, the Masons who know the secret, say that this statement is not true (even Mr. Pike contradicts himself on this issue.) The following quote comes from Manly P. Hall, from page LXXX of his book entitled SECRET TEACHINGS OF ALL AGES:

"Despite statements to the contrary [here Mr. Hall admits that the Masons are lying to the public when they say that "masonry is not a religion,"] Masonry is a religion seeking to unite God and man by elevating its initiates to that level of consciousness whereon they can behold with clarified vision the workings of the Great Architect of the Universe." [219]

In the quotation that follows, Mr. Pike admits that he is lying as well when he makes the statement that "Masonry is not a religion:"

"Every Masonic Lodge is a temple of religion; and its teachings are instruction in religion." [220]

In fact, according to Albert Pike, the Mason is asked about religion during "the Reception" of the 18th Degree. His book reports that the candidate is asked:

> "My Brother, there are several questions that you must answer sincerely and truly . . . .
>   1st: What is your religious belief?" [221]

But Mr. Pike clears up the mystery as to why they ask this question:

> "So every Masonic Lodge is a Temple of Religion; its officers, ministers of religion; its teachings, instruction in religion." [222]

The reader might wish to ask how it is that the same author can say that "Masonry is not a religion" and then say that their lodges are "a temple of religion." One can only conclude that this is intentional, and that its purpose must be to further cloud the issue for both the Mason and non-Mason. But only Mr. Pike and the other Masons who know the secret know for certain.

But, it is clear that "Masonry is a religion."

chapter 22
THE "TRUTH"
IS "LIGHT"

The Mason is told in the Blue Lodge initiation ceremonies that the "Light" that he is seeking is "Masonic truth." But the Masons who know the secret know that this statement is not true.

Albert Pike wrote that the candidate in the 18th ceremony, and then in the 29th Degree, is taught:

> ". . . since what any man believes, is Truth, to *him*: and none can say with certainty that he hath the same possession of Truth as of a chattel [defined as: "sometimes, a slave; in Law, any item of immovable property except real estate."]" [223]

> "No man can say that he hath as sure possession of the truth as of a chattel.
>   When men entertain opinions diametrically opposed to each other, and each is honest, who shall decide which hath the Truth; and how can either say with certainty that *he* hath it!
>   We know not what *is* the truth. [This statement should offend both the Christians and the Jews, because they believe that "the truth" is "knowable" because it has been released in the Bible.]
>   That we ourselves believe and feel absolutely certain that our own belief is true, is in reality not the slightest proof of the fact, seem it never so certain and incapable of doubt to us. [This last part of the last sentence of this quotation appears to have used the

word "seem," which appears to be an inappropriate word. I checked again and it is an accurate quotation.]" [224]

So it appears that Mr. Pike is teaching the Mason that there is no truth, even the Masonic "truth." But, in other writings, he has one of the officers of the Lodge ask another officer the following questions in the 14th Degree, the purpose of which appears to inform the candidate that there is only one "truth:"

Q: "What are you, my Brother?
A: I *am* your Brother; a Gr∴, El∴, Perf∴ and Sub∴ Mason [that means Grand, Elect, Perfect and Sublime Mason;] who have undergone all the tests and trials, and obtained the reward of my labours.
Q: What is your reward?
A: The knowledge of the True God . . . ;" [225]

It is interesting to note that these questions and answers occur in the 14th Degree. Here the candidate who is listening to these words learns that the Mason will learn "the knowledge of the True God."

It is certainly not a coincidence that it used to be after the candidate completed the 14th Degree that he was given a copy of Albert Pike's book entitled MORALS AND DOGMA, the book that reveals the fact that "Lucifer, the light-bearer" is the God of the Masons. So the "knowledge of the True God" is given to the Mason in the book entitled MORALS AND DOGMA, and as we have seen, he cannot learn that in the rituals he is proceeding through.

This is an amazing revelation by Mr. Pike. He just admitted that "Lucifer, the Light-bearer" is "the True God," and that truth, that "knowledge," is the reward for the Mason who figures it out!

No, the Masons are wrong.

Masonry IS a religion: the religion of Lucifer!

The "second layer" Masons have said it themselves!

chapter 23
THE WARFARE

The next step in the Masonic literature in partially exposing the Secret inside the Lodge occurs when the Mason is told that what he has involved himself in is a war. Mr. Pike informs the reader that:

> "You see, my Brother, what is the meaning of Masonic Light. You see why the East of the Lodge, where the initial letter of the Name of the Deity overhangs the Master, [I believe it is the letter "G", variously described by the Masons as standing for "God," "geometry," or "gnosis," the last of which is defined as: "the positive knowledge of spiritual truth"] is the place of Light.
>
> Light, as contradistinguished from darkness, is Good, as contradistinguished from Evil: and it is that LIGHT, THE TRUE KNOWLEDGE OF DEITY, THE ETERNAL GOOD, for which Masons in all ages have sought.
>
> Still Masonry marches steadily onward towards that Light that shines in the great distance, the Light of that day when Evil, overcome and vanquished, SHALL fade away and disappear forever, and Life and Light be the one law of the Universe, and its eternal Harmony." (I added the emphasis to show that they believe they shall be victorious in this war.) [226]

Notice here how Mr. Pike seems to be saying exactly what any moral person would say when committing his life to the opposition to "evil." That is, who amongst a moral society would not be in favor of opposing murder, plunder, etc. And to those who have read Mr. Pike's admonition about reversing things, it makes sense to reverse the meaning of this statement: when he refers to "evil," he is referring to "good," and when he says "good," he is referring to "evil."

The Mason is then encouraged to become "a soldier" in this warfare. According to Albert Pike, the initiate is asked this question:

> "Are you willing to become the soldier . . . and enlist in this new crusade against the powers of evil, and all the wrongs that vex and afflict humanity?"

And the candidate is encouraged to answer:

> "I am." [227]

The Mason takes at least two oaths, the first at the 18th Degree, and the second at the 30th Degree:

> "Kneel with us, then, my Brother, and unite with us in imploring the assistance, protection and support of Him to whom we owe our Being; and to who alone can make Darkness Light, and bring the tyranny of Evil to an end." [228]

The Candidate then kneels on one knee before the Gr∴ Commander (apparently this refers to the Grand Commander, one of the officials in the Masonic Lodge) who says to him:

> "My Brother, you desire to unite yourself to an Order which has labored in silence and secrecy for more than 500 years for the attainment of a single end [here the Masons acknowledge that they have only one goal,

one that I believe I have found and will reveal a little later in my book,] in which it has as yet only partially succeeded [they have been working at it, but the day of final victory is still in the future,] and to which, if you join us, you must devote yourself."

And then he takes the following oath:

"Do you promise and swear, by all that you hold most dear and sacred, that you will hereafter consider your-self the Soldier of Truth, Justice, Order, Law, and Suffering Humanity; and that YOU WILL WAGE CONTINUAL WAR, by all legitimate and proper means that may comport with the character of a Mason, a Knight and a gentleman,

I would like to interrupt the quotation at this point to remind the reader that the Mason has been taught that there are no "moral absolutes," and that "Often one man and many men must be sacrificed, in the ordinary sense of the term, to the interest of the many." This teaching now has extra importance when the Mason is told that he is involving himself in the "waging [of a] continual war." He is telling the Mason how they are to fight "the war." Now, back to the quotation:

against all tyranny over the mind or body, temporal [defined as: "civil or secular rather than ecclesiastical"] or spiritual, and all ignorance, fraud and wrong-doing . . . ;" (I placed the emphasis in the quotation.)

In his book entitled MAGNUM OPUS, Mr. Pike gives a little different version of the same oath taken at the 30th Degree.

This is how he reports it in this book:

"We do most sacredly and solemnly vow, and to each other renewedly pledge our Masonic and Knightly Word, that we will, by all legal and honourable [his spelling of the word] means, avenge the murderers of our predecessors of this Order . . . ." [229]

Notice that the Mason takes a "solemn vow" to avenge the murderers of their Masonic predecessors. Each and every Mason takes this vow at the 30th Degree, even those who claim that they did not understand the concealed meaning.

As mentioned earlier, Henry C. Clausen, like Mr. Pike, a former Sovereign Grand Commander of the Southern Jurisdiction of the Scottish Rite, wrote a book entitled CLAUSEN'S COMMENTARIES in 1974. His book, like some of the ones written by Mr. Pike, is official Masonic literature, since it was published by the 33rd Degree Council. He also informs the Mason just how important it is that they vow to oppose "spiritual despotism." This is what he wrote:

"This is one of the mandatory Degrees that humanizes the old lesson of vengeance. The candidate vows in the solemn presence of death that he will oppose spiritual despotism and political tyranny . . . . [that means that he will oppose religion and government.]
. . . symbolic action is taken to spurn all attempts of any church or state [here he confirms that "religion" and "government" are the correct interpretations of the two symbols of "despotism and tyranny"] to crush man's liberty, lessen his freedom, or degrade and detract from his worship of the supreme spiritual power or his choice" [meaning that they believe that man's freedom is restricted by the "moral absolutes" of God.] [230]

But the initiate must read the following explanation in one of Mr. Pike's books to assist him in understanding the nature of the battle he is engaging himself in. Mr. Pike wrote:

"Behold the object, the end, the result, of the great speculations and logomachies [defined as: "contention in or about words; a war of words"] of antiquity: the ultimate annihilation of evil [meaning the annihilation of religion and government,] and restoration of Man to his first estate [meaning the re-creation of The Garden of Eden,] by a Redeemer, a Christos, the incarnate Word, Reason or Power of Deity." [231]

So the Mason learns that the purpose of Masonry is to replace "evil," meaning the God of the Bible and His teachings, with Lucifer, the "good" god of "Light." And to re-create Heaven on this earth, such as was in the Garden of Eden where Man lived in the presence of God. But in this case, the new "God" will be Lucifer!

And the following quotation illustrates the motive for the Mason's desire to dethrone the God of the Bible. Albert Pike wrote:

"Men are good. Evil institutions [meaning religion and government] alone have made them bad [by setting up standards that teach them that man sins when he violates God's law;] and it is the duty of Masonry and of every Knight to aid in leading them back to the truth [meaning that the Mason should be free of God's restraints on his freedom.]

For much still remains to be done. Tyranny is startled and weakened, but not overthrown. The chains still weigh on human thought and conscience . . . .

187

It is the old contest between Good and Evil, between the Sons of Light and the Children of Darkness,
between Hercules and the giant Antaeus." [232]

The dictionary says that Antaeus was "a giant wrestler who
was invincible while he touched the earth. Hercules strangled
him while holding him off the ground." Is it possible that this
symbolically means that Hercules is the ancient mystery religion and that Antaeus is God's religion, powerful on earth,
but powerless in heaven?

The Mason is then brought step by step to the position of
knowing just who or what his fraternity believes is the "enemy" in this "war." He is first taught that he might have to
"punish" the enemy at the 30th Degree, the degree called the
Knight Kadosh degree. Mr. Pike wrote:

"To be true, just, and upright is the basis of all virtue
and excellence, without which neither of these can exist. Especially these qualities are essential to the character of a true Knight Kadosh, who must be always
frank and true, and even called on to punish, must not
forget that justice is never to be violated." [I added the
underlining.] [233]

The Mason even makes this "war" in which the Mason will
"punish" the "evil-doer" the subject of prayer. The following
quotation is taken from the invocation in the Thirtieth Degree
ceremony:

"Oh! Omnipotent and Infinite Wisdom and Reason,
Holy and Merciful! . . . Source and Sovereign of the
Universe! . . . Eternal Reason Absolute! [Here the
Mason acknowledges his belief that no God has the

right to interfere with his right to totally control his "reason."] . . . Thou art the only Light whose splendors can dissipate the darkness that vails [spelled this way in the book entitled LITURGY] Nature from our gaze . . . . Purify us and give us strength, and let Thy Holy Kingdom come at last [the Masons are praying for a kingdom where there will be neither religion nor government, a NEW WORLD ORDER] and with it the end of all the wrongs that oppress and crush Humanity! AMEN! So mote it be!" [234]

So the Mason becomes a "soldier" in a war. He prays to the Masonic god that he will be victorious in the conflict. He is then provided with a sword:

"Receive this sword, . . . with which you are hereafter to war against error, vice, wrong and injustice, and defend the rights of men, and the cause of the oppressed against the oppressor." [235]

So the Mason is slowly being brought to the position of knowing that he can be expected to use violence against "those who oppress humanity." The sword appears to be symbolic of his permission to use violence if it is needed to conquer the enemy in this "war."

He is also told about a symbolic axe that he can use in this warfare. This quotation comes from Rex Hutchens:

"The axe should remind the Mason of the march of civilization and progress which requires him to hew the poisonous trees of intolerance, bigotry, superstition, uncharitableness and idleness to let in the light of truth and reason upon the human mind." [236]

189

Pike starts explaining who the real enemy is in the 19th Degree:

> "In the NINETEENTH degree you were taught that . . . the Human Race must wait with patience for the comin of the eternal reign of Good, when the feet of Truth, Honor and Charity SHALL have crushed the triple-headed serpent of Falsehood, Baseness and Intolerance." (I added the emphasis once again to illustrate the fact that they believe that they will be successful in their quest.) [237]

Notice that Mr. Pike refers to the "triple-headed" serpent. It appears as if the Mason is being conditioned, I believe, to see the connection between these "three" serpents and the "triune God" of the Bible.

And that conditioning continues because it is here that he officially learns for the first time just who his oath of action is against:

> "The Serpent, writhing in chains, has to us a particular signification. It was promised that the offspring of the woman should bruise the Serpent's head. Fulfill thou the prophecy!" [238]

To the casual observer somewhat familiar with the Bible, this part of the ceremony appears to be in accordance with Genesis Chapter 3, Verse 15. But on closer examination, the reader will observe that this Masonic quotation is different from the quotation in the Bible. I will first quote the entire Biblical verse, and then dissect it by explaining what I believe it means. Then, I will compare it to the Masonic version. The Bible reads in Genesis Chapter 3, Verse 15:

"And I will put enmity between thee and the woman, and between thy seed and her seed; it shall bruise thy head, and thou shalt bruise his heel."

This is what I believe that Scripture teaches:

"And I [meaning the Lord God, the God of the Bible] will put enmity [defined as: "the bitter attitude or feelings of an enemy; hostility; antagonism"] between thee [meaning the Devil] and the woman [meaning Eve, but actually she represents all of mankind]; and between thy [the Devil's] seed and her [meaning Eve's] seed [the word "seed" as used here means the future seed of Eve: Jesus Christ, for reasons that are discussed in the following paragraph;] it [this enmity between the Devil and mankind] shall bruise thy head [meaning the head of the woman's seed, meaning in this case Jesus Christ,] and thou [the woman, or her seed] shalt bruise his [meaning Lucifer's] heel."

So the Bible teaches the reader that Satan will bruise "the woman's head." There is nothing in that Scripture that teaches that "the offspring of the woman should bruise the Serpent's head." So, the Masons have added a completely different line to these verses of Scripture, perhaps in an attempt to convince the Christian or the Jew who is not totally aware of the correct Scripture that their statement is in accordance with those Scriptures.

Dr. Henry Morris, the President of the Institute for Creation Research, and a Christian, wrote that the Bible's reference to "the seed of the woman" can only be an allusion to a future descendant of Eve who would have no human father. He explained that:

> "Biologically, a woman produces no seed, and except in this case Biblical usage always speaks only of the seed of men. This promised Seed would, therefore, have to be miraculously implanted in the womb . . . .
>
> This prophecy [that Satan would bruise Eve's head] thus clearly anticipated the future virgin birth of Christ." [239]

So the Bible teaches that Satan will "bruise" Jesus Christ, and that He in turn will "bruise" Satan's heel. Biblical scholars interpret this to mean that Satan will later arrange for the crucifixion of Jesus, but that in the end, He will remove Satan from the world scene. The Masons seem to be saying that Lucifer will resist and be victorious.

But notice that the Masons have it backwards. The Bible teaches that it is the devil who will bruise the woman's seed, meaning Jesus Christ. Yet they wish that the "offspring of the woman should bruise the Serpent's head." This can only mean that they consider themselves to be the "offspring of the woman" who is to "bruise" the head of the woman, meaning Jesus Christ. So they consider Jesus to be the "Serpent." That is what Mr. Pike was saying in this verse.

There can be no doubt about it. The Masons are telling their members that they are to bruise the future offspring of the woman: Jesus Christ!

Once again, the Masonic quote is as follows:

> "The Serpent, writhing in chains, has to us a particular signification. It was promised that the offspring of the woman should bruise the Serpent's head. Fulfill thou the prophecy!" [240]

So, to make the point again, they are saying that they consider themselves to be "the offspring of the woman," and that sometime in the future they are to bruise the "head" of the Serpent," meaning that they consider "the Serpent" to be the "head" of the woman, meaning Jesus. There is nothing in the Bible that teaches this, so they have stated their own "prophecy" and then they tell the Mason to "fulfill" it.

So, once again, we are to reverse the thought, as we have been taught by Albert Pike:

> "*What is Superior is as that which is Inferior, and what is Below is as that which is Above . . . .*" [241]

We, the average people, are to reverse things, and then what Mr. Pike is saying makes sense.

And for the third time, so there can be no doubt about what he means, Mr. Pike is saying that they consider themselves to be the "offspring of the woman" and the "woman's offspring" is to bruise "the Serpent's head," meaning that they must consider the Christian religion to be the "Serpent," and Jesus, its head, to be their target. And they are told to "fulfill the prophecy!" And that it is a "war" they are engaging themselves in.

Later in the ceremony, the Mason is told that he is to "bruise" three heads. The quotation continues as Mr. Pike explains the ritual inside the first and last brackets. The brackets inside the others are mine:

> "[The candidate is caused to step in succession on the three heads: and as he does so, the Th∴ P∴ [I can find no direct explanation of who this officer of the Masonic Lodge is, because Mr. Pike does not explain

193

what the "Th∴" stands for, but he does explain that the "P∴" stands for "Puissant." According to Mr. Pike, these two abbreviated words stand for the title of "the Master" for this degree, apparently referring to the Worshipful Master, the "President" of the Lodge. The dictionary defines "puissant" as: "strong, powerful"] says, at each step respectfully]:

> *So shall the foot of* TRUTH *crush* ERROR!
> *So* HONESTY *and* HONOUR [his spelling in the original] *trample on* FALSEHOOD!
> *So* CHARITY *tread in the dust* INTOLERANCE!" [242]

So the initiate Mason is asked to "crush" three skulls during the 19th Degree of the Ritual. The reader will learn in a later chapter of this work that the Mason will once again see three skulls at the 30th Degree

He is then told two things: one, that the war is ongoing, meaning that it is something he must commit to for the long haul, and two, he learns that the ultimate goal is the conquest of the world. First, Mr. Pike tells the Mason:

> "For these outrages we righteously swear to detest these monsters and to wage eternal war against them. There shall be no peace, no truce, no armistice between them and us, henceforward forever." [243]

Then he tells him:

> "And thus the warfare against the powers of evil [it appears as if he is referring to "government" and "religion"] that crushed the Order of the Temple [meaning the Knights Templar, the grandfather to Masonry]

194

goes steadily on, and Freedom marches ever onward toward the conquest of the world." [244]

So there will be no accommodation between the two warring sides. There will be no compromise. The Mason will not rest until their opponent is totally destroyed.

Notice that Mr. Pike stated that the opponent in this battle was a "monster." This is how he views "religion" and "government."

So the Mason takes an obligation that commits himself to battle for the rest of his life. He takes this obligation in the Knight Elu degree, the 9th of the 32:

> "I furthermore promise and swear that I will ever maintain the cause of the oppressed against the oppressor; of every people that struggles against Tyranny [meaning "government" and "religion"] . . .; of all who defend . . . Free Thought, Free Conscience and Free Speech [meaning those who wish to free themselves so that they can freely use their "reason."]" [245]

The word "elu," according to Mr. Mackey in his ENCYCLOPEDIA, is French and means "elected." These are the Masons "whose object is to detail the detection and punishment of the actors in the crime traditionally related in the Third Degree." They were "those of the Craft [meaning of Masonry] chosen or elected to make the discovery [of the criminals] and to inflict the punishment." [246]

So, the Elus are the Masons in the "second layer" who will punish the enemies of the Masonic Lodge: the "government" and "the church.."

195

And the reason he is taught these things is because it is his "duty" to mankind to involve himself in this war:

> "Masonry teaches . . . that resistance to power u-surped [defined as: "seized"] is not merely a duty which man owes to himself and to his neighbour, but a duty which he owes to his God . . . ."[247]

Keep these thoughts in mind as you read the following quotations taken from the 15th Degree Ritual (I am hopeful that the reader is now beginning to see what these references to "free thought, free conscience," etc. really mean):

> "The transition from slavery to liberty, or that from political or religious subservience [meaning both government and religion] to freedom of Thought and Conscience, is not to be effected instantaneously or even quickly, but only by a great and persistent struggle, in which there are often repulses and reverses, discouragements and apparent defeat . . . ." [248]
>
> "The restitution to men of the Primitive Truth, of rational and regulated Liberty, of Free Thought and the rights of Conscience; the regeneration of the Nations, and the establishment of that state of Toleration and Peace, which will make earth a fit temple for a God of Mercy and Loving-kindness [so Lucifer is now called "a God of Mercy and Loving-kindness."] [249]

In the opening of the Twentieth Degree, the *"Ven∴ M∴"* (it appears that this means the "Venerable Master," one of the officers,) asks the other Masons in the room:

> "Brethren in the North, what seek you to attain in Masonry?"

And the Orator, another Masonic official, responds:

> "LIGHT! The Light of *Liberty, Free Thought, Free Speech* for all Mankind: Free *Conscience,* Free *Action,* within Law the same for all [meaning freedom without constraints from religion and/or government.]" [250]

The exact nature of this battle should be clearer now in the mind of the student of Masonry. He is learning that this "war" is not against a standing army or revolutionaries equipped for battle. It is against the "TYRANNY" of those who oppose "free thought, free conscience and free speech."

The Mason has been taught in MORALS AND DOGMA that there are no moral absolutes. Those who wish to structure their society around a conviction that the God of the Bible demands a system of justice that convicts guilty people, are guilty of "despotism and tyranny" against the Mason and others who believe that their "free choice" allows them to make all decisions themselves, including such things as their own morality, punishment, and conscience.

The member of the Masons is beginning to learn that he has now engaged himself in a "war" against those who wish for a moral society. Manly P. Hall explained why:

> "The religious motion in the modern world is away from theology and all the artificial limitations set up by creeds and dogmas." [251]

So there you have it. Religion has "artificial limitations."

And because certain men on this earth believe that, they plan on creating a world without "religion."

197

chapter 24
VICTORY
IS CERTAIN

The soldier in the Masonic war is taught that "victory is certain:" his side will conquer their enemy. And the Mason can know for certain because he can read these quotations from Albert Pike's works:

". . . we can look on all the evils of the world, and see that it is only the hour before sunrise, and that the light is coming . . . ." [252]

". . . no true Mason despairs of final victory." [253]

"Light will finally overcome Darkness. [This is] . . . the religion and Philosophy of Masonry." [254]

". . . the doom of Tyranny is near at hand." [255]

"Ultimately, Good will prevail, and Evil will be overthrown." [256]

" . . . The ultimate disappearance of political and religious despotism, though perhaps remote, is certain . . . . The result is certain as the lapse of time." [257]

". . . the rule of Evil and Darkness is but temporary, and that that of Light and Good will be eternal." (Mr. Pike wrote the double "that.") [258]

"That the doctrines of Masonry will ultimately rule the Intellectual world, is certain . . . ." [259]

The Masons do not have a problem with knowing which side will win in this "war." Manly P. Hall wrote:

> ". . . the Mysteries must win, for they are on the side of the Great Plan." [260]

This was the first time I found the evidence that the Masons had a "Great Plan" for the world. I believe I have found out what it is as well, and I cover it in my booklet entitled AMERICA'S SECRET DESTINY. This would not be the place to discuss it since it is altogether a completely different subject and it takes some foundational work to understand. However, all should know what it is, and how it is going to affect our future.

But, it is appropriate that I continue my explanation of what is "evil" and what is "good."

chapter 25
SYMBOLISM

Adam Weishaupt, the founder in 1776 of a secret society known as the Illuminati, called himself by the secret code name of Spartacus, who led a revolution against the Roman government around 70 B.C. John Robison quotes Weishaupt under this name in his book entitled PROOFS OF A CONSPIRACY, and provides the reader with the reason that secret societies have prospered for centuries. He wrote:

> "Of all the means I know to lead men, the most effectual [defined as: "producing the desired result"] is a concealed mystery." [261]

Masonry is certainly aware of this truth, as they have often admitted that their entire system is complete with symbols concealing mysteries.

This quotation comes from Manly P. Hall:

> "The arcana [defined as: "a secret mystery"] of the ancient Mysteries were never revealed to the profane [defined as: "not initiated into the inner mysteries"] except through the media of symbols.
> Symbolism fulfilled the dual office of concealing the sacred truths from the uninitiated and revealing them to those qualified to understand the symbols." [262]

As we have examined the matter previously, the Masons admit that their symbols have multiple interpretations, and that the Mason is 1. instructed to discover what the other interpretations are that they might have and 2. given permission to lie in order to conceal their true meaning. (See the quotation on pages 77 and 78 by Albert Pike. This is the quotation that I previously cited that explained that the Masons who know the secret are "intentionally misleading" their fellow Masons in the explanations provided during the course of their initiation ceremonies.)

Manly P. Hall amplified this thought a little further in his book entitled THE LOST KEYS OF FREEMASONRY:

"The leading Masonic scholars of all times have agreed that the symbols of the Fraternity are susceptible of the most profound interpretation and thus reveal to the truly initiated certain secrets concerning the spiritual realities of life.

Freemasonry is therefore more than a mere social organization a few centuries old, and can be regarded as a perpetuation of the philosophical mysteries and initiations of the ancients." [263]

And Mr. Pike explained how the symbols were used:

"Symbols were used, to a great extent, to *conceal* particular truths from all except a favored few, who had the key to their meaning . . . .

The meaning of the Symbols of Masonry is not unfolded at once. We give you hints only, in general. You must study out the recondite [defined as: "hidden from sight"] and mysterious meanings for yourself. A single symbol often has several meanings." [264]

The Mason is also instructed with similar thoughts in "THE INTERROGATION" of the first degree of the Blue Lodge, called the Entered Apprentice Degree. Albert Pike wrote this to show just how important these symbols are:

"In whatever you see or hear in Masonry you will find a meaning. If it is hidden from you, search and you shall find it [here he is confirming that it is possible for anyone, including a non-Mason, to discover THE SECRET.]

Every symbol and all the ceremonial are replete with significance, and have a reason for being found here." [265]

So the Mason who does not read Masonic literature after he has completed his initiation ceremonies is missing the entire point, and he will never learn "the true knowledge of Deity."

But, as we have seen, it is something that "the second layer" of the Masons are challenging him to discover on his own.

chapter 26
THE ENEMY OF MASONRY

The fact that the Mason is at war with an enemy is made abundantly clear during the rituals between the 4th and the 32nd Degree of the Scottish Rite. But exactly who that enemy is, or, more importantly, what that enemy represents, is not made clear, and must be sought out by the Mason through "study and reflection." As the Masons have written, one of the sources of that information is the material that the Masons have published.

So, it is possible to determine just what the Masons mean by their symbols if only the student will take the time to read through the Masonic literature. And that is what I have done.

And the answer to that inquiry is startling, indeed. But, as will be demonstrated, it is something that anyone can know if they will only look hard enough.

Albert Pike started explaining just who, or what, the Masons consider to be their enemy in his discussion of the 30th Degree in his book entitled LITURGY:

> "You already know that Scottish Masonry is the enemy of all oppression, injustice, and usurpation.
> . . . she labors to emancipate men from their own ignorance, prejudices, and errors, which enslave them, in order that they may emancipate themselves from the bondage of despotism and the thraldom [defined as: "state of servitude, slavery"] of spiritual tyranny." [266]

So the candidate is once again exposed to the idea that the government and the church are the enemies of the Masons.

The initiate is told that he must "punish" his enemies as early as in the degree of Master Mason, meaning the third degree. Mr. Pike tells his readers that the Venerable Brother Senior Deacon asks the candidate:

"Why do you seek advancement when all the Craft is in distress?"

And the candidate answers:

"To be the better able to serve the Order, avenge innocence, and punish crime." [267]

In fact, he is told that he is not only to "punish" his enemies, he is to "destroy" them. In his book entitled A BRIDGE TO LIGHT, Rex Hutchens has the "candidate recite the duties taught him in the previous Degrees." The ninth of these "duties" is that he obligates himself to "destroy ignorance." [268]

In fact, in a quotation already cited, at the 17th Degree, the Mason prays for the victory over "darkness." This is how Mr. Pike wrote it:

"HEAR us, our Father . . . . BE GRACIOUS UNTO US, OUR FATHER!
We wander in the Desert in darkness, and turn anxiously to the East, and look longingly for the promised Light.
SEND US THE DAWN OF DAY, OUR FATHER!
SEND US THY LIGHT, OUR FATHER . . . . THY LIGHT, TO BE THE LIFE OF MEN!"[269]

In fact, this "Father," this "God of Light," is a good "god" according to this quotation, already cited, from Mr. Pike:

"The restitution to men of the Primitive Truth, of rational and regulated Liberty, of Free Thought and the rights of Conscience, the regeneration of the Nations, and the establishment of that state of Toleration and Peace, which will make earth a fit temple for a God of Mercy and Loving-kindness." [270]

Mr. Pike explained the reason for their concern in this quote, taken from the 30th Degree ritual of the Masonic Lodge:

"This Order has for its mission the avenging of an awful crime; not by the punishment of those that committed it; for they have long since gone before the Judge of all mankind [but] . . . by the destruction of that of which those men were but the miserable instruments; of arbitrary and irresponsible power, of tyranny over the conscience, of bigotry and intolerance; and by the establishment everywhere of well-ordered liberty . . . .

We work in secret, because we can so work more efficiently . . . .

Are you willing to devote yourself to the great purposes that I have indicated, and to become the sworn servant of the Order . . . ?" [271]

And the candidate answers: "I am."

It is important that I point out again that these Masons are out to destroy government and religion "in secret." This becomes important when you ask your friend or relative who is a Mason if my charges are correct. You cannot expect him to confirm my contentions. He must answer in the negative because of the oaths that he has taken as a Mason not to reveal any of their secrets.

So the only way you will know that I am right is to read their literature, because that is not secret, and as we are seeing, it truly informs all who read it what their goals are.

The "awful crime" that Mr. Pike referred to concerns the fate that befell Jacques deMolay, the twenty-second and last Grand Master of the Templars, in the fourteenth century. The Encyclopaedia of Freemasonry, written by Albert G. Mackey, 33rd Degree Mason, says this about Brother deMolay:

> "In 1298, . . . he [meaning deMolay] was unanimously elected Grand Master . . . .
>
> On the 12th of September, 1307, the order was issued [by a Pope] for the arrest of the Templars, and deMolay endured an imprisonment for five years and a half . . . .
>
> . . . he was subjected to the utmost indignities and sufferings for the purpose of extorting from him a confession of the guilt of his Order.
>
> . . . on the 11th of March, 1314, he was publicly burnt in front of the Cathedral of Notre Dame, in Paris." [I believe that the date of March 11th was also picked because of its symbology. March is the third month of the year, and that number times 11, the day on which the stake burning occurred, is 33, a key number to the Masons.]" [272]

Henry Wilson Coil adds a few additional details to the story of Jacques deMolay (the name is spelled a variety of ways: deMolai, deMolay, DeMolay, de Molay, etc.) by pointing out that he was:

> "the 22nd and last Grand Master of the Medieval Knights Templar. He was born about 1240 in Bur-

gundy and was burned at the stake at Paris, March 11, 1314.

> . . . when about to die at the stake, he cursed the Pope and King Philip the Fair, co-conspirators, [the two individuals that deMolay felt were responsible for his predicament, representing "religion" and the "government"] predicting the death of the former in 40 days and the latter within a year. His prophecy was vindicated [that means that they died within the predicted times.]" [273]

So another Mason teaches that it is their contention that Pope Clement V, the representative of the church, and Philip the Fair, according to Mr. Mackey, "the treacherous King of France," were "guilty of the most infamous deceit" and ultimately the death of Brother deMolay. But, even more importantly, notice once again that the two "tyrants" died within the predicted dates of deMolay's "prophecy." One can only presume that the Templars sought their vengeance against the two "tyrants" for the death of their leader, and succeeded in making his "prophecy" about their deaths come true.

But Mr. Pike points out that the king and the Pope were not the guilty ones, but that they were the representatives of the powers of the king and of the clergy for all time.

> "The good De Molay was a victim; but there was a nobler victim than he, the Order itself, of which he was but a part. In the persecution and destruction of that Order we have seen renewed, under another form, the legend, ever varying, yet ever the same, of Hiram and his assassins, [apparently meaning that the Masons intend to avenge the deaths of both Jacques deMolay and Hiram Abif. They have determined that they wish

to avenge the murder of Hiram, under a legend, because they know that there is no direct evidence of this
murder in the Bible] of Osiris and Typhon, of the Light
and the Darkness, of the Good Principle and the Evil.

And the three assassins of the Widow's Son [ap-
parently meaning Hiram Abif, called "the Widow's
son" by the Masons] we see reproduced in the Royal
Power of France, embodied in Philip le Bel; the Papal
Power, in Clement the 5th; and the rapacious [defined
as: "given to extorting what is coveted"]Order of the
Knights of Rhodes, or the Order of St. John of Jerusalem." [274]

So it appears as if the Masons are out to avenge the real murder of Jacques deMolay, and the imagined murder of Hiram
Abif.

But deMolay, the leader of the Knights Templar, and the mar-
tyr of the Masonic Lodge, did something else that also stands
as a symbol of the Masonic warfare. And as confirmation that
this interpretation is correct, another key Masonic writer, Kenneth MacKenzie, added his thoughts:

". . . he was burnt on the 12th September, 1314, in
front of the Cathedral of Notre Dame de Paris. He
summoned his murderers before the tribunal with his
dying breath - - [Pope] Clement [V] in forty days, and
Philip [le Bel, King of France] within a year; and it is
an historical fact that they obeyed the summons. [The
"they" who obeyed the summons must mean the
Knights Templar. It certainly could not refer to the
two men because that would mean that they committed suicide, and that seems to be extremely unlikely.
So the inference is that the Knights Templar murdered

them to fulfill the prophecy of their leader. So Mr. MacKenzie is confirming that they were murdered by the Knights Templar. This Mason has just made an amazing admission.]" [275]

And the Mason is told that he must also avenge the death of Jacques de Molay:

"Vengeance is symbolically invoked in certain of the high degrees [meaning in today's rituals] upon the murderers of James [James is the English name for the French name Jacques] de Molay." [276]

So the Masons are not through yet in avenging the murder of Jacques deMolay.

The circle, or is it a noose, is beginning to tighten.

chapter 27
THE ENEMIES

So far, the reader has been exposed to only a series of small clues as to who the combatants are in this struggle.

It now becomes appropriate to more clearly identify the two sides.

One who attempted to do that, albeit in symbolic language, was Albert Pike in his book entitled LITURGY. This is what he wrote:

> "The long war between the Evil and the Good, between MICHAEL and his angels, and the Dragon and his angels, shall end; and the Serpent and his angels shall be overcome, and shall pass away and be seen no more forever; . . . .
> Thou wilt, in due time, assert Thy power . . . when evil shall no longer reign." [277] (Emphasis in original)

This is an extremely important quotation from Mr. Pike. Notice that he is separating the warring factions into two sides in the heavenly war before Satan was expelled from heaven. He is saying that "Michael and his angels," meaning the forces of God, were at war with the forces of "the Dragon," meaning the Devil. (The Devil is referred to as "the dragon" in the Book of Revelation, the final book of the Bible.) But he does not say either of these forces will be "overcome;" he says that the "Serpent and his angels" shall be "overcome." He does not say which of the two sides he considers to be "the Serpent and his angels." It could be "Michael's" side or it could be "the dragon's" side. So, Mr. Pike is not saying which side he considers to be "the Serpent and his angels."

But Mr. Pike does provide two clues that he does not believe that "Michael and his angels" are the "good" forces in this "long war," but are the "Serpent and his angels."

First, notice that he states that this is the "war between Evil and Good." Most Bible scholars traditionally call this "the battle between Good and Evil," choosing to put "Good" first and "Evil" second." But Mr. Pike has reversed it. He has "Evil" first and "Good" second.

Then Mr. Pike identifies the combatants: he puts "Michael and his angels" first, and ""the Dragon and his angels" second. That could mean that he considers "Michael and his angels" to be the forces of "Evil," and "the Dragon and his angels" to be the "forces of "Good." That would mean that he is calling "God's" forces the side of "Evil," and "the Dragon's" side the "forces of Good." This, of course, would be consistent with some of the other writings of Mr. Pike that we have examined.

So he appears to be predicting that the "forces of Evil," mean-in the forces of God will be overcome by the "forces of Good," meaning those of the Devil.

But more importantly, this is an excellent opportunity to apply Mr. Pike's strategy in reversing things in accordance with his teaching:

> *"What is Superior is as that which is Inferior, and what is Below is as that which is Above . . . ."* [278]

If the student applies this thought to this quote, the result is that "Michael and his angels," thought to be the "the Good" side, become "the Evil" side. In other words, reverse what you traditionally believe to arrive at the truth.

So Pike is saying that the God of the Bible, symbolized as "the Serpent," will be overcome at the end of this war. (Remember that Pike told his readers to "reverse" things: if you read the quotation with a Biblical mind, you think that it means that God will overcome the devil. But when you understand what I have chosen to call "the principle of Reversal," you can understand what Mr. Pike is saying. Quite clearly, but in symbolic language, he is saying that "Michael and his angels" are Lucifer and his angels, and it is "the Serpent and his angels," meaning the God of the Bible and his angels, who will be overcome. It appears to be the reverse of the casual reading of the quotation.)

So he is saying that the vanquished foe, the God of the Bible, is "evil" and will "no longer reign."

So, according to Mr. Pike, the Christians have it backwards when they claim that God, in the form of Jesus, will return to save this world from Lucifer, Satan, also called the devil. They believe that Satan will triumph when he, meaning the Devil, returns.

Mr. Pike continued in his book entitled LEGENDA:

". . . the mitre of the one [the mitre, or miter, is defined as: "a headdress; specifically a tall, ornamented cap with peaks in front and back, worn by the Pope" of the Catholic Church as "a mark of office"] and the crown of the other [meaning the crown of a King] were the symbols, and remain the symbols of the enemies whom it is the purpose of the Order of the Temple of Solomon, of the Holy House, or Hierodom, of Jerusalem, [these terms will be explained a little later in this work, but basically, Mr. Pike is saying that the

other combatant is the Masonic Lodge and others who
believe in Lucifer] to war against without remission or
relaxation." [279]

So, it appears as if this battle is between the Catholic Church,
allied with the government, and the Masons.

But there is still more to the secret.

And the Masons keep releasing the clues.

chapter 28
THE OATH

It becomes important to know that even if the member of the Masons does not understand the information that will follow, he is bound by an oath to enforce it should he ever be given an order from his Masonic superiors to do so. This is the oath, called an "obligation," that the Mason takes at the 18th Degree, according to Albert Pike:

> "I, [the initiate provides his name] furthermore promise and swear that I will observe and obey all the rules and laws of this order of Knights of the Rose Croix, [the title of the 18th Degree] and the decrees and manates that may be transmitted to me by the Sov∴ Inspector Gen∴ [apparently this means the Sovereign Inspector General] in Sup∴ [apparently meaning Sureme] Council of the 33rd Degree in whose jurisdiction I may reside . . . ." [280]

So, the 33rd Degree Council has the power to order any Mason in their "jurisdiction" to obey their orders.

This will become significant later.

214

chapter 29
HIRAM ABIF, LEGEND

The Masonic "war" revolves around a legend surrounding the building of King Solomon's temple as recorded in the Old Testament of the Holy Bible. The Masons have added their claim that this legend started in the year 1012 B.C.

This story of the building of the temple starts in 1 Chronicles, chapter 28 of the Bible when David, the King of Israel, spoke to his people and said:

> 28:2: "*As for me*, I *had* in mine heart to build a house of rest for the ark of the covenant of the LORD . . . .
> 28-3: But God said unto me, Thou shalt not build a house for my name, because thou *hast been* a man of war, and hast shed blood.
> 28-4: [But] the Lord God of Israel
> 28:5: . . . hath chosen Solomon my son to sit upon the throne of the kingdom of the LORD OVER ISRAEL.
> 28-6: And he said unto me, Solomon thy son, he shall build my house and my courts . . . .'
> 28-10: Take heed now; for the LORD hath chosen thee to build a house for the sanctuary; be strong, and do *it*."

According to II Chronicles, Chapter 3, Solomon accepted the command of God and:

> 3-1: ". . . began to build the house of the Lord at Jerusalem . . . ."

He sent for the king of a neighboring country, according to other chapters in II Chronicles, to assist him:

215

> 2:3: And Solomon sent to Hu'-ram [the name is variously spelled Hiram, Huram, Khirum, etc.] the king of Tyre . . . ."

Tyre was the capital of Phoenicia in what today is southern Lebanon. The King sent his father, also named Huram, or Hiram, Abif (as I said, there are various spellings of his name, as shall be shown in this book,) to Solomon. The Bible says in I Kings chapter 7, verse 14, the father "was a worker in brass." The Masons have added that he was also a stone-Mason, meaning a worker in stone as well. There is no Biblical authority for this addition.

And when he completed his work for Solomon, the Bible in I Kings chapter 7, verse 40 says that Hiram:

> "made an end of doing all the work that he made king Solomon for the house of the LORD . . . ."

Hiram's occupation, and the fact that the Bible states that he completed his work and returned to Tyre, becomes important for reasons that follow, as the reader shall see.

The Bible variously calls Huram, the king of Tyre, Hiram as well, and it appears as if the Masons have almost universally adopted the name Hiram. Albert Pike wrote about this in one of his books:

> "In 2 Chronicles] [Chapter] iv. [verse] 16, we find Khurum Abiu [here Mr. Pike calls him Khuram Abiu, but it is the same individual,] which our translation renders, 'Khuram, his father.' The last word, Abiu, has been transformed into Abiff, [also spelled Abif] and become part of the name, which it is not." [281]

216

Mr. Pike adds one additional detail about King Hiram that apparently is not in the Bible. He wrote that this King said that he:

". . . sent thee [meaning King Solomon] Hiram, my father . . . . [and that] we [apparently referring to the fact that both King Hiram and his father, Hiram] were brothers in the Sacred Mysteries." [282]

The claim by the Masons that King Hiram and his father were both believers in the Sacred Mysteries is an amazing revelation. This thought clearly links them to a belief in a god other than the God of the Bible. And Albert Pike put that declaration in writing. Yet the Bible and the Masons both say that King Solomon asked for King Hiram to assist him in the buildin of the temple.

The Masons also say that some of the story of Hiram is a "legend." This quote comes from Rex Hutchens, in his book entitled A BRIDGE TO LIGHT:

"Thus the Biblical account of the story of Hiram is occasionally at variance with the legend as told in Masonic instruction.

For example, we are told in 1 Kings 7:40 that Hiram [meaning Hiram Abif] finished all the work he had been commissioned to do by King Solomon and presumably returned to his own country, but Masonic tradition asserts the death of Hiram during the construction of the Temple." [283]

So what Mr. Hutchens is saying is that the Masons have built a legend around an event that did not happen: the alleged death of Hiram Abif. That means that they are knowingly not telling the truth to their fellow Masons when they make certain claims in their story about the death of Hiram Abif.

For example, the Bible says that Hiram Abif completed his work and returned to his home. And the Masons have constructed a legend that says that he was murdered at the temple site before it was finished. This is called "intentionally misleading" the "first layer."

Mr. Hutchens confirmed the thought with this quotation:

"The legends of the degrees are all symbolic and allegorical [defined as: "a veiled presentation in a figurative story."] We are urged to learn the allegorical meaning of this degree [the 12th,] in particular what the Master Hiram symbolizes." [284]

And, in keeping with all of his other statements about "reading, studying and reflecting," Mr. Pike, and others, are loyal to this promise: the Masons will reveal the true meaning behind the symbol to anyone who cares enough to make the effort of finding the truth behind the symbol. They will reveal "what Master Hiram symbolizes."

Albert Mackey confirmed all of this with this quotation:

"There is in Freemasonry a legend of certain unworthy Craftsmen [the three assassins, who will be identified later in my book] who entered into a conspiracy to extort from a distinguished brother [Hiram Abif] a secret of which he was the possessor.

The legend is altogether symbolic, and when its symbolism is truly comprehended, becomes surpassingly beautiful." [285]

And then Mr. Pike explained that the legend of Hiram is also symbolic. He wrote this in his explanation of the 30th Degree:

> "If you have reflected upon the Degrees that you have received, you must have long since concluded that the legend of the death of Khurum [meaning Hiram Abif. His death will be discussed in the following paragraphs] and the mourning of Masons for his tragical fate, had some deeper meaning than appeared on the surface . . . ." [286]

So the tale told by the Masons has a symbolic meaning. It is not true that Hiram was murdered by three human assassins, nor that he died before the temple was completed, but these parts of their "legend" are symbolic, concealing a meaning that they are encouraging their members to discover.

Other Masons have confirmed Mr. Pike's comments. The first quotation I would like to offer is this one from Mr. Hutchens who confirms Pike's assertion that Hiram himself, as a man, is but a symbol of something else:

> ". . . the Master, Hiram is the symbol of intelligence, liberty and truth . . . ." [287]

Additional details as to what Hiram is and what he symbolically represents were provided by other Masons, in this case by Carl Claudy, who wrote:

> "The legend of Hiram Abif [meaning the man who respresents all of mankind] is at once the tragedy and the hope of man; it is virtue struck down by error, evil, and sin, and raised again by truth, goodness, and mercy." [288]

219

The following explanation comes from Albert Mackey:

> "The Masons are therefore perfectly correct . . . in
> preserving . . . the word *Abif* as an appelative [defined
> as: "a title, or a descriptive name," meaning that the
> word Abif is not Hiram's last name, but it is a title, in
> this case it means "father," the father of King Hiram,]
> surname, or title of honor and distinction bestowed
> upon the chief builder of the Temple . . . ." [289]

Mr. Pike also explained that Hiram was a symbol of something
else:

> "Hiram not only represents the Sun, and the Good
> Principle, but the Eternal, never-dying, primitive
> TRUTH, ever struggling for the victory." [290]

And then he takes the explanation of the symbology behind the
legend of Hiram a little further. He wrote that Mr. Pike explained what the true symbology of Hiram is to Masonry:

> *"Whatever Hiram really was, he is the type, perhaps
> an imaginary type, to us, of humanity in its highest
> phase; an exemplar* [defined as: "one who serves as a
> model or pattern, an ideal model"] *of what man may
> and should become . . . , in his progress toward the
> realization of his destiny; . . . an earnest* [defined as:
> "being an indication or assurance of what is to come"]
> *of what humanity may be . . . ."* [291]

So Hiram is not "a man;" he is "humanity," meaning he represents all of mankind.

He symbolically represents all of the humans on the earth.

Mr. Pike confirmed these thoughts in some of his other books:

> "Of the *Masonic* legend, the Hero [meaning Hiram
> Abif] . . . represents the people at large. . . .
> The Master Hurom [another spelling of the name
> Hiram] is a symbol of THE PEOPLE, and of a free
> STATE, and, therefore of LIBERTY itself." [292]

> "Hiram is *Man* attaining Empire by means of Knowl-
> edge and Sagacity [defined as: "keenness of discern-
> ment or judgment."]" [293]

Albert Mackey also confirmed the symbolism behind the individual known as Hiram Abif. He wrote:

> "Hiram Abif is the symbol of man in the abstract sense,
> . . . ." [294]

So Hiram represents all of the people of the earth, all of mankind, not just one man by that name. This is the true meaning
of Hiram, the symbol.

Stated in my own words, Hiram symbolically represents all of
mankind in the battle between good and evil. He symbolically
represents the thought that mankind has been cheated by the
God of the Bible when he was removed from Heaven for deciding that he should decide for himself what was right and
wrong.

And Masonry is now engaged in a battle with the God of the
Bible to bring man back to the perfect paradise, called heaven,
on earth. If only man can attain a condition where there will be
no moral absolutes, then man can attain a perfect state on the
earth.

That is the symbolic meaning behind the legend of Hiram Abif.

I have "read, studied and reflected" on these things as Albert Pike suggested.

Their secret has been revealed.

Because I have found it.

But it has not been completely revealed as yet.

There is more to come.

chapter 30
THE DEATH OF HIRAM

The Masons have told their initiates that there is more to their legend than they have been told. This quotation comes from Albert Mackey:

> "Masonic writers who have sought to interpret the symbolism of the legend . . . have finally arrived at the same result, namely, that it has a spiritual signification." [295]

The death of Hiram is covered in the last part of their legend. And a good place to obtain the details is in Coil's Masonic Encyclopedia, written in 1961. On page 307 of Mr. Coil's book, under the heading of "Hiram Abif," the author quotes a portion of the ritual in a Blue Lodge relating to Hiram's death (the spelling in this quotation is exactly as it was recorded in the quotation from Mr. Coil's book.) It appears to be in the form of a question and response:

> Q: "How came he [meaning Hiram Abif] by his Death? R: In the Building of *Solomon's* Temple, he was [a] Master-Mason [today the equivalent of a Third Degree Mason,] and at high 12 or Noon, when the Men [who were building the Temple] were gone to refresh themselves, as was his usual Custom, he came to survey the Works [apparently meaning when Hiram went to the temple to see the progress of that day's work] and when he was enter'd into the Temple, there were Three Ruffians, suppos'd to be Three Fellow-Crafts [meaning three First Degree Masons,] planted themselves at the Three Entrances of the Temple, [apparently there were only three doors of the Temple. The

missing one, in my estimation, or at least the fourth one not mentioned in this scenario, was the Northern door for reasons already examined] and when he came out, one demanded the Master's Word [in other works by other Masons, this Master's Word is identified as the true name of God. The Masons are saying that Hiram, as a Master Mason, was in possession of this secret which was only possessed by "Master Masons" and could not be given to "Apprentice Masons"] of him, and he reply'd he did not receive it in such Manner, but Time and a little Patience would bring him to it: He, not satisfied with the Answer, Give him Blow . . . , [which means he struck him] which made him reel; he [Hiram Abif] went to the other Gate, where being accosted in the same manner and making the same Reply, he received a greater Blow, [meaning the second man struck him as well] and at the third his Quietus [this part of the story ends with Hiram Abif being murdered by the third "ruffian" at "the third gate."]" [296]

The Masons are claiming that Hiram Abif was beaten by the first two "ruffians," and was then killed by the last of the "three ruffians," but Mr. Coil did not name them. In other Masonic writings, however, the reader learns that the three men were named Jubelo, Jubela and Jubelum.

Nowhere in my research can I find just what the Masons believe these three names mean. But, I have found the evidence that these names, like the name of Hiram Abif, are symbolic and conceal a larger secret. Mr. Mackey in his Encyclopedia, under his heading for "Jubela-o-um," tells the student a little about these three men:

"Jubela-o-m. The mythical names of assassins, the true interpretation of which is only known to the initiate who is an esoteric [defined as meaning: "one skilled in the secret, or hidden"] student." [297]

It is my best estimation that these three names are somehow connected to the Masonic search for the "Light." And the reason I believe this is because it appears as if they are derived from the Latin word meaning "light."

I checked a recent Latin to English dictionary and it defined the word JUBAR as: "a booming light, radiance, literally the light of the sun."

When I was a student of the Spanish language during two of my three years in high school, we learned that there were similarities between the Spanish language and the Latin language. One of the things I was being taught was "how to conjugate" words in Spanish, from their root, such as "I run, he runs, we run, etc." So it is my opinion that these three names of these "ruffians," Jubelo, Jubela, and Jubelum, have a root in the Latin word "jubar." And I am guessing that they mean "I am the light of the sun, you are the light of the sun, and we are the light of the sun." But that is just my opinion, it is not contained in any of the Masonic writings that I have read.

Mr. Pike tells his readers that there were originally 15 "ruffians" who wanted to know the secrets of Hiram Abif, the Master Mason, but that some of them did not wish to become involved with this attempt to obtain this secret by violence. He wrote in Chapter 10 of a book that he wrote to be given to an initiate "before investiture [meaning before he is given the degree] with the fourth degree," that the Worshipful Master tells the Candidate:

"Twelve of the Conspirators . . . failed to meet the other three in the Temple at the time agreed upon for putting their wicked plot into execution.

The other three, though disappointed, persisted. Their names are *said* to have been Yubela, Yubelo, and Yubelom [apparently a different method of spelling the names Jubelo, Jubela, and Jubelum.]

In these a mystery is concealed." [298]

So, it is possible that the secret within the secret about the names of the three assassins of Hiram Abif is that they are somehow symbolically connected to the worship of the Sun God.

Mr. Pike provided the reader with some more details about the three assassins:

". . . . . [Mr. Pike placed these dots here] According to the sentence of the court, the two assassins of the Master have been executed, confessing their guilt in the hearing of all the people; and their heads, struck off after life was extinct, have been set, with that of Abairam, over the East, West and South gates of the city. [Notice that there were no "heads" placed at the North gate of the city. This must mean that they did not want to place a "head" on the gate of the "darkness"] . . . .

Henceforward let our departed brother and revered Master [Hiram Abif] be unto us and unto all Masons the symbol of Liberty, Intelligence and Truth, and his assassins of Ignorance, Tyranny and Intolerance . . . ;

that the freedom of the State can only be attained and perpetuated, by instructing the people, by following Ignorance into its darkest dens, and there smiting it mortally and mercilessly." [299]

So the Masons wish to "smite" religion and government "mortally and mercilessly." And once again, Mr. Pike explains that religion is "Ignorance."

And this quotation adds additional details to the murder of Hiram:

"This degree [the tenth, called Elu of the Fifteen] . . . . . [these dots were placed there by Albert Pike] is devoted . . . to the cause of human freedom, corporeal [defined as: "bodily, physical"] and mental, against tyranny exercised over the soul or body.

The two assassins of the Master Khirum (who is to us the symbol of that freedom), whose capture and execution are recounted in this degree, are the symbols of those special enemies of freedom, *Ambition*, of which *Tyranny* or *Despotism* is born, and *Fanaticism*, from which spring *Intolerance* and *Persecution*." [300]

Mr. Hutchens goes a little further than did Mr. Coil in his explanation of the death of Hiram and the attack upon him. He wrote this on page 66 of A BRIDGE TO LIGHT:

"2. What are the symbolic meanings of the attacks upon Hiram . . . ?

Hiram is first accosted at the south gate of the Temple where the instrument of the attack is the rule. In Greek the word for a 'rule,' whether a measuring instrument or a code of conduct, is *canon*.

Thus we see the bureaucracy of the early Church establishing the Canon Law [it is to be remembered that Adam Weishaupt taught Canon Law at the University of Ingolstadt, a Catholic university. Canon Law is defined as: "the laws governing the organizational affairs of a church."] to regulate conduct. This law was to be obeyed with unquestioned loyalty, hence it is an apt symbol of the suppression of freedom of speech which might question the divinity and justice of these laws; therefore, Hiram, with the rule, is struck where the organs of speech are." [301]

This comment by Mr. Hutchens is puzzling. When I was a member of the Catholic Church for some 36 years, I did not "obey the Canon Law with unquestioned loyalty." I was free to accept or reject the teachings of the Church. And when I finally put my concerns about the precepts of the Catholics to a test of the Bible, and found no Scriptural authority for much of what I believed as a member, I freely left the Church.

There was no retribution on the part of the Church. I was free to go and when I thought it was appropriate to leave, I left.

The point I wish to make is that nowhere in Mr. Hutchens' book is he equally critical of the Government of the United States. As a student of the Constitution, I have put some of the laws passed by Congress to a test of this document, and found that much of what Congress is doing today is not authorized by its provisions. I consider this to be "tyranny," and if I attempt to withdraw as I did when I was a Catholic, I will soon discover that I am not free to leave. (For example, if I protest the evidence that most of the money that I pay in federal taxes is being used for unconstitutional purposes, and that I wish to object by not paying those taxes, I am not free to do so. There would be retribution on the part of the government if I do not send in my taxes to the Internal Revenue System.

I would go to prison. This act of government would be called "tyranny," meaning that you will do what you are told by the government, but you are not under any such compulsion by the Catholic Church. And yet Mr. Hutchens claims that he is in opposition to all forms of "tyranny."

So, in my opinion, Mr. Hutchens is wrong. He fails to see tyranny when it permeates the government of the United States, but sees tyranny where there is none in the Catholic Church.

There must be a reason for this: why does he see tyranny when there is no tyranny, and no tyranny when there is tyranny.

This is extremely hard to understand. I have spent nearly all of my adult life exposing a conspiracy in government to deprive us of our very freedom. And it is this conspiracy that created the tyranny in our government today. This conspiracy controls "Communism" like it controls "Capitalism." It finances both sides of wars, including the financing of Adolf Hitler's "Socialist" government before and during World War II. They financed both sides in that war that killed over 50,000,000 people. Yet I can find not one word of opposition to that conspiracy and their control of governments worldwide in Mr. Hutchens' book. Yet he claims to be in opposition to all forms of "tyranny."

You the reader will have to answer this question: What could be the motive of Mr. Hutchens when he sees tyranny where none exists, and cannot find tyranny where it does exist?

And there is an answer to this question.

And I am hopeful that I will make the answer clear to the reader a little later in this book.

Mr. Hutchens continues:

> "The instrument of attack at the west gate of the Temple was the square, an implement formed of two rigid pieces of metal at right angles to each other; it represents the merger of civil and religious power intending to control man's emotions, telling him not only what he can do but also what he can believe . . . .
>
> Thus Hiram is struck near the heart, the traditional seat of the affections." [302]

Here Mr. Hutchens appears to be referring to the Christian Church, because it dares to tell mankind that God has a plan for their life. God has instructed man in the Bible that there is a right way, and a wrong way, to live their lives. God is the author of "moral absolutes," which are to teach man "to control [his] emotions, [and] tell him not only what he can do but also what he can believe." For instance, God tells man that he is not to commit the crime of rape, even though that thought of anticipated pleasures may appeal to his "emotions."

However, man is free to accept or reject the principle. Mr. Hutchens is saying that man should reject all that God teaches mankind.

He is also saying that the church and the government have "merged" to punish the person who wishes to exercise his free choice as to whether or not he should forcibly take a woman.

I also find this hard to understand. Is it possible that Mr. Hutchens is suggesting that "civil and religious power" should not merge to punish the crime of rape? Should they not tell the prospective rapist "not only what he can do but also what he can believe" about the act of rape? It is true that the punishment of this "crime" "intends to control man's emotions" and therefore, according to Mr. Hutchens, should not be punished, because government and the church do not have the right to "merge" to "control man's emotions."

He continues:

> "The setting maul, an instrument of brute force, is a fitting symbol of the blind, unreasoning mob. [In my classes and lectures, I frequently call the "blind, unreasoning mob" a "democracy," which has been the definition of a "democracy" for about 5,000 years. Here Mr. Hutchens apparently calls "the will of the majority" "the people telling him not only what he can do but also what he can believe."] It fears the force of the intellect and seeks the destruction of the products of the mind . . . . Hiram is killed at the east gate by a blow to the head, the seat of the intellect." [303]

So the people, "the blind, unreasoning mob," acting together and pooling their individual right to self-defense, create a government to punish those who commit crimes against others. They base their reasons for this action upon the Commandments and Laws given to mankind by the God of the Bible.

Yet, Mr. Hutchens speaks out against these actions, because it is his opinion that they represent "the merger of civil and religious power intending to control man's emotions, telling him not only what he can do but also what he can believe."

It is remembered that Mr. Hutchens speaks for all of Freemasonry on this subject, since his book was published by the 33rd Degree Council. So this must be the official position of all of the Masons worldwide.

231

It might be appropriate here to quote the second paragraph of the Declaration of Independence issued on July 4, 1776 by the "founding fathers" of the united States of America. The words in this paragraph very clearly explain why men create governments. They read:

"We hold these truths to be self-evident that all men are created equal, that they are endowed by their creator with certain unalienable rights, that among these are life, liberty, and the pursuit of happiness.

That to secure these rights, governments are instituted among men . . . ."

This nation's founding fathers believed in a creator God (they referred to God as "their creator,") and that this God had given them "unalienable rights" (that means that they believed that no one, no government, no majority, no minority, no individual can take them away.)

That means that they believed in moral absolutes (because they believed that God taught man "Thou shalt not murder," for instance, meaning that they recognized that all men had an equal right to life.)

That means that they recognized that they had the right to protect that right, called the Right to Self-Defense, and that is why they created government. The Right to Self-Defense means that it is the right of every individual to hire a bodyguard, called government, to protect his God-given rights to Life, Liberty and Property, the three basic and essential rights of all humans.

So government is created by men who recognize that their rights can be violated only by other men or by tyrannical governments. And to protect those rights, they create government, and give that government the right to use their individual, and then their collective, right to use force in defense against those who wish to violate those rights.

I can remember reading many of the works of Ayn Rand, a major writer during the 1960's and 1970's. She separated force into two categories: what she called Initiatory Force and Retaliatory Force. It was her position that no one has the right to initiate force against anyone else, under any circumstances. Conversely, all men have the right to use Retaliatory Force, called the Right to Self-Defense.

It is the individual's right to use Self-Defense against one who comes to violate that individual's rights. That individual can pool his or her Right to Self-Defense with others who have an equal right, and hire a bodyguard that will protect each of them individually or collectively. We call that hired bodyguard "Government."

This Right to Self-Defense is based upon a Moral Absolute that reads: "Thou shalt not murder."

If no one has the right to murder, it follows that each of us has the right to protect ourselves against the murderer.

Yet the Masons are saying that there are "no moral absolutes," and therefore there is no need for man to create governments.

I do not want the majority of the people deciding what my rights are. I do not want the Masons saying what my rights are. I do not want Mr. Hutchens saying what my rights are. My rights come from God, therefore they are unalienable, meaning that no man, no Mason, no majority, no government can take them away. And because I feel that way and have a right to protect my rights, I create government.

I acknowledge that these rights come from God and that only God can take them away. I do not acknowledge that any one else can deprive me of them.

But I do not wish the Masons, or anyone else, to say that I do not have any rights because there are no "moral absolutes" upon which I can base my claim to unalienable rights. And I want my government to punish murderers, thieves and rapists, because these individuals destroy my rights to life, liberty and property. That is why men create governments: to protect their God-given, unalienable rights.

But returning to the assassination of Hiram Abif, the names of the three assassins have a far more important hidden or concealed meaning, just like the name of Hiram Abif itself. And the following Masonic writers have explained just what the symbolism is behind the names of these three murderers:

To start, Manly P. Hall wrote this:

> "When the mob governs, man is ruled by ignorance; when the church governs, he is ruled by superstition; and when the state governs, he is ruled by fear.
> Before men can live together in harmony and understanding, ignorance must be transmuted into wisdom, superstition into an illumined faith, and fear into love." [304]

Albert Pike took a similar tack with his understanding of the symbolic meanings of the three assassins by explaining this in his LECTURE during the 10th Degree:

"This Degree, my Brother, . . . is devoted . . . to the cause of Toleration and Liberality against Fanaticism and Persecution, political and religious; and to that of Education, Instruction and Enlightenment against Error, Barbarism and Ignorance." [305]

And this further explanation comes from the opening of the 10th Degree:

"To the cause of every people that struggles against oppression!

To the cause of all who defend right and justice against tyranny!

To the cause of toleration against intolerance and persecution!

To the cause of free thought, free speech, free conscience!

We devote ourselves, our hands, our hearts, our intellects, now, henceforward and forever! Amen!" [306]

As the student continues his reading, the explanation becomes a little clearer. Take, for instance, this quotation from Mr. Pike's book entitled LITURGY:

"You will hereafter learn who are the chief foes of human liberty, symbolized by the assassins of the Master Khirum; [once again, another way of referring to Hiram Abif] and in their fate you may see foreshadowed that which we earnestly hope will hereafter overtake those enemies of humanity, against whom Masonry has struggled so long." [307]

The concealed symbolism behind the names becomes a little clearer with this quotation from Mr. Pike:

235

"The colors of the apron and collar [worn by the Mason in the fourth degree, called the Secret Master degree] -- white edged with black . . . are also symbolical of the contest, in the Universe of things . . . between Light and Darkness, Good and Evil, Truth and Error, a struggle which commenced with time, and is typified in Masonry by the efforts and anxiety of the aspirant to attain the light." [308]

Here Mr. Pike reveals that this "contest" dates back to the very beginning of time (he wrote that the "struggle commenced with time.") This is completely consistent with the A.L. calendar, which dates to the time when Lucifer was cast out of heaven, the "beginning of time," as they see it [I will discuss the A.L. calendar in a later chapter. But at this point, let me explain that it is the Masonic calendar, and starts with the year "0," when they believe Lucifer fell to this earth.]

And, finally, the symbolism becomes a great deal clearer with this quotation by Mr. Pike:

". . . [these dots were placed here by Mr. Pike] Clothed in the habiliments [defined as: "the dress or attire"] of mourning, [apparently the Masons are not mourning the death of Hiram, but symbolically the death of mankind at the hands of "government" and "religion"] the columns of the Temple shattered and prostrate, [apparently referring to Heaven, after man and Lucifer were expelled by God] and the Brethren bowed down in the deepest dejection, represent the world under the tyranny of the Principle of Evil [the "merger" of church and state] . . . ; where King and Priest [the representatives of Church and State] trample on Liberty and the rights of Conscience [man's right to decide what is right and wrong.]" [309]

So the symbolism of Hiram and the three assassins now becomes clear: Hiram is "mankind," murdered by the three assassins, symbolically representing the hands of "the church" and "the government," the "abusers" of human free choice.

Now the student must learn what the Masons plan on doing about this situation.

Hold on, it gets worse!

chapter 31
JOHN ROBINSON

I would now like to discuss additional details of the meeting I had with Mr. John Robinson, the author I briefly discussed in the early parts of this book. It is interesting that Mr. Robinson, who admitted to me that he was not a member of the Masons, later joined the Lodge. And I believe that I was the reason that he did.

Before the television program on which we were to conduct the debate on the Masonic Lodge that I discussed earlier, Mr. Robinson and I were left alone in a conference room adjacent to the studio. I asked him why he was interested in Masonry but was not a member of it. His response was something to the effect that he was an historian and felt he had found the tracks of a secret society in history all the way back to the 11th or 12th century. He then identified that society as the Knights Templar and their descendant, the Masons. He also claimed that they had a connection to modern day Masonry. He decided to write a book about what he had discovered entitled BORN IN BLOOD, which I had already read by the time we met in Tampa, Florida.

I told him that I too had discovered their importance in the affairs of the world, and that this discovery frightened me. I then suggested that he read my book entitled THE NEW WORLD ORDER, to learn just what the Masons believed in. I told him that my book had been praised as being quite possibly the finest book ever written about the Lodge by a non-member. I attempted to convince him that he should study their secret beliefs and then join me in exposing them for what they were, and exactly how they had affected history against the best interests of the people.

The program's producer then entered the room and the three of us walked into the studio. I did not have a chance to meet with Mr. Robinson again, and had no further contact with him until the day he called me possibly a year or two later.

He told me he had called because he had read Pat Robertson's book entitled THE NEW WORLD ORDER and suggested that I "sue him [Mr. Robertson] for plagiarism [the act of copying another writer's material and then claiming it as your own,]" since he felt that Mr. Robertson's book, published months after mine, had stolen my research. I told him that I would not do such a thing because I had read Mr. Robertson's book and did not feel that he had stolen my material. And secondly, I told him that I felt that his book would assist me in selling mine because I believed that people would go into a bookstore and ask for his book, and quite possible end up with mine because it had the same title. Since I felt that his television ministry could sell a lot more books than my advertising efforts, I felt his book, with the same title, could only help the sale of my book.

Furthermore, I told him that Mr. Robertson's book was only a shadow of mine. My book by the same title goes much deeper into the mysteries of not only Masonry, but other secret societies as well. In addition, I detail the nature of THE NEW WORLD ORDER far more extensively than does Mr. Robertson. (Write me for a booklet that I've written entitled "Pat, Can We Talk?" that addresses the serious problems with Mr. Robertson's book.)

A short time later, Mr. Robinson wrote another book about his research into the Masonic Lodge, called A PILGRIM'S PATH. It appears that in addition to reading my book, he had read others on the subject, but he must have had trouble accepting our research. The book cover on his second book reads, in part:

> "Freemasonry has never lacked for detractors. Ene-
> mies of the organization have included the Roman
> Catholic Church, the Communist Party, and the Nazis
> [meaning the Socialist Nazi Party of Adolf Hitler, the
> leader of Germany in World War II.]
>
> It has been denounced by popes and kings, by the
> ignorant [apparently this is what Mr. Robinson consid-
> ered me and the other non-affiliated critics to be] and
> by those who felt threatened by the fraternity's reputa-
> tion for secrecy. [I certainly cannot speak for others,
> but I can attest that I do not feel threatened by their
> "secrecy." I am not a pope, a member of the Catholic
> Church, a Communist, and am not now, nor have I
> ever been, a member of the Nazi Party! That only
> leaves me, one of the more modern critics of Masonry,
> as being termed "ignorant."] [310]

Mr. Robinson did refer to me once, however, in his second book. This is what he wrote:

> "One special aspect of Robertson's [book entitled]
> *The New World Order* seems to have gone unnoticed.
> A couple of years before Robertson's book, a book
> was published by an Arizona author named A. Ralph
> Epperson. [In truth, it was not "a couple of years" be-
> tween the publication dates of our two books. I sent
> Mr. Robertson a copy of my book before his was pub-
> lished, and to the best of my knowledge, his book
> came out about 10 months later.]
>
> It [my book] was based on the same central thesis:
> a Masonic conspiracy to rule the world. As its 'ev-

idence,' it cited some of the same writings that Robertson used later. It even discussed the same alleged Masonic symbolism in the design of the Great Seal on the U.S. dollar bill, although Robertson appears to present it as his own original thinking. [There is nothing "alleged" about the Masonic symbolism in the design of the Great Seal. It is all Masonic. Should you be interested in not only the Masonic symbolism here but in how the Masons who created this nation set it up to fail, may I suggest that you read my booklet entitled AMERICA'S SECRET DESTINY, available through the catalog from the publisher.]

I'm quite certain that Mr. Robertson, if questioned on these points, would claim that they are simply innocent coincidences, although he might take a deep breath before asserting that stand on Epperson's title, which was *The New World Order* - - precisely the same title Robertson used." [311]

I want the reader to know that I am not offended by the number of misstatements Mr. Robinson made in those two paragraphs, but it does offend me that he did not include my name in this paragraph that he wrote in his book:

"It serves no purpose to make direct appeals to Pat Robertson, James L. Holly [a doctor who challenged the nationwide Southern Baptist Church to study Masonry. The Church did conduct their study, and in my opinion, white-washed the truth,] or John Ankerberg [a television evangelist who did a short series of television programs exposing the rituals of the Blue Lodge of Masonry. I met him in Phoenix a year or two later, and personally asked him to read my book entitled THE NEW WORLD ORDER if he cared about ex-

posing Masonry. I gave him a copy, personally autographed, as I remember, but I never heard from him.
To my knowledge, he has never exposed more than
the basic rituals of the first three degrees, which, although interesting, only scratch the surface of the truth
about Masonry.]

It is a waste of time trying to find an opening into
closed minds." [312]

Apparently Mr. Robinson did not include me in his list of ex-
posers of the Masonic Lodge because he felt that I, like him,
had figured the secret out. I believe that these gentlemen that
he mentioned have only studied the preliminary evidence, and
have not gotten into Masonry like I believe I have. So, I guess
his mentioning of my name has mixed blessings.

In any event, Mr. Robinson ended his book, after he apparently had done enough of his own research into Masonry, with
this statement:

"By the time this book [PILGRIM'S PATH] goes on
sale, I expect to be a Master Mason [a Third Degree
Mason, in the Blue Lodge.] The one person I know
that will please is me." [313]

Apparently he had read the book entitled A BRIDGE TO
LIGHT, because he listed it as one of three "recommended
reading" books at the end of his book. I can only presume that
he read it because he found it quoted frequently in my book
entitled THE NEW WORLD ORDER, which I must presume
he read shortly after our Tampa meeting.

I made an attempt to contact Mr. Robinson after I read his
second book. I was going to discuss the possibility of the two

of us joining together to offer ourselves as a team to conduct a series of debates on Masonry on the radio talk programs all over America, since I had the evidence to prove my claims. I called his publisher and asked if they would forward information on to him that I was asking him to call me, and the receptionist informed me that he had passed away. I was sorry to hear that, since I felt that if I was instrumental in peaking an interest on his part in Masonry, and that he had apparently done so because of my urging, then he would be willing to assist me in participating in a series of debates between the two of us on the two opposing views on Masonry. But he was gone and that obviously would not be possible.

It is interesting that Macoy Publishing & Masonic Supply Co. reported in their September, 1994 catalog that his book entitled A PILGRIM'S PATH would "soon be available," in October, 1993. They reported that he had discussed,

> "debated, and gone head to head with anti-Masons in over 100 radio and television appearances." [314]

Neither his publisher, nor Mr. Robinson himself, nor the Masons ever invited me to "discuss, debate or go head to head" with Mr. Robinson between the time of our meeting in Tampa probably in 1990, and his death a few years later, even though he knew that we had debated the issue on television BEFORE he decided to join the organization. Yet he had done "over 100" such debates since we met to debate the subject of Masonry in Tampa! It appears as if they were very selective as to who they wanted Mr. Robinson to debate. It was not me, the "anti-Mason" with what I consider to be the most complete evidence against the Masons! The reader can decide for themselves just what their motive was when they decided not to invite me to debate him.

But the reason that they might have chosen not to invite me is because of the views Mr. Robinson expressed in his book BORN IN BLOOD:

> "As this book is being written, religion, the love of God, [it appears as if he was referring to the God of the Bible, although he did not say it] is still the major problem in many lands. It is the basis for political turmoil, terrorism, and outright war and carries the potential for much more of the same in the future." [315]

I certainly do not agree with this assessment, having spent over 30 years of my life proving that an international conspiracy is in truth "the [real] major problem in many lands." And I have also debated those who claim that "the love of God" is the problem that causes war. This is also a common charge of the atheists, those who do not believe in a God.

For instance, once at a street fair in Tucson, I discussed this charge with an atheist in the booth manned by The Tucson Atheist Association (that might not be their name because I do not exactly remember the group's official name.) The gentleman, just like Mr. Robinson, claimed that Christianity had caused all of the wars of the past 2,000 years, and I argued that it was another religion, called "atheism," that had been "the problem."

I made the claim that it was their belief system, which is part of Humanism, officially cited as a "religion" by the United States Supreme Court, that was behind the Communist revolutions in China and Russia.

I informed him that the Russian Revolution was led by Nikolai Lenin, an atheist, who wrote:

"We [the Communist atheists] must combat religion. Down with religion. Long live atheism. The spread of atheism is our chief task!" [316]

Lenin also wrote in these two quotations attributed to him::

"Our power does not know liberty or justice. It is entirely established on the destruction of the individual will.

We are the masters.

Complete indifference to suffering is our duty. In the fulfillment of our calling, the greatest cruelty is a merit." [Cruelty isn't cruelty if there are no moral absolutes preventing it.]

"Through a systematic terror, during which every breach of contract, every treason, every lie will be lawful [meaning that since "moral absolutes" are "dead," the Communists could use any means to achieve their goal] we will find the way to abase humanity down to the lowest level of existence. That is indispensible to the establishment of our dominance."

I can say as a Christian of over 25 years that I have never found one word in the words of Jesus that teaches anything like this. Yet we can read the words of Lenin, one of the lead-in atheists of his day, and see that he preached it as part of his belief system. He believed it because he did not believe in God, and therefore did not believe in His absolutes.

His religion murdered and starved more than 40,000,000 persons, all in the name of "atheism." After its successful revolution, over 6,000 concentration camps were created all over the nation, and at one time housed over 6,000,000 people. Avraham Shifrin, a Russian Jew who was allowed to emigrate to Israel after spending 14 years in one of these camps, estimated that about one half of those people were there because they chose to worship a God in a country whose government professed to its citizens that there was no God. That is a major tenet of a religion called atheism.

Mr. Shifrin's crime, as he told me when we met back in 1985, was that he was working for the benefit of the Jewish people in Russia, when his homeland was officially atheist. And they, the atheists in charge of the government, determined that this was a punishable crime and he spent 14 years of his life in one of their concentration camps.

The Chinese atheists who started a revolution in their country between the years of 1923 and 1949, the one fought "to make China safe for atheism," brutally murdered and starved as many as 80,000,000 people. The fundamental religion of the Chinese at the time was not enough to stop the Chinese atheists. They, too, did not believe in God, and in His absolutes. And 80,000,000 people are dead because of it.

I can remember calling this same leader of the Tucson atheists on a telephone talk program once and I asked him if he could recommend a book that I could read that would clearly teach me just what the morality of their religion was. He stated that there was no such book, that each man was to decide for himself. (It sounded to me as if this man was also a member of the Masons!)

So the Christian religion that teaches its believers that they cannot murder others because they will not accept Christianity, receives the blame from some of the atheists who do preach that they can murder those who will not accept atheism. This is very confusing to the observer, but it is what this atheist told me.

If you want to know who taught Lenin that it was acceptable to murder those who would not accept atheism, may I suggest that you find the writings of Sergei Nechayev, the "revolutionary" who taught that murder was acceptable if it furthered the aim of the Communists. One quotation of his is this one:

> "The object is perpetually the same: the surest and quickest way of destroying the whole filthy order. The revolutionary . . . must be tyrannical toward others.
>
> All the gentle and enervating [defined as: "to deprive of nerve, force, or strength"] sentiments of kinship, love, friendship, gratitude, and even honor must be suppressed in him and give place to the cold and single-minded passion for revolution."
>
> "Do not pity . . . . Kill in public places . . , kill in houses, kill in villages . . . . Whoever is against us is our enemy.
>
> And we must destroy enemies by all means."

These thoughts come from the man who taught Lenin. And the only reason Mr. Lenin could accept these views as the fundamental basis of his revolution was because he was an atheist: he had rejected the moral absolutes of God because he did not believe in them. So the teachings of Nechayev became his freely chosen morality.

I think it would be a fair statement to make that any critic would not be able to find similar thoughts to these in the words of Jesus, as recorded in the Bible. Yet, here we see the teacher of the atheist Nikolai Lenin teaching him that he must learn to kill in order to promote the atheist agenda.

The student can read the thoughts of the atheist Nikolai Lenin and the writings of Nechayev in my books entitled THE UN-SEEN HAND and THE NEW WORLD ORDER, and discover additional information about just what it is that these atheists believe in, and why they believed that they could murder millions of people to achieve their goals.

To say that something is wrong in the view of the atheists is an understatement. Yet they contend that "it is the Christians who cause wars."

Remember that the Masons claim to "shape the destinies of worlds." That means that they must have been supportive of the atheist revolutions in Russia and China, because they did nothing to prevent them. If they truly do "shape the destinies of worlds," and they were opposed to these revolutions, the atheists would not have succeeded.

Nothing else makes sense, unless the English language means nothing.

Therefore, I would agree with Mr. Robinson's position if you just inserted two words before the word religion:

> "As this book is being written, THE ATHEIST religion is still the major problem in many lands. It is the basis for political turmoil, terrorism, and outright war and carries the potential for much more of the same in the future."

But back to the issue at hand.

The December, 1993 edition of The PHILALETHES, a Masonic research organization that publishes a newsletter, stated that Mr. Robinson had indeed become a Master Mason before he died. And the Masons had decided that his second book had great merit. Macoy's, the Masonic supply store and catalog outlet, urged the Mason to read his book with this endorsement:

"With Freemasonry facing its most vicious attack in 100 years, [meaning that those who print what they have found about what the Masons actually believe in are having some effect] A PILGRIM'S PATH is a must-read book . . . ." [317]

Yes, Mr. Robinson figured it out.

And joined the Masons. In fact, he was apparently so impressed with what he found, he actually continued on and became a 33rd Degree Mason! He bought the entire package!

I too have figured it out. I will not become a 33rd Degree Mason.

Because I have chosen to expose them!

The world must ask which of us did the right thing!

chapter 32
THE THREE CROWNS

John Robinson inserted one key quotation into his book about what the three assassins symbolize:

"In the Southern Jurisdiction 30th degree, the ceremony that recounts this historical drama [both of the symbolic murder of Hiram Abif, and the actual murder of Jacques de Molay,] the candidate is led into a tomb with three skulls on display. The skull on the left wears a crown; the one in the center bears a laurel wreath; and the third wears a papal tiara.

The skull bearing the wreath of the hero is Jacques de Molay. The skull with the crown represents Philip IV, a secular tyrant, while the third represents Clement V, a religious tyrant.

The candidate is told that he should always oppose tyranny in whatever form, whether it emanates from a government or from a religion." [318]

As was previously discussed when I wrote about the apparent problem with Mr. Hutchens' failure to speak out against real tyranny in government, this statement of Mr. Robinson's is simply not true. The Mason does not "oppose tyranny in whatever form, whether it emanates from a government or from a religion." They turn a blind eye towards government tyranny when atheists rule the nation, and see tyranny in religious organizations when there is none.

The best way I can illustrate this is to suggest to the reader that they read my booklets entitled THE UCC CONNECTION, and AMERICA'S SECRET DESTINY, because these two works clearly show that the government of the United States is a "tyranny" today, and that the Masons who wrote the Constitution in 1787 wrote that tyranny into the very Constitution itself.

I wrote those booklets to discuss the evidence that our found-in fathers, who were in the main members of the Masons, institutionalized tyranny in a particular clause of the Constitution itself. The document is a "false front," meaning that this tyrannical power has been basically concealed from the reader. This provision is called Article 1, Section 8, Clause 17, and it created a hidden tyrannical government, called "the government of the United States." And this is the government running America today. [319]

Those who believe that the government today is being run by a group of "misguided liberals" who do not understand the Constitution are simply wrong.

I believe that these members of Congress know that they have had the power to do anything they wanted since our "founding fathers" gave them that tyrannical power back in 1787.

And Rex Hutchens says nothing in his book.

Everything that the government is doing today is Constitutional: the power was given to them by our founding fathers.

In other words, they have the power to do whatever they want, including even suspending the Constitution itself. The power is that broad! That means that the founding fathers lied to us. That means that the founding fathers, the majority of whom were Masons, did not tell us the truth when they claimed to have "freed us" from tyrannical government.

They, in fact, created it!

This shocking proof is now documentable: it can be proven in the words of the Constitution itself.

But Masonry, which claims to "shape the destinies of worlds," is strangely silent, even today, about the tyrannical "government of the United States."

They see tyranny in the Church, where there is none, but do not see it in the government, where it is rampant! So, just like Mr. Hutchens, Mr. Robinson did not see the truth. In other words, both of these men were wrong!

And this would be a good time to repeat Albert Pike's teachings about how to conceal things. This quotation comes from page 324 of MORALS AND DOGMA:

> *"What is Superior is as that which is Inferior, and what is Below is as that which is Above . . . ."*[320]

That means in this case that the Masons who wrote the Constitution made us believe that the Article meant one thing, when it meant exactly the opposite. They hid it with clever wording. And we got tyrannical government when we thought we were getting limited government. And this is in keeping with the teaching of their Sovereign Grand Commander.

But continuing with the main issue being discussed, Mr. Hutchens confirmed that there are various crown symbols in what he called "the fourth apartment:"

> "A mausoleum shaped like a truncated pyramid [meanin one that has had its top cut off, like the pyramid on

the back of the American dollar bill] displays a funeral urn wreathed in laurel, a regal crown and a Pope's tiara." [These three symbols represent the "hero's wreath" worn symbolically by Jacques deMolay, the "crown" worn by a king, and a "tiara" worn by a pope.] [321]

Mr. Pike reported that there are other "apartments" in the Masonic ritual. This is what he wrote in his books entitled LITURGY and MAGNUM OPUS about the first, second and fourth "apartments" in the Thirtieth Degree:

"THE FIRST APARTMENT:
On the platform of the tomb are three skulls. The middle one, wreathed with laurel . . . . Upon the one on the left is the triple crown of the Pope, and on the one on the right a regal crown . . . ." [322]

"The second apartment . . . represent[s] the world . . . . where King and Priest [meaning government and religion] trample on liberty and the rights of conscience." [323]

"THE FOURTH APARTMENT:
On the platform of it is a funeral urn, covered with a black veil. This is encircled by a wreath of laurel. On the right of the urn is a regal CROWN [signifying government;] on the left, a Pope's TIARA [signifying religion.]" [324]

Notice that the skulls have disappeared in this apartment. The skull representing Jacques deMolay has been replaced with an urn, a receptacle intended to hold the cremated remains of the deceased. That must mean that this urn represents the cremated remains of their martyred hero. It will be remembered that the Catholic Church burned the leader of the Knights Templar at the stake.

There are no skulls for the other two crowns, either. It might well represent the day in the future when religion and government have been destroyed and buried.

But, as we shall see, even this explanation about what the crowns represent does not go far enough. Mr. Pike amplified the meaning of these symbols in the following two quotes:

> "The *Crown* itself is but a symbol, and Royalty is but the most common type of tyranny." [325]

And this explanation:

> "The Mitre and Tiara also are but symbols, and the Pontificate [defined as: "the office of the Pope"] but the most usual mode in which spiritual despotism manifests itself." [326]

So here the reader sees that the symbols represent "religion" and "government:" the Mitre and Tiara are starting to come into focus as the symbols of the Catholic Church, presumed by Pike and others to be the official representative of Christianity, and the crown symbolically represents the government.

And this further confirmation comes from Mr. Hutchens:

> "Again the skull, tiara and crown are the objects of discourse . . . .
>   The crown represents all those kings and emperors [meaning representatives of government] who have

usurped or abused power, reigned for themselves and not the people and robbed a free people of their liberty . . . .

The tiara is not a symbol of any particular religion or creed [I will let the reader decide whether this is true or not, since Mr. Pike has said elsewhere that it is a "Pope's tiara"] but of the patron of ignorance and ally of despotism which in every age has made dupes of men and enslaved humanity through fear and superstition [meaning, as we shall continue to see, that it represents all of religion, but more specifically Christianity.]" [327]

And this quotation from Albert Pike

"Civil and religious freedom, emancipation of both the muscles and the mind of all who are fit to be free, education and enlightenment, and the raising up of the oppressed masses of humanity to that level of equality on which they ought to stand; that is the mission in which Masonry is to co-operate:

and to fulfil which it must necessarily labour for the overthrow and extermination of Kingly tyranny [meaning government] and Priestly oppression [meaning religion,] as well as the exclusive Privileges of rank and caste [those who benefit by the merger of religion and government.]" [328]

And Mr. Pike actually identifies these as "the enemies of Humanity:"

". . . the same three Powers which wrought the death of Jacques de Molay; the despotic power . . , the insolence, cruelty and blood-thirstiness of the Sacerdotal

[defined as: "relating to the priestly office or function"] power . . . and the bitterness of rank, caste and
privilege . . . . These three have ever been the enemies
of Humanity . . . ." [329]

And Mr. Pike added this:

" . . . we remember . . . the same enemies of human
freedom that sacrificed the Templars [meaning the
merger of religion and government that, according to
him, murdered the master of the Templar organization,] and that still wage war against Free Thought,
Free Action and Free Conscience . . . ." [330]

And another quotation, of a similar vein, taken from the 15th
Degree, reads:

"Qu∴ Of what are the chains of the captives, with
their triangular links, an emblem?
Ans∴ Of the three powers that have in all ages imposed fetters on the human intellect . . . -- the Kings
[meaning government,] Priests [meaning religion] and
Nobles, [those who benefit from the merger of state
and religion] -- or TYRANNY, SUPERSTITION and
PRIVILEGE." [331]

Here the reader learns a little more about the three enemies in
the Tenth Degree:

"Qu∴ How many Elus were at first received?
Ans∴ Fifteen . . . .
Qu∴ On what occasion were they received?
Ans∴ When King Solomon despatched [the spelling
in the original] them to search for and apprehend the

256

two murderers [notice that there were only two murderers of Hiram Abif] of our Gr∴ Master Hiram Abi [once again, another spelling of the name of Hiram Abif,] who still remain at large . . . .

Qu∴ Did the Fifteen succeed in apprehending the murderers?

Ans∴ They did . . . .

Qu∴ Of what do the three heads upon the apron and collar [worn by the Masons during initiation ceremonies] represent?

Ans∴ Tyranny, Fanaticism and Ignorance: the three enslavers of mankind, smitten by the sword of freedom . . . .

(The Brethren all assemble around the altar in a circle . . . with their swords drawn, and [various members] repeat as follows) . . . :

To the cause of Free Thought, Free Conscience and Free Speech! [meaning freedom from "religion" and "government," the "oppressors" of "free thought, free conscience and free speech!"]" [332]

So here the Mason learns that he must symbolically "behead" the three (or in some cases, two) enemies of the Lodge.

And they draw their swords as a sign that they are willing to accomplish this task by using violence.

But Mr. Pike told us that we were not wrong in our assessment:

"It is the old contest between Good and Evil, between the Sons of Light and the Sons of Darkness.

. . . we advance the cause of human progress, and labour to enfranchise human thought, to give freedom

257

to the human conscience, and equal rights to the people everywhere . . . . [by abolishing "religion" and "government."]

This, my Brother, is the true Vengeance . . . . We have not hesitated to make known to you the true purpose of our Order." [333]

So, now we are starting to see the "true purpose of our [Masonic] Order."

It is a world filled with violence, murder and bloodshed.

It is a world filled with vengeance against "religion" and "government."

chapter 33
WHEN 3 OR 2 EQUALS 1

That there are three, or possibly two, enemies of Masonry is certain, at least at this point in our study.

But, as we continue, we shall see that there is only one.

The following quotations are taken, once again, from the pens of Rex Hutchens and Albert Pike, their major writers. This first one is from Albert Pike:

> "Hiram not only represents the Sun, and the Good Principle, but the Eternal, never-dying, primitive TRUTH, ever struggling for the victory.
>
> The Three assassins are *Ambition, Falsehood*, and *Ignorance*; the *ambition* of a corrupt Priesthood [by which he means religion,] who concealed the Truth from the Masses, [meaning that they have concealed "the true knowledge of God" from the people] that by means of debasing superstitions they might subjugate them more completely to their will;
>
> the *falsehood* of their myriad fictions and fables that soon become absolutely inexplicable, a mere jargon and chaos of confusion;
>
> and the *ignorance of the Masses*, that caused them to believe in error, and forget the truth [meaning government and religion, merged together, to force moral absolutes upon the unwilling people.]
>
> Such is the Masonic Myth." [334]

Rex Hutchens: ". . . the assassins are the symbols of tyranny, ignorance and intolerance or fanaticism." [335]

Albert Pike: "Behold, my Brother, the true explanation of the Master's Degree.

The Respectable Master Hiram, assassinated in the Temple, is the Grand Master of the Templars [apparently Mr. Pike is saying that Hiram and Jacques de-Molay are the same individual, at least symbolically] . . . . The three assassins are the King [meaning government,] the Pope [meaning religion] and the imprisoned Knight [representing the class that benefits from the merger of religion and government] . . . .

After these events, my Bro∴ [apparently referring to "my Brother,"] many Knights of the Temple were dispersed in all parts of the world, and established themselves as Knights Kadosh [the title of the 30th Degree, where the Mason is first taught officially that the "tyrants" represent religion and government.]" [336]

In this quotation from the 22nd Degree, Albert Pike explains that the apron, worn by the Mason as a symbol, has an important concealed meaning:

"The Apron is white lined and bordered with purple . . . . On the flap is a serpent with three heads." [337]

So here we see that Mr. Pike says that the three heads are on one serpent, presumably referring to the three-Gods-in-one God, meaning the God of the Bible. This would certainly be consistent with his other writings on the subject.

He added this thought:

"The three murderers [notice here that there are three murderers, perhaps meaning the three-in-one God] symbolize the chief causes of the loss of liberty of Nations [as we have seen, some of his other writings state that he considers the God of the Bible to be the cause of the "loss of liberty," or of representing government, religion and those who benefit from the merger of the two.]" [338]

So, once again, the Mason learns that he has permission to use violence in the war against "state" and "religion." But, notice that Mr. Pike's claims that there are three enemies is repeated later in the lecture of the twentieth degree:

Albert Pike: "The leading ideas in the Second Class, or that of *Instructors*, are:

In the ninth degree; That Masonry is the implacable antagonist of the three great evils that afflict humanity; the three great powers of darkness and evil, Falsehood, Fanaticism and Ignorance [religion, government, and the class that benefits from the merger of the two;]

and that its mission upon earth [meaning the Masonic mission, of the Knights Kadosch, the 30th Degree of Masonry] is ultimately to exterminate the first [meaning religion,] that inciter of the second [meaning government, created by those who wish for a moral world because of their religious teachings,] and of whom the third is the blind and stupid instrument [meaning the class that benefits from the merger of the two.]" [339]

Mr. Pike then brings in another symbol into the discussion: the Serpent. He wrote an explanation into the 19th Degree Ritual:

"The Serpent, writhing in chains, has to us a particular signification. It was promised that the offspring of the

261

woman should bruise the Serpent's head. Fulfill thou
the prophecy!

[The following sentence was placed in the brackets
by Mr. Pike:]

[The candidate is caused to step in succession on
the three heads: and as he does so, the Th∴ P∴ says, at
each step respectfully]:

So shall the foot of TRUTH *crush* ERROR!

So [shall] HONESTY *and* HONOR *trample on*
FALSEHOOD!

So CHARITY *tread in the dust* INTOLERANCE!" [340]

This quotation comes from Mr. Pike from his explanation of
the Ninth Degree, called the Knight Elu of Nine: This is what
he wrote:

Qu∴ "What was the first duty assigned to you?
Ans∴ To search for and apprehend the murderers of
our Gr∴ Master Hiram Abi, that they might be
tried and punished.
Qu∴ Did you find them?
Ans∴ One of them only; Abiram, their Chief and leader
. . . .
Qu∴ Of what is Abiram the type, to the Knights Elu?
Ans∴ Of Tyranny, chief assassin of Free Thought." [341]

So, here we see that there is in truth only one assassin: "tyranny." It appears as if all of what we have seen to far boils down
to there being just one enemy: anything or anybody that restricts man's freedom to express their own individual "free
thought." This thought is continued into the 10th Degree:

"This degree [the tenth, called by the title Elu of the
Fifteen] . . . . . [these dots were placed there by Mr.

Pike, the writer of the book] is devoted . . . to the cause of human freedom, corporeal and mental, against tyranny exercised over the soul or body.

The two assassins [in this explanation, Mr. Pike says that there are two assassins] of the Master Khirum (who is to us the symbol of that freedom), whose capture and execution are recounted in this degree, are the symbols of those special enemies of freedom, *Ambition,* of which *Tyranny* or *Despotism* is born [presumably meaning government,] and *Fanaticism*, from which spring *Intolerance* and *Persecution* [presumably meaning religion.]" *342*

And it is in the 30th Degree that the Mason learns that he will be a soldier in this warfare for the rest of his life. Albert Pike wrote this:

"In this chamber a grave voice announces the duties of a philosopher and a Knight Kadosh [the 30th Degree Mason.] The candidate learns that the Knight Kadosh 'now pursues with feet that never tire and eyes that never sleep, the personification of the three assassins [now there are three assassins] of Hiram, the Incarnations of Evil which these three were but the tools; and so labors unceasingly for the good of Mankind' [meaning the abolition of religion and government, and the class that benefits from the merger of the two.]" [343]

And he learns that this is a mortal combat, with total victory over the enemy the certain end result, even if it takes violence:

"Henceforward let our departed brother and revered Master be unto us and unto all Masons the symbol of Liberty, Intelligence and Truth, and his assassins of Ig-

norance, Tyranny and Intolerance; . . . that the freedom of the State [meaning the freedom from govern-
ment] can only be attained and perpetuated, by instructing the people, by following Ignorance [meaning
religion] into its darkest dens, and there smiting it
mortally and mercilessly." [344]

And the thought is repeated in the tenth degree, called the
ELU OF THE FIFTEEN:

"The apron [worn by the Mason in this degree] is
white, lined, edged and fringed with black; the flap also is black. In the center are painted or embroidered
three gates, and over each gate a head impaled on a
spike . . . .

The heads themselves represent ignorance [mean-
ing religion,] tyranny [meaning government,] and fanaticism [apparently meaning the merger of the two.]
It is against these vices that Masonry is particularly
opposed . . . .

The heads . . . [were] smitten by the sword of freedom." [345]

It might be somewhat illustrative of all that I've covered in
this chapter to quote a little poem that Thomas Paine included
to his book entitled THE AGE OF REASON in 1794. It is un-
clear in his writings whether or not Mr. Paine understood the
symbolism behind the words, but they do seem to have been
written by a Mason who did. The poem is entitled THE
DRAGON OF WANTLEY:

"Poor children three devoured he,
That could not with him grapple;
And at one sup [supper] he ate them up,

As a man would eat an apple." [346]

So the people of England spoke or sang the words to this little poem over two hundred years ago, not knowing (presumably) that they were speaking about a "dragon," meaning Masonry, that devours "three children," meaning Religion, the Government, and the Caste System that benefitted from the merger of State and Religion. This is probably a prime example of how they get us to mouth their words, without understanding their real meaning.

The symbols can be explained. 3 enemies, or 2 enemies, really equals 1 enemy.

We shall see who this "1 enemy" is.

chapter 34
THE 33RD DEGREE RITUAL

What you are about to read is perhaps the most controversial material I have included in this book. And it is because it summarizes everything that I have written so far. This information, if it is correct, is the piece that brings all of the other pieces of the puzzle together.

I believe the final proof of all that I have just covered is found in a book not written by a Mason. This book is called OCCULT THEOCRASY, written in 1933 by a woman author named Edith Starr Miller, also called Lady Queenborough.

She claimed that she was quoting a Mason when she inserted what she called the "Official ritual of the 33rd and last degree of [the] Ancient and Accepted Scottish Rite" into her book. It must be presumed that the Masons will claim that this rendition of the 33rd Degree Ritual, (maybe it is only a part of the entire Ritual,) is a fraud, since their Ritual is secret and has not been made public. I am including it in my book because I believe that it is an accurate reproduction of a part, if not all, of the 33rd Degree ritual. And I believe that the reader will see the amazing similarity between it and what we have just read from the major Masonic writers of the last 100 years.

I will leave the final verdict up to you, the reader. You can decide if you feel the following "ritual" is basically what the Masons have taught in their other writings. The "ritual" is covered on pages 363-364 in her book and reads as follows:

> "For the Sovereign Grand Inspector General the 33rd is the last degree of the Rite. The Order is the Great

Avenger of the assassinated Grand Master and the great champion of humanity, [this could be either Hiram Abif or Jacques deMolay] for the innocent Grand Master is man, man who is Master, King of Nature, man who is born innocent and unconscious. [As we have seen, these sentences are representative of what we have found in our research into the Masonic material.]

"Our innocent Grand Master [once again, this individual could be either Jacques deMolay or Hiram Abif. Both of these men have been called their "Grand Master"] was born for happiness and for the enjoyment of all rights without exception.

"But he has fallen under the blows of three assassins, three scoundrels have thwarted his happiness and rights and have annihilated him. [Once again, this sentence could be about either deMolay or Abif. So this sentence is also accurate. We have seen that they have written that both Jacques deMolay and Hiram Abif were murdered by three assassins.]

"The three infamous assassins are Law, Property and Religion. [Here Lady Queenborough identifies the hidden meaning behind the Masonic assertion that the three assassins are "Ignorance, Tyranny and Intolerance." So, this is the first time her rendition of the ritual varies with what the Masons have written. However, this does not mean that what she claims to have found is incorrect. She could have actually found the true ritual and made it public. My research will continue to reveal that these are the true meanings of the three symbols of the assassins.]

"Law, because it is not in harmony with the rights of the individual man and the duties of social man in society, rights which belong to all. Duties are but the immediate consequence of the right inherent in all for the enjoyment of all rights. [Here she claims that the ritual proclaims that the Masons are opposed to government, because it is government that passes "laws." This is the assertion made by the Masonic writers that I have examined. So this statement is accurate.]

"Property, because the earth belongs to nobody and its fruits belong to all in proportion as they are required by each for the needs of his own well being. [Here the ritual explains that "private property" is one of the targets of the Masons, as it is with Karl Marx, the so-called "father of Communism." This connection between the Masons and the Communists will be examined in an upcoming chapter.]

"Religion, because religions are but philosophies evolved by men of genius and adopted by the people in the belief that they would increase their well being. [We have already seen that this sentence is accurate. The Masons have repeatedly written about their desire to abolish religion.]

"Neither law, property nor religion can be imposed on man as they annihilate him by depriving him of his most precious rights. They are assassins on whom we have declared war to the death and without quarter. [We know that Masonry has vowed to avenge the death of their "master" and that there are "three" assassins, and Lady Queenborough has explained just what these three assassins represent.]

"Of these three infamous enemies [there are three enemies] it is on religion [but there is really only one enemy] that we must concentrate our most deadly attacks, because no people has ever survived its religion. Once Religion is dead, Law and Property will fall to our mercy, and we shall be able to regenerate society by founding on the corpses of the assassins of man, Masonic Religion, Masonic Law and Masonic Property." [347]

This last paragraph should convince even the skeptic. It appears as if Lady Queenborough found the real ritual, because it appears to reveal the true meaning behind the symbology of the three assassins. And the reason we can know for certain is that the Masons have written similar words, as we have seen in our study.

And it would be appropriate for the 33rd Degree Ritual writer to have written that their "most deadly attacks" should be concentrated on religion because, as this writer has suggested, once "religion falls, Law and Property" will follow as well. This hypothesis will be examined in the following chapter of my work.

Lastly, it should be remembered that Mr. Pike "wrote the rituals for all 33 Degrees." And Lady Queenborough's book was written in 1933, about 75 years after Mr. Pike completed the task. And if he was the "leader of the world wide Masonic movement," and if she found the 33rd Degree ritual as she claimed, then it had to be Mr. Pike's rendition. And, as we have seen, it compares favorably with the information he provided in his other works.

If it is his ritual, then it provides the final interpretation of the symbol of the three assassins. So it is a reasonable position to take that Mr. Pike has extended the meaning one step further than either the writings of the others, or of his own previously recorded writings. He states that the three assassins are "law, religion and [private] property," and not "religion, government and those who benefit by their merger."

It appears to me that what Lady Queenborough wrote is a valid transcription of the 33rd Degree Ritual, even if it is over 64 years old. It does, however, add something new to the discussion: it claims that the three assassins are Law, Property and Religion.

But, first let me examine the presumed Masonic objection to my quoting of this ritual. If the Masons are "a society with secrets," any Mason who claims that this "ritual" is not accurate, could not tell us if the quotation was accurate even if it was, because he had taken an oath of secrecy not to reveal the exact nature of any of their rituals. So, his denial would not necessarily be the truth, because it is still possible that this "ritual" was real and that he could not tell us that it was. And, if he knew that this was not the real ritual, he would deny it as well, because it was not the true rendition.

So, no matter what any Mason says, it does not mean anything, because of their "oath of secrecy."

The only "proof" that we have as to its accuracy is the fact that we have been able to prove that about 75% of it is reliable through the writings of key Masonic writers. We have read the works of Rex Hutchens, Albert Pike, Henry Wilson Coil, Albert Mackey and Manly P. Hall, amongst others. And their writings show the reader that Lady Queenborough was on the right track.

So my charge to the Masons still holds: Mason, show me where I am wrong!

Open up all of your rituals, especially the 30th and 33rd Degree ceremonies, so that I can attend! Let me see where I am wrong! But I believe there will be no such invitation.

And if there is no invitation, then accept my challenge to debate any Mason, anywhere, anytime, so that I can prove that I am right! As I wrote earlier in this book, no member of the Masons has yet accepted this challenge and I have been making it for over 10 years!

But the student of Masonry can know that neither of my challenges will be accepted! They cannot open up their secret rituals, and they cannot debate me on the subject, because I have used their own literature to discover THE SECRET!

chapter 35
THE ANTI-MASONS

In 1994, Art deHoyos and S. Brent Morris, two writers who also happen to be Masons, (Mr. Morris claims to be, in fact, a 33rd Degree Mason) wrote a book entitled IS IT TRUE WHAT THEY SAY ABOUT FREEMASONRY? This book claims to be a book about the "methods of [the] anti-Masons," those who write books discussing the negative aspects of Masonry.

The first complaint that I have about the book is that they did not include me as one of the "anti-Mason" writers that they named! My book entitled THE NEW WORLD ORDER, a thoroughly documented exposure of the Masonic ideas from official Masonic sources, was published in August of 1990, and their book was published four years later, in 1994. So they had approximately four years to find my book and critique it as they did several other books by other authors on the subject of Masonry.

One of those books they claim to have reviewed was Pat Robertson's book entitled THE NEW WORLD ORDER, published months after I published my book. So, they certainly could have known about my book by the same title, and quite possibly even the 14 hour lecture video series that I produced in 1994 with the same name, the year they published their findings, that more completely documents the problems I have with Masonry.

These two authors are very critical of us "anti-Masons," because we "are often dishonest in both little and much." They cite as an example the fact that many of the "anti-Mason" authors cite a letter by Albert Pike that they claim is bogus.

This is called the "Pike Luciferian Letter" that many believe was written by Mr. Pike on July 14, 1889. It was in this letter that Mr. Pike admitted that Lucifer, the devil, also called Satan, was a God, and that "the Masonic religion must be . . . maintained in the Luciferian doctrine."

That letter, according to those who use it, reads as follows: (it is taken from pages 220-221 of Lady Queenborough's OCCULT THEOCRASY:)

"That which we must say to the crowd [meaning the people of the world] is -- We [the high ranking Masons] worship a God, but it is the God that one adores without superstition. [As we have seen in other writings by Mr. Pike, he has stated that their belief in a God is based upon "reason," and not "faith." So, those who worship the God of the Bible do so without evidence. So, this "God" that they "adore" cannot be the God of the Bible, whom they claim is worshiped without any evidence of His existence.

Secondly, since Mr. Pike believes that it is an act of "faith" and not of man's ability to "reason" to believe in the God of the Bible, those who do worship a "creator God," "adore with superstition." His "God" is "adored "without superstition," because he is adored with "reason."]

To you, Sovereign Grand Inspectors General [the book claims that Mr. Pike wrote the letter to the leaders of the 23 Supreme Councils of the world,] we say this, that you may repeat it to the Brethern of the 32nd, 31st and 30th degrees [it is at the 30th Degree, called the Knight Kadosch degree, that the Mason learns the real secret of the Masons. That means that if you know the secret at the 30th, you will know it at

the next two higher degrees, the 31st and the 32nd] --
The Masonic religion should be, by all of us initiates of
the high degrees, maintained in the purity of the Luciferian doctrine.

If Lucifer were not God, would Adonay (The God
of the Christians) whose deeds prove his cruelty, per-
fidy and hatred of man, barbarism and repulsion for
science, would Adonay and his priests calumniate [de-
fined as meaning: "to accuse falsely and maliciously of
a crime or offense; to slander"] him?

Yes, Lucifer is God, and unfortunately Adonay is
also God. [Here the author of the letter proves that he
believes that there are two Gods in the universe. But
we have seen previously, and we shall see it again, that
Mr. Pike has written this as well, although in truth, he
does not believe in the Creator God.]

. . . the true and pure philosophical religion is the
belief in Lucifer, the equal of Adonay [the God of the
Bible;] but Lucifer, God of Light and God of Good, is
struggling for humanity against Adonay, the God of
Darkness and Evil." [348]

For those who claim that Mr. Pike did not write this letter,
they must deal with the following quotation from his book
entitled MAGNUM OPUS. Because he believes that there are
two "gods" in the universe, one more than the Bible teaches:

"All have admitted two gods with different occupations, one making the good and the other the evil
found in nature. The former has been styled 'God,'
and the latter 'Demon.' The Persians or Zoroaster
named the former Ormuzd and the latter Ahriman; of
whom they said one was of the nature of Light, and
the other that of Darkness. The Egyptians called the

former Osiris, and the Latter Typhon, his eternal enemy." [349]

So any fair individual would have to conclude that the last paragraph of the letter that Mr. Pike allegedly wrote, about Lucifer and Adonay, is totally consistent with the quotation just cited. And other parts of the letter are consistent with other writings of Mr. Pike.

Now the question should be asked as to how anyone could know for certain whether or not Mr. Pike wrote the letter. Certainly Mr. Pike is no longer living, so he cannot testify as to whether or not he wrote it. And no Mason, nor for that matter, any "anti-Mason," has ever claimed, as far as I have been able to determine, that Mr. Pike denied that he wrote it in the two years before his death. So, I believe it is fair to claim that no one, on either side of the issue, knows for certain whether the letter is valid.

Also, I have never read where the Masons sued Lady Queenborough for her claim that Mr. Pike wrote the letter.

This lack of such evidence is certainly not conclusive either way, but if such a lawsuit exists, no one that I can find has ever written about it.

So, the only way we can know if the letter is valid is to compare it to other known writings of Mr. Pike and see if the letter appears to be real because it shares similar thoughts to those expressed in known writings of Mr. Pike.

And that has been done.

And they do.

Because one can be certain that Mr. Pike did agree that Lucifer was "the Light-bearer" that "brings the Light" to the Mason who asks for it. Because he was the one who wrote that he was! And he is the one who wrote that each Mason states that "Light" is what he most desires.

Both Art deHoyos and S. Brent Morris, the two writers who wrote the critical book about the "Anti-Masons," were very critical of those "anti-Masons" who used this quotation in their literature. (I was one, but they did not mention that. I explained my use of the quotation in my book entitled THE NEW WORLD ORDER in 1990, on pages 63 to 66, and explained it much the same way that I did above.)

But, and this is very important, they found no fault with anyone using the first quotation, the one that I call "the 33rd Degree ritual" quotation, taken from OCCULT THEOCRASY. These two authors cite no objection to any "Anti-Mason" writer using this quote.

Now, there are only two possibilities as to why they chose not to be critical of those who quote Lady Queenborough's citation of the 33rd Degree Ritual.

One: it is conceivable that they know that this quotation is accurate, so they can not criticize any researcher when he uses it, or two: they did not know of its existence.

However, one would assume that the second option simply could not be the case. They cite the source of the "Lucifer" letter as being Lady Queenborough's book entitled OCCULT THEOCRASY. So they certainly could have objected to anyone's use of the "33rd Degree Ritual" as well, because it is in the same book. But they did not.

They had, for reasons cited above, known about me and my research, that is, if they had read John Robinson's book entitled A PILGRIM'S PATH. Mr. Robinson discusses my book in his book (see pages 240 and 241 above for the entire discussion of this fact.)

So, if they had heard of my book, and they believed that the 33rd Degree Ritual was not valid, they should have been critical of me for using it. However, their book takes no position on my quoting of this ritual. And in fact, they are not critical in their book of anyone using the quotation. So, it must be that they believe that it is an accurate quotation, especially when one of the two authors is a 33rd Degree Mason himself.

So, it appears as if Lady Queenborough found the truth when she repeated the ritual for her readers.

But, now back to their book.

As I said, there are clues that they knew about me and my research prior to their writing of their book. It is particularly interesting to note that they dedicated their book "to the memory of John Jamieson Robinson, Researcher, Author, [and] Master Mason." (It will be remembered that Mr. Robinson was the man I had my television "debate" with in Tampa, Florida.) That must mean that they were familiar with both of his books, the last one of which was published in 1993, maybe as much as a year before they published their book.

Yet, they made no mention of me and my work of many years of involvement in exposing the Masons.

And Mr. Robinson wrote about me directly in his second book!

Could it be that they did read my book and felt that I had accurately portrayed the hundreds of quotations taken from major Masonic sources? And then they chose to be critical of those researchers who had not been as thorough?

It is possible that they felt that I had done as James T. Tresner, II, a "Master Mason" who wrote the Foreword to their book, suggested on page x:

> "Examine us in depth -- we have nothing to hide." [350]

(It is ironic: if you do examine the Masons in depth, and report what you find, they call you "an anti-Mason!" Or, as in my case, they simply ignore you and pick on others who might not have "examined [the Masons] in [great] depth.")

Maybe they knew that I have spent about 12 years examining the Masons "in depth." And, secondly, they are right in one sense of that phrase: "they have nothing to hide" because they have made it public in their own materials!

But they have plenty "to hide" from the people of the world.

Yes, Mr. deHoyos and Mr. Morris, I have "examined [your organization] in depth."

And I have found "the secret."

And I am not wrong by citing your own evidence.

In fact, I am duty bound to expose it!

chapter 36
OTHER ANTI-MASONS

These two Masonic writers, Art deHoyos and S. Brent Morris, somehow failed to mention that there have been numerous "Anti-Masons" writing for many years about their concerns with Masonry. These two writers have been very selective as to who they wrote about. The following comments are taken from my personal files on the subject, and they are not very extensive. However, they are reflective of the concern that many others have had with the Freemasons in the past.

On April 20, 1884, Pope Leo the Thirteenth of the Catholic Church issued a papal encyclical entitled HUMANUM GENUS, which was extremely critical of Freemasonry. It appears as if the Pope issued his paper during the time when Albert Pike was busy managing the affairs of the "worldwide Masonic movement." The Pope wrote this:

> "At this period, however, the partisans of evil seems to be combining together, and to be struggling with united vehemence, led on or assisted by that strongly organized and widespread association called the Freemasons. No longer making any secret of their purposes, they are now boldly rising up against God himself." [351]

He continued:

> ". . . that which is their ultimate purpose forces itself into view -- namely, the utter overthrow of that whole religious and political order of the world [meaning that he had discovered the secret goal of the Masons: the destruction of the church and the government] which the Christian teaching has produced, and the substitu-

tion of a new state of things in accordance with their ideas, of which the foundations and laws shall be drawn from mere naturalism.

Then he connected what he had learned about Masonry with a religion known as "naturalism:"

"Now, the fundamental doctrine of the naturalists . . , is that human nature and human reason ought in all things to be mistress and guide [this is the same goal that I found when I studied the works of the Masons] . . . . it is against the Church that the rage and attack of the enemies are principally directed [it is clear that he found the stated goal of the Masons.]" [352]

". . . their [the Freemasons] endeavor [is] to obtain equality and community of all goods by the destruction of every distinction of rank and property. [Here the Pope shows that the Masons are out to destroy private property as well. This is also what the ritual that Lady Queenborough quoted in her book entitled OCCULT THEOCRASY says.]" [353]

It is obvious that the Pope had figured it out: he was aware that the Masons were out to destroy Christianity, including the God-given right to private property, and the government created by the people to protect that right.

What possibly happened to the Pope after he wrote these warnings to the world was perhaps revealed in a Time magazine article on June 18, 1984. The article said this:

". . . there were whispers about how poison killed Leo XIII in 1903 . . . ."

Another famous "Anti-Mason" was John Quincy Adams, the sixth President of the United States. He wrote this in 1833, after he was President:

"I do conscientiously and sincerely believe that the Order of Freemasonry, if not the greatest, is one of the greatest moral and political evils under which the Union is now laboring." [354]

He continued by saying that Masonry was: "A conspiracy of the few against the equal rights of the many; anti-Republican [here he was not referring to the Republican Party, but to a concept of a republic as a form of government] in its sap [meaning in its vitality] . . . ." [355]

"I am prepared to complete the demonstration before God and man, that the Masonic oath, obligations and penalties cannot by any possibility be reconciled to the laws of morality, of Christianity, or of the land." [356]

Millard Fillmore, the thirteenth President of the United States, voiced his concerns as well:

"The Masonic fraternity tramples upon our rights, defeats the administration of justice, and bids defiance to every government which it cannot control." [357]

Another who spoke out against the Masons was the eighteenth President of the United States, Ulysses S. Grant, who has been quoted as saying this:

"All secret oath-bound political parties are dangerous to any nation, no matter how pure or how patriotic the motives and principles which first bring them together." [358]

Masonry is certainly not a "political party," but they are "se-cret [and] oath-bound," and they claim to "shape the destinies of worlds." Therefore, it is reasonable to presume that he was talking about them, and not the Democrats or the Republicans.

John Marshall, the Chief Justice of the Supreme Court in the early days of this nation, was a member of the Masonic Lodge. Apparently he changed his mind, and later recanted. He made this charge:

> "The institution of Masonry ought to be abandoned as one capable of much evil, and incapable of producing any good which might not be effected by safe and open means." [359]

Another warning came from John G. Stevens, a Baptist cler-gyman, who denounced his Masonic ties by publishing his views in AN INQUIRY INTO THE NATURE AND TEND-ENCY OF SPECULATIVE MASONRY. Included in his wri-tings were these conclusions:

> "Masonry was a state within a state and that one day Masons would overthrow the democratic government of the United States and would crown one of their 'grand kings' as ruler of this nation." [360]

This quotation is reminiscent of the one that Albert Pike used as being typical of those that the "anti-Masons" would make against the Masons:

> ". . . the World will soon come to us [apparently meaning the Masons] for its Sovereigns [apparently meaning its governmental leaders] and Pontiffs [appar-ently meaning its religious leaders.]

> We [the Masons] shall constitute the equilibrium
> of the Universe, and be rulers over the Masters of the
> World." [361]

So, someone else believed that this quotation was valid!

Another minister who came out of the Masonic Order was
Charles G. Finney, who left the Order in 1826. He wrote a
little pamphlet entitled WHY I LEFT FREEMASONRY, in
which he made these observations:

> ". . . in taking these oaths, I had been grossly deceived
> and imposed upon [the reader might remember Albert
> Pike's quotation stating that the Adept Masons "inten-
> tionally mislead" the initiate Masons.] Indeed I came
> to the deliberate conclusion that my oaths had been
> procured by fraud and misrepresentations; that the in-
> stitution was in no respect what I had been informed
> it was; and . . . it has become more and more irresist-
> ibly plain to me that Masonry is highly dangerous to
> the State, and in every way injurious to the Church of
> Christ [so another "anti-Mason" points out that the
> Masons are out to destroy Christianity and the govern-
> ment.]"

Another who attempted to warn the world about the Masonic
Order was Bernard Fay, who wrote a book entitled REVO-
LUTION AND FREEMASONRY.

This is why he shared his concern:

> "The New Masonry did not aim to destroy churches,
> but, with the aid of the progress of ideas, it prepared
> to replace them." [362]

Even some Christian denominations have voiced their concerns. The Orthodox Presbyterian Church met at Rochester, New York, on June 2-5, 1942, and they issued a report on the Ancient Order of Free and Accepted Masons. The following was part of their conclusions:

> ". . . Masonry is a religious institution and as such is definitely anti-Christian. Membership in the Masonic fraternity is inconsistent with Christianity." [363]

The Eastern Orthodox Church issued a book on the subject of Masonry called CHRISTIAN-ORTHODOX LIGHT ON SPECULATIVE FREEMASONRY in 1948. It was their conclusion that:

> "Freemasonry is anti-christian in both theory and practice; it fights national governments, especially in Christian countries."

The authors of this book quote Metropolitan Anthony, the leader of all European Russian Orthodox Churches outside of Russia, who issued a position paper on August 15, 1932. This report said this about Freemasonry:

> "Freemasonry is a secret international organization struggling with God, Christianity, and all national governments, and especially Christian governments."

So, it does not appear as if anything has changed since then.

But one of the more dramatic studies of the Masons occurred a short time ago in England, when the Church of England released a report on the Lodge after they convened a summer session intended to examine the Order. The article that appeared in the Arizona Daily Star, released by the Associated Press on July 14, 1987, said that:

> "Church of England leaders overwhelmingly endorsed a report yesterday that called Freemason rituals blasphemous [defined as: "uttering blasphemy," which is defined as: "irreverence toward anything regarded as sacred."]
> The report [entitled] FREEMASONRY AND CHRISTIANITY: ARE THEY COMPATIBLE? said some Christians found Masonic rituals disturbing and 'positively evil.'" [364]

Perhaps the best summary of the whole concern about the Masonic Order came from another ex-Mason, Edward Ronayne, in his book entitled THE MASTER'S CARPET. Mr. Ronayne said that Masonry:

> ". . . is a system which has not the least shadow of support, either from history, from scripture, from reason, or from common sense, but, in fact, is diametrically opposed to them all." [365]

But for some unknown reason, Art deHoyos and S. Brent Morris failed to mention these "anti-Masons" in their book.

It would certainly be appropriate to ask them why.

chapter 37
BIRDS OF A FEATHER

There are other people, and other organizations, besides the Masonic Lodge, that wish to abolish "law, religion and property."

Two of these men were Karl Marx, the so-called "father of communism," and Frederick Engels who together wrote a book entitled THE COMMUNIST MANIFESTO in 1848. The 100th anniversary edition of the book, published in 1948, contains several pages of information about their organization called The Communist Party in addition the basic beliefs of Communism.

It is important for the student of Masonry to review the contents of this book because the reader will discover that they, and the other Communists who followed them, share the same goals as do the Masons: the abolition of Law, Religion and Property. These men wrote:

> "In this sense, the theory of the Communists may be summed up in the single sentence: Abolition of private property.
>
> We Communists have been reproached with the desire of abolishing the right of personally acquiring property as the fruit of a man's own labour [their spelling of the word "labor,"] which property is alleged to be the ground work of all personal freedom, activity and independence." [366]

> "In one word, you reproach us with intending to do away with your property. Precisely so: that is just what we intend." [367]

But not only were the Communists intending to do away with "private property," they also were out to destroy religion, primarily Christianity. In the introduction to a book entitled CAPITAL AND OTHER WRITINGS BY KARL MARX, Max Eastman states that:

"Marx was an implacable enemy of religion . . . ." [368]

In 1964, The Committee on the Judiciary of the United States Senate commissioned a subcommittee to study what it called THE CONTRADICTIONS OF COMMUNISM. This report of 64 pages examines many of the quotations taken from the major Communist writers. And they reported on the views of the Communist leaders on the major issues of the day.

The writers of this report confirm the above quotation with this one of their own:

"Marx has branded religion as 'the opium of the people.'" [369]

Marx was commenting that opium, a narcotic and habit-forming drug, was analogous to religion, a man's method of getting closer to God.

But, here he is saying that it is his opinion that religion drugs mankind, and clouds his mind from seeing the truth.

According to Marvin S. Antelman, a Jewish Rabbi in his book, Marx's entire quotation is:

"Religion is the lament of the oppressed, the soul of a world that has no soul, the hope of a humanity which has lost all hope; it is the opiate of the people." [370]

287

Nikolai Lenin, an atheist, the leader of the Bolshevik faction of the Communist Party in Russia, and the leader of the Bolshevik Revolution and ultimately the head of the Russian government itself, shared Marx's view. The report stated that Lenin in fact had carried this thought further:

> "Religion is the opium of the people. Religion is a kind of spiritual gin in which the slaves of capital drown their human shape and their claims to any decent life . . . this dictum of Marx's is the cornerstone of the whole Marxist view on religion.
>
> Marxism has always regarded all modern religions and churches and all religious organizations as instruments of bourgeois reaction that serve to defend exploitation and to drug the working class." [371]

So Lenin took Marx one step further. He not only wished to abolish religion, he desired to "combat" it. The Report quotes him as saying:

> "Atheism is an integral part of Marxism." [372]

> "We must combat religion [this is the same goal of the Masons] . . . . The fight against religion must not be confined to abstract ideological preaching or reduced to such preaching. The fight must be linked up with the concrete practical work of the class movement . . . . " [373]

Reverend Richard Wurmbrand is a Christian Minister from Romania, a Communist nation until the Berlin Wall came down in the 1980's, and he was imprisoned for 14 years in his native land because of his outspoken views against Communism. He has written that:

". . . Lenin, at the age of sixteen, tore the cross [meaning the symbol of Christianity] from his neck, spat on it, and trod it underfoot, a very common Satanist ceremony.

There is not the slightest doubt that Lenin was dominated by Satanist ideology [here Rev. Wurmbrand is saying that Lenin was a believer in Satan, another name of Lucifer, the devil.]" [374]

Joseph Stalin was another Communist, and the successor to Nikolai Lenin as the premier of Communist Russia. According to the Senate Report, he repudiated any idea of neutrality toward religion when they quoted him as saying:

"The [Communist] Party cannot be neutral towards religion, and it does conduct antireligious propaganda against all and every religious prejudice [just like the Masons] because it stands for science while religious prejudices run counter to science, because all religion is something opposite to science." [375]

Once again, this is wrong. True science proves the existence of God, it does not disprove it. I wrote a chapter on Evolution in my book entitled THE UNSEEN HAND that charges that Evolution is a fraud and a hoax. Lenin certainly lived after Charles Darwin admitted that his theory was wrong himself (see THE ORIGIN OF SPECIES in which he states several times that it is not true) so it is impossible for Lenin not to have known that. Yet he charges that science disproves "religion," when just the opposite is true.

So it becomes apparent from this brief review of the writings of the major Communists of this era, that they embrace a philosophy that teaches the destruction of religion and private property. Their last target, like the last target of the Masons, was government.

Max Eastman explained that Marx had very specific goals for the Communist society of the future. He stated that Marx's goal was:

> ". . . a society without classes and without government by force . . . ." [376]

The Report connects all three of these Communist leaders with the last of the three goals: the destruction of government. They say that:

> "Marx, Engels, Lenin, and Stalin all considered the state under capitalism as an instrument of class repression. This characterization they applied to both democracies and monarchies. Lenin put it this way:
>
> 'According to Marx, the state is an organ of class rule, an organ for the oppression of one class by another . . . .'" [377]

They promised the victims of their propaganda that, under communism, the state, that hated instrument of capitalist repression, would be done away with. Their logic for this theory was formulated by Engels:

> "Insofar as, at long last, the State becomes truly representative of society at large, it renders itself superfluous. As soon as there is no longer any social class which has to be kept in subjection, . . . there will be nothing left to repress, and therefore nothing which will necessitate the existence of a special repressive authority, a State . . . .

The Government of persons is replaced by the administration of things and by the management of the processes of production. The state is not 'abolished,' it dies out." [378]

This idyllic picture was amplified by Lenin in an authoritative work entitled THE STATE AND REVOLUTION in which he wrote:

". . . . there will vanish all need for force, for the subjection of one man to another, and of one part of the population to another, since people will grow accustomed to observing the elementary conditions of social existence without force and without subjection." [379]

The student of Masonry can see the "logic" of these Communists: if man abolishes religion, there will no longer be any crime. If there is no private property, there will be nothing to steal. If there is no marriage, there will be no adultery. If no man has the right to life, there will be no need for courts and prisons to punish those who wrongfully take the life of another. If there is no need for government, it can and will be allowed to wither away.

This is the same thinking of the Masons. They wish to abolish religion, and when they do, there will be no need for government.

The fact that Karl Marx wanted to "abolish private property," "the family," "national borders," etc., is no surprise to the student of Communism. And the answer is simply unbelievable: it was because Karl Marx, apparently like Lenin, a fellow Communist, was a Satanist: he knowingly worshiped Satan, also known as Lucifer, or the Devil.

291

This startling conclusion was reached by Reverend Richard Wurmbrand, the Christian Pastor from Romania briefly discussed above. He is the author of many books on the subject, but the two that are pertinent to this study are WAS KARL MARX A SATANIST?, published in 1976, and MARX AND SATAN, published ten years later, in 1986. These two books build a case that young Karl was a member of a Satanic cult during his college years.

And to prove that is so, it is possible to glean this information from the writings of Karl Marx himself. Marx wrote not only about the need to destroy "religion," but the Christian religion in particular:

> "The abolition of religion as the illusory happiness of man is a demand for their real happiness." [380]

> "We make war against all prevailing ideas of religion .... The idea of God is a keynote of a perverted civilization. It must be destroyed." [381]

According to Rev. Wurmbrand, Marx wrote the following in a poem:

> "I wish to avenge myself against the One who rules above [meaning the ruling God in the Bible who gives man "moral absolutes."]" [382]

George Jung, a contemporary of Marx's and a personal friend, wrote in 1841 that:

> "Marx will surely chase God from his heaven .... Marx calls the Christian religion one of the most immoral of religions." [383]

And now history knows why Marx turned against Christianity. He joined a Satanic cult when he went away from home to a college. Rev. Wurmbrand writes that Marx's long hair (pictures of Marx show him with long hair and an unkempt beard) was a:

"... characteristic of the disciples of Joanna Southcott, a Satanic priestess who considered herself in contact with the demon Shiloh." [384]

Mikhail Bakunin, a Russian anarchist, meaning he favored the complete dissolution of all governments, explained the attraction that Satan had to young college minds like Marx's:

"Satan is the first free-thinker and Saviour [the spelling used in the quotation] of the world. He frees Adam [the first man in the Bible, and presumably a symbol of mankind, at least in the thinking of Bakunin] and impresses the seal of humanity and liberty on his forehead [the forehead is the location of the "mind's eye," meaning the direct passage to the interior brain,] by making him disobedient." [385]

So, young college students, in many cases away from the influence of their God-fearing parents for the first time, were being taught that they were no longer to listen to their parents and their outmoded religion, but to Satan who was to be the positive influence for all of mankind. So here we see the reason that Marx was also out to destroy the family: parents were commonly the source of the teaching about morality. The students who were away from their parents were being taught that this being was the first "rebel," and that he should become the model for their lives. The thinking that God was an evil force and that his civilization had to be destroyed so that man could be totally free was the philosophy taught at college to impressionable minds like those of Marx and Bakunin.

Marx bought into the lie. He wrote:

> "Communists preach absolutely no morals." [386]

Morality was the constraint on mankind's freedom, and it had to be abolished. Christian-style civilization, based upon a belief in private property, nationalism, freedom and the right to life, especially became the target of the young students.

But, now, looking backward to the years when Marx wrote, it is revealing to learn that only a small percentage of the written ideas of Marx have ever been allowed to surface in history.

> "In *The Revolted Man,* Albert Camus [the author of the book] stated that thirty volumes of Marx and Engels have never been published . . . ." [387]

That means that the complete thoughts of Marx have never been made available to the public. It can only be presumed that someone does not want the world to know exactly what Marx believed in. The motive must be the thought that if the world could read his complete works, they would probably understand the complete depravity of this man's ideas, or that they would discover Marx's belief in the Devil as a god. So, someone has decided that the world cannot learn what Marx truly believed. His ideas would apparently disgust even those who believe his theories.

But Marx and Frederick Engels, his co-author of THE COMMUNIST MANIFESTO, did not come up with this document on their own: they were hired by an existing organization of

very rich and powerful men. That organization was known as
The Communist League, whose history is detailed in the 100th
Anniversary Edition of the Communist Manifesto, previously
discussed. This review of their history was written on page xi
of that book:

> "The Communist League sprang from what was
> known as the League of the Just. The latter, in turn
> was an offshoot of the Parisian Outlaws' League,
> founded by German refugees in that city. After a tur-
> bulent ten-year period the League of the Just found its
> 'center of gravity,' as Engels put it, in London, where,
> he added, a new feature came to the fore: 'From being
> German, the League became *international.*'" [388]

Many historians are convinced that the "German refugees"
who formed the organization that was the foundation of the
Communist League were members of the Illuminati. The members of this secret society had fled Bavaria, now part of Ger-
many, after their plans for revolution had been discovered by
the Bavarian government.

One who saw the connection between Karl Marx and the Illuminati was Winston Churchill, the Prime Minister of England during and after World War II. Mr. Churchill was also a
member of the Masonic Lodge, and was certainly in a position
of leadership so that he would know enough to make comments like this one:

> "From the days of Spartacus -- Weishaupt [Spartacus
> was the secret code name Adam Weishaupt, the foun-
> der of the Illuminati, used to conceal his identity inside
> the order] to those of Karl Marx [the "father of Com-
> munism," who wrote the COMMUNIST MANI-

FESTO,] to those of Trotsky [meaning Leon Trotsky, the Communist active in the two Russian Revolutions] . . . this world-wide conspiracy for the overthrow of civilization [the goal of all of these secret societies, including the Communist Party] . . . has been steadily growing." [389]

So, Mr. Churchill, an extremely powerful man, certainly saw the power of this conspiracy in the affairs of his day. And he linked the Illuminati of 1776, to Karl Marx of 1848, and to the Communist Revolutions of 1905 and 1917.

As just mentioned, the founder of the Illuminati was Adam Weishaupt, born on February 6, 1748, a professor of Canon Law at the University of Ingolstadt. That means that the Professor taught his students just what the official position of the Catholic Church, called The Canon Law, was on the moral questions of the day.

This school was operated by the Jesuit Order, part of the Catholic Church, and there are many historians who feel that he was a Jesuit priest himself. One such comment was made by Albert Mackey, the Mason, who wrote this in his section on the "Illuminati of Bavaria:"

"Weishaupt . . . had originally been a Jesuit . . . ." [390]

There are Catholics today who deny that this could be true, but it certainly goes without saying that no one on either side of this issue can say for certain, because Weishaupt has since passed on, and left no comment himself that I am aware of as to the accuracy of the claim. Nor has anyone that I know of found evidence to either support or reject the statement. All that is known, as far as my research has shown, is that he was a teacher at a Jesuit school in Bavaria, teaching the Catholic morality to college students.

Professor Weishaupt founded the organization on May 1, 1776, and secretly started recruiting initiates. Within two years of its founding, all of the Professors at the University, with two exceptions, were members of the Illuminati. But membership lists captured by the Bavarian government after its existence had been discovered, showed that lawyers, counselors, counts, clergymen, priests and barons had joined. In other words, the "common man," supposedly yearning to be free of religion and government, was not joining the Illuminati. It was the upper class and the intellectuals of the day, yearning to be free from the oppression of "religion and government."

In 1783, the Bavarian government convened an investigation of the Illuminati when four professors were summoned to a Court of Enquiry. They confessed that they were members of the Order and they revealed for the first time in public what the goals of the Order were. The Elector of Bavarian government ordered the Illuminati abolished on June 22, 1784, and their members, including Weishaupt, fled the country. The Professor, after being banned from Bavaria:

> ". . . repaired to Gotha, [apparently a city in Germany] where he was kindly received by Duke Ernest, who made him a counselor and gave him a pension. There he remained until he died in 1811." [391]

This is why many historians feel these fleeing members of the Illuminati were the "German refugees" who would later form the Communist League. And the reason they do so is because they have discovered that the Communists perpetuate the ideas of the Illuminati.

297

Weishaupt put his views in writing for others to see. He directly stated what their plans were and how he hoped to function in the society. He wrote:

> "Of all the means I know to lead men, the most effectual is a concealed mystery." [392]

> "The great strength of our Order lies in its concealment; let it never appear in any place in its own name, but always covered by another name, and another occupation." [393]

So it was always their purpose to conceal their activities inside other organizations. That means that the members were instructed to infiltrate other groups and take over the roles of leadership in the second organization. And then he detailed how he would succeed in his endeavor in at least one field of activity:

> "We must do our utmost to procure the advancement of Illuminati into all important civil [defined as: "of a citizen or citizens, their government"] offices." [394]

The Professor revealed to the world what his philosophy was when he wrote this:

> "Man is not bad except as he is made so by arbitrary morality. He is bad because Religion, the State, [here Weishaupt states that his two enemies are the same as those of Masonry, religion and the government,] and bad examples pervert him." [395]

So Weishaupt was claiming that the problem of mankind was "religion," and once it was removed from the face of the earth, mankind could live in a paradise. And to eliminate the problem, he formed a secret society with that motive as its dominate activity. He felt that if you could eliminate religion, you would eliminate the need for a government. It is the church that sets up standards for behavior, and if you remove those standards, you remove the need for people to protect themselves from those who would violate those standards. Religion leads to crime. Eliminate religion and governments created to punish crime and you will live in a paradise.

This is the essence of what the Professor was writing.

One of those great secrets that Weishaupt was keeping from the world is this one, revealed to their initiates in the Second degree ritual:

> ". . . nations must be brought back to that state, by whatever means are conducible -- peaceably, if it can be done; but, if not, then by force -- for all subordination [defined as: "being submissive to authority"] must vanish from the face of the earth." [396]

So tyranny is any action by a government or a religion. And it is religion that causes people to form governments.

This, in turn, sets up standards for man to follow, and these are the "bad examples" that the Professor wrote about.

Because he believed that when man:

> "lives under government, he is fallen . . . ." [397]

Can you imagine a time when there would be no crime, no sin, because there would be no guilt because you harmed someone else? All of mankind could live guilt-free because there would be no crime and no sin. He would live without "tyranny" because there would be no government and no religion. This is "the utopia" envisioned by this dreamer.

But there is a price to pay for this paradise.

Some men would feel it was acceptable to rape, or to steal, or to murder.

So the society these dreamers will build will be free of government and religion, but there will be abundant rape, murder and plunder, because there will be no restrictions placed on man.

Fortunately for mankind, two great researchers wrote books around this time exposing the Illuminati and their beliefs. One was a book written in 1798 by Professor John Robison entitled PROOFS OF A CONSPIRACY, and the other was a four volume set entitled MEMOIRS ILLUSTRATING THE HISTORY OF JACOBINISM, which in part covers this author's research into the Illuminati. This second book was written by the Abbe Augustin Barruel, a Jesuit Priest of the Catholic Church, in 1797-98. The ironic thing is that both men, without the one knowing the other, reached the same conclusions about the Illuminati.

Prof. Robison was Professor of Natural Philosophy at Edinburgh University in Scotland, and a member of the Masonic Lodge. He was the general secretary of the Royal Society in that city, and some of his contemporaries labeled him as "one of the leading intellects of his time."

James Watt, the inventor of the steam engine, called the Professor:

"a man of the clearest head and the most science of anybody I have ever known." [398]

Professor Robinson was asked to join the Illuminati and it is presumed that he was because he was a member of the Masons. He was very cautious and proceeded to investigate their organization prior to his joining, and he decided to make his research available to the public.

And the reason he made that determination was because he discovered the true purpose of the Order: it was not as they had stated. This is what he wrote:

> "The great aim professed by the Order is *to make men happy*; and the means professed to be employed as the only and surely effective, is *making them good*; and this is to be brought about by *enlightening the mind*, and *freeing it from the dominion of superstition and prejudices* [meaning that Weishaupt wanted to free man from the moral constraints of religion. This was the identical thought to that of Karl Marx who wrote about 70 years later. We have seen that there are ties between the Illuminati and the Communists.]
>
> This purpose is effected by its *producing a just and steady morality*. This done, and becoming universal, there can be little doubt but that the peace of society will be the consequence -- that government, subordination, and all the disagreeable coercions of civil governments will be unnecessary -- and that society may go on peaceably in a state of perfect liberty and equality." [399]

The Professor explained to its members that the Illuminati had two goals:

"AN ASSOCIATION HAS BEEN FORMED for the express purpose of ROOTING OUT ALL THE RELIGIOUS ESTAB-LISHMENTS, AND OVERTURNING ALL THE EXISTING GOVERNMENTS OF EUROPE." [400]

". . . their real intention was to abolish *all* religion, overturn every government, and make the world a general plunder and a wreck . . . ." [401]

So, here we see that the Illuminati had the same goals as the Masons: the destruction of religion and government.

But, the Professor went on to identify just how the Illuminati wished to "make men happy:"

"But to do this, . . . this must be . . . suggested . . . by removing the restrictions of religion . . . .
. . . to accomplish this, they want to abolish Chris-tianity." [402]

And the Professor reported that his research went further:

"It surely needs little argument now to prove, that the Order of the Illuminati had for its immediate object the abolishing of Christianity . . . with the sole view of overturning civil government." [403]

He further linked the desire to destroy Christianity and gov-ernment with their desire to destroy property rights. He wrote:

". . . they meant to abolish the laws which protected property accumulated by long-continued and success-ful industry; and to prevent for the future any such ac-cumulation.

They intended to root out all religion and ordinary morality, and even to break the bonds of domestic life, by destroying the veneration for marriage vows, and by taking the education of children out of the hands of the parents," [404]

And to remind his readers just how they were going to accomplish their task, he informed us that they intended to go underground, especially into government:

"By this plan we shall direct all mankind . . . . The occupations must be so allotted and contrived, that we may, in secret, influence all political transactions." [405]

So that there may be no doubt that this is what he desired for mankind, Weishaupt put it into writing:

"There must . . . not a single purpose ever come in sight . . . that may betray our aims against religion and the state . . ." [406]

So there is no question: the Illuminati wanted to destroy religion, especially Christianity, and government. And we can know that for certain because the founder put his goals into writing.

On page 393 of Abbe Barruel's book, in a section entitled THE ANTISOCIAL CONSPIRACY, the Abbe says that he:

"denominated *the conspiracy* [meaning the Illuminati] *of the Sophisters* [defined as: "a teacher or thinker"] *of Impiety* [defined as: "irreverence, or ungodliness"] *and Anarchy* [defined as: "a state of society where there is no law or supreme power"] *against every religion na-*

303

tural or revealed; not only against kings, but against
every government, against all civil society, even
against all property whatsoever. " [407]

The priest then summarized the goals of the Illuminati very
succinctly when he wrote this:

"Princes [meaning governments] and Nations [with
their Christian style civilizations] SHALL disappear
from the face of the Earth . . . and this REVOLUTION
SHALL be the WORK OF SECRET SOCIETIES." [I added
the emphasis] [408]

So the priest had discovered the goal of the Illuminati: the destruction of law, religion and property, the same goals as those
of the Masonic Lodge. These two books were written to expose the Illuminati as an anti-Christian group out to destroy,
not just religion, but specifically the religious teachings of
Christ. In fact, the Abbe wrote about their goals repeatedly:

"We SHALL therefore begin with the conspiracy
against the whole religion of the Gospel, and which we
have styled the ANTICHRISTIAN CONSPIRACY." [I added the emphasis to show that they believe that they
will be successful in their endeavors.) [409]

". . . each individual [member of the Illuminati] . . .
had . . . secretly concurred in that wish, to destroy the
religion of Christ . . . . My proofs shall be drawn from
. . . the records of the conspiracy . . . ." [410]

". . . the grand object of the conspiracy, ... to crush
the Christ whom they pursued with unrelenting hatred
. . . ." [411]

"The religion which is to be destroyed is the religion of
Christ . . . ." [412]

And in a section that appears to be a long quotation from the
writings of Weishaupt himself, the Abbe says that their leader
wrote this:

"If, to overturn Christianity, and every Religion, we
pretended solely to possess true Christianity, the true
Religion [meaning that the Illuminati would infiltrate
even the very churches that they were out to destroy.
This is why some members of the conspiracy join local
churches, sometimes in a position of leadership, such
as a pastor or priest. They do not believe that Jesus is
the son of God, but they attend church regularly. It is
an enormous cover, intended to give respectability,]
remember that the *end sanctifies* [defined as: "to make
holy, to make free from sin"] *the means*, [Weishaupt
was instructing his members that they would not have
to restrain their activities by any sense of morality. If
the contemplated action furthered the goals of the Illuminati, the members had permission to perform it, no
matter what means they used] that the sage *must make
use of all those means for good purposes, which the
wicked do for evil.*" [413]

So, if this is a quotation from Weishaupt himself, it would
appear that he also had bought the philosophy of the Masons
that there are no moral absolutes; that each member of the Illuminati may do as he sees fit to advance their cause.

That thought is familiar, because it the exact teaching, said in
other words, of Albert Pike, the "leader of the world-wide
Masonic movement."

And to show the reader that these comments made about the anti-Christian nature of the Illuminati are not based on speculation, Arthur Edward Waite, a believer in the occult, ancient mystery religion connected to both the Masons and the Illuminati, and a leading Masonic writer, wrote this about the Illuminati:

> ". . . the Order [of the Illuminati] was anti-Christian . . ." [414]

Both Robison and Barruel connected the Illuminati directly to the Freemasons. The Abbe connected the two by showing that they both had the same objects: the destruction of religion and government. This is what he wrote:

> ". . . the grand object of Masonry [and the Illuminati] . . . is, to rid the earth of this double pest [meaning the two "assassins of mankind," religion and government,] by destroying every altar which credulity and superstition had erected [meaning religion,] and every throne on which were only to be seen despots [meaning government] tyrannizing over slaves." [415]

But Professor John Robison went further. He showed how and when the two secret societies had merged. He wrote that the Illuminati had infiltrated the Masons at their convention at Wilhelmsbad in 1782, only five years after the Illuminati was founded:

> "Baron Knigge [a high ranking member of the Illuminati] . . . had now formed a scheme for uniting the whole Fraternity, [meaning the Masons and the Illuminati] for the purpose of promoting his Utopian plan . . . ." [416]

However, not all of the Masons of the day agreed with the motive of the infiltrators in the Illuminati. One member, the Comte de Virieu, a Freemason of the Martiniste Lodge at Lyons, France, could not conceal his alarm at what he had observed. Returning from the Congress of Wilhelmsbad, he declared:

> "I can only tell you that all this is very much more serious than you think. The conspiracy which is being woven is so well thought out that it will be, so to speak, impossible for the Monarchy and the Church to escape from it [so this Mason saw that the conspiracy was out to attack the church and the state, and he believed that they would succeed in their goal.]" [417]

Professor Robison confirmed the conclusions of the Abbe when he stated that he also had discovered the intent of the Illuminati:

> ". . . the express aim of this Order was to abolish Christianity, and overturn all civil government. . . .
> The Order was said to abjure [defined as: "to renounce, disavow, or repudiate"] Christianity. . . .
> The baneful [defined as: "causing distress, or ruin"] influence of accumulated property [meaning the universal, unalienable right to private property] was declared an insurmountable obstacle to the happiness of any nation whose chief laws were framed for its protection and increase." [418]

> ". . . they meant to abolish the laws which protected property accumulated by long-continued and successful industry; and to prevent for the future any such accumulation. They intended to root out all religion and

307

ordinary morality, and even to break the bonds of domestic life, by destroying the veneration for marriage vows, and by taking the education of children out of the hands of the parents." [419]

"The true purpose of the Order was to rule the world. To achieve this it was necessary for the Order to destroy all religions, overthrow all governments, and abolish private property." [420]

The Abbe wrote that the Illuminees, by which he meant both the Illuminati and the Freemasons, were:

" . . . the most unrelenting enemies of the alter [meaning Christianity,] of the throne [meaning government,] and of all society." [421]

But even more succinctly, Barruel showed his readers that he had indeed found the secret of the Freemasons. He revealed this truth on page 320 of his book:

". . . on his reception of *Kadosch* [once again, the 30th Degree of Masonry,] he learns that the assassin of Adoniram [apparently meaning Hiram Abif] is the King [meaning the symbol of government,] who is to be killed to avenge the Grand Master Molay [meaning Jacques deMolay,] and the order of the Masons successors of the Knights Templars.
    The religion which is to be destroyed . . . is the religion of Christ . . . ." [422]

So the Abbe, in 1798, had found the secret of the Masonic Lodge: they were out to destroy the "religion of Christ" and the government that is based upon God's law. And the reason they had this goal was because they were infiltrated by the Illuminati in 1783.

The professor then linked the Illuminati with the Freemasons in a very unusual way. He reported that the initiate into the Illuminati was taught that one of the two secet societies was the superior to the other:

> "In the bond of No. IV [presumably the 4th degree of the Illuminati] the candidate binds himself to 'consider and treat the Illuminati as the Superiors of Free Masonry.'" [423]

And:

> "The founder [meaning Adam Weishaupt] . . . says that his doctrines are the only true Free Masonry." [424]

And as would be expected, it appears as if the key Masonic writers have read the works of both Robison and Barruel, And as would be expected, they have attacked their conclusions.

Perhaps the final evidence that the Masons are "out to destroy Christianity," lies in the meaning behind the symbology of the hat worn by the members of the Shriners, probably the most visible of the the Masonic groups.

The Shrine is the organization that both 32nd Degree Scottish Rite Masons and 13th Degree York Masons can join. That red hat, shaped like an upside down clay flower pot, is called a "fez," after the town of Fez in Morocco. Macoy, the "Masonic supply company," sells a maroon fez that they call the "NOBLE FEZ." [425] The use of the word "NOBLE" to describe the "fez" appears to refer to the Shriner, who is called a "Noble," but it also might refer to how they view the fez itself: it is a "noble" hat.

The Shriners' explanation of the "fez" was written in a book issued by the local Shrine in Tucson, Arizona, in 1977 entitled SABBAR TEMPLE [the name of the Shrine temple in Tucson] PICTORIAL HISTORY FROM 1966 - 1977. This book was a history book for those 12 years of their local history. Included in its pages was a two page "History of Shrine" section. These two pages contained a brief explanation of the signification of "the fez:"

> "The fez, which Nobles of the Mystic Shrine of North America have the privilege and honor of wearing, has been handed down through the ages [the Shrine was formed in 1872, not thousands of years ago, so they are reporting that their use of this hat predates the founding of the Shrine] as one of the most significant of headdresses. The fez derives its name from the place where it was first manufactured commercially -- the holy city of Fez, in Morocco." [426]

But there is more to the story than this. Remember that the Shriner Masons acknowledge that their "fez" has been handed down from centuries ago and that they "have the privilege and honor of wearing" it. And that it was manufactured in "the holy city of Fez."

A good explanation of this "noble headdress" comes from Mick Oxley, a native of England, a former Mason, and a student of both Islam and Hinduism as he traveled to various parts of the world before he retired from the Royal Air Force. He heard the story of "the fez" in Egypt from some of his Muslim friends, called Mullahs, the Islam teachers, who had:

"bragged that at Fez, the Moslems took revenge for their losses during the Crusades by executing fifty thousand Christian men, women and children. [This event, as I recall, took place around 800 A.D., which would make it a story "handed down through the ages."] The Mullahs said that even unborn babies were murdered . . . .

They boasted that the blood of the slaughtered Christians was running deep in the streets of ["the holy city" known as] Fez and the Moslem executors dipped their white hats [called turbans] into the Christian's blood and proudly placed the now blood-red hats on their heads as symbols of their triumph. [Although Mr. Oxley was told they attacked the "Christians" in Fez as an act of revenge against the "Christians" for their losses during the Crusades, one can just as easily presume that the reason they attacked the Christians was because they did not wish any "non-believers" in their "holy city."]

These red hats were known as Fezes from that time forward." [427]

And the Shriners call those who wear the fez a "noble." Yet the hats are in truth a symbol of the Muslim's victory over Christianity in the town of Fez, Morocco. And they claim that they have the "privilege and honor" of wearing this "symbol of a victory over Christianity."

Perhaps you might ask a Shriner about this. But do not expect him to answer. Because he cannot. He probably does not know. And even if he did, he wouldn't tell you.

But he continues to wear this symbol of a "victory over Christianity."

I would now like to quote some of their comments about the writings of Professor Robison and of the Abbe. Arthur Edward Waite wrote about the two men:

"[Barruel's book] remains a very serviceable history of German Illuminism; and if in respect of Masonry he distorted facts and ascribed bad motives in the absence of adequate evidence . . . ." [428]

"In 1797 appeared the notorious work of John Robison, entitled *Proofs of a Conspiracy*. . . .
    Robison was a gentleman and a scholar of some repute, a professor of natural philosophy, and Secretary of the Royal Society of Edinburgh.
    . . . his theory is based on false premises and his reasoning fallacious and illogical . . . ." [429]

Kenneth MacKenzie wrote that the Professor was:

"The author of a silly and self-contradictory book about Freemasonry, in which he has the effrontery [defined as: "impudence, shameless boldness"] to say that he sought admission into the Order [of the Illuminati] on purpose to betray it . . . ." [430]

He added the thought that he considered that:

". . . the nauseating nonsense with which Robison decks his book is only to be compared to the more virulent [defined as: "extremely bitter"] and subtle sarcasm of Barruel." [431]

Masonic author William Hutchison was another who wrote about the Professor. He added his thoughts:

"Professor Robison, amongst a great deal of trash which he collected or invented as evidence against Freemasonry . . . ." [432]

But it was not only the Professor who drew the ire of the Masonic writers. It was the Abbe as well. Albert Mackey wrote these disparaging comments about the priest:

"In this work he charges the Freemasons with revolutionary principles in politics and with infidelity in religion." [433]

Then he charged his work with being in error with "its extravagant assertions." And:

"No work, perhaps, was ever printed which contains so many deliberate misstatements as disgrace the pages of Barruel." [434]

Mr. MacKenzie in his CYCLOPAEDIA also joined in the repudiation of the Abbe's work. He wrote:

"[The] French abbe . . . was the author of an infamous book on Masonry. . . .
    In this work he wilfully distorted the truth, and promulgated views having no foundation save in his own truculent [defined as: "feeling fierceness; savage; cruel"] mind. He accused the Freemasons of having been the instigators of the horrors of the French Revolution, and sought in every way to discredit the Fraternity. His book is now a dead letter." [435]

The reader might remember that Albert Pike wrote that Masonry "aided in bringing about the French Revolution" so the

Abbe was right when he claimed that the Masons were the "instigators of the French Revolution." It was Mr. MacKenzie who "distorted the truth" when he was critical of the Abbe for making the same statement. That means that Mr. MacKenzie was wrong and the Abbe was right.

Sometimes the Masonic writers write about both of the critics. Albert Mackey wrote that both the Professor and the Abbe were wrong. He claimed that:

"The original design of Illuminism was undoubtedly the elevation of the human race." [436]

If both the Abbe and the Professor are correct, the Masons believe that the destruction of religion and government would "elevate the human race." This is strange reasoning, but, as we have seen, completely consistent with the views of the Masons. Mr. Mackey continued:

". . . yet the coarse accusations of such writers as Barruel and Robison are known to be exaggerated, and some of them altogether false." [437]

". . . the ponderous effort of the Abbe Barruel, published in four volumes, in 1797 . . . .
     The general scope of his argument was the same as that which was pursued by Professor Robison; . . . both were false in their facts and fallacious in their reasoning. . . ." [438]

So it is quite clear that some of the key Masonic writers have attacked the works of both Professor Robison and the Abbe Barruel. And they have then written words of praise for Professor Weishaupt. Mr. MacKenzie was one who had kind words for the founder of the Illuminati:

> "Weishaupt was a much belied man; and the best proof that the infamous reports circulated against him were not true, is to be found in . . . the statements . . . made by impartial contemporaries." [439]

> "The founder of this celebrated society was Adam Weishaupt . . . .
>
> Its object was the advancement of morality, education, and virtue, by the mutual assistance of good men. It can hardly be called a] Masonic institution [as discussed previously, it might be remembered that the Illuminati infiltrated the Masons, not the other way around] but its members were selected from the ranks of the fraternity.
>
> . . . the Order finally became extinct at the close of the last century [meaning 1800. This is the typical position that the Masons take, but at least one Masonic writer, Kenneth MacKenzie, has said that they remain today, inside the Masons. I'll discuss that in a few paragraphs.]
>
> Had the Order been allowed free scope, much good would have resulted [he is saying that much good would come from the abolishment of Christianity,] as the members were, as a rule, men of the strictest morality and humanity, and the ideas they sought to instil were those which have found universal acceptance in our own times." [440]

The statement that the Illuminati had ceased to operate after its exposure by the Bavarian government is a common one made by not only the Masons but by many contemporary historians. But, at least one Masonic writer has reported that this statement is not true. He wrote that the Illuminati had perpetuated itself by infiltrating the Masonic Lodges. Kenneth MacKenzie defined the term "Adept" in his "Cyclopaedia:"

"A name given to the Order of the Illuminati." [441]

I have chosen to call this group of Adepts inside the Masonic Lodge "the second layer." It will be remembered that Mr. Pike wrote frequently about these men inside the Lodge in his book entitled MORALS AND DOGMA. This quotation is typical of the many that he wrote:

"It is for the Adepts to understand the meaning of the Symbols." [442]

That means that this "second layer," as I have chosen to call it, still exists. It is just that the first layer does not know it.

And Mr. MacKenzie says that those "adepts" are the members of the Illuminati. This organization did not become "extinct," it apparently went underground inside the Masonic Lodge.

But, continuing on the writings of Masons about Adam Weishaupt, let me quote Henry Wilson Coil who also praised the founder of the Illuminati:

"The most objective writers on the subject give Weishaupt credit for being of high moral character and a profound thinker . . . ." [443]

And Albert Mackey added these words of praise for the professor: he stated that Weishaupt was:

"celebrated in the history of Masonry as the founder of the Order of Illuminati of Bavaria, ..." [444]

"Weishaupt [was] . . . a Masonic reformer." [445]

". . . Weishaupt could not have been the monster that he has been painted by his adversaries." [446]

"Illuminism . . . its founder had hoped by it to effect much good . . . ." because "Weishaupt's . . . honest desire [was] to do good." [447]

"The original design of Illuminism was undoubtedly the elevation of the human race." [448]

So the student can see that the key Masonic writers have praised Weishaupt and condemned both John Robison and Abbe Barruel.

There are others, however, who do not agree.

Gary Allen, a "revisionist historian" of great note (a "revisionist historian" is one who corrects the record of history back to the truth,) attempted to set the record straight about the infiltration of the Illuminati into the Masonic Lodge. He described the convention at Wilhelmsbad with these words:

"The power and influence of the Illuminati achieved a great leap forward through a formal alliance with continental Freemasonry that was sealed during the Congress of Wilhelmsbad which began July 16, 1782, when representatives of some three million members of Europe's secret societies met and adopted organizational plans formulated by the Illuminati." [449]

Alan Stang, another "revisionist historian" of great repute, looked into this period of Illuminati history, also wrote about the Convention. This is what he added:

> ". . . Weishaupt decided to infiltrate them too [meaning the Masonic Lodges.] In the summer of 1782, Masonic leaders from throughout Europe met in Wilhelmsbad . . . .
>
> Weishaupt recruited them, thereby winning control of German Freemasonry. Only a few years later, there were already at least two thousand members of the Order in the German-speaking lands." [450]

However, as could be expected, the Masons do not agree with these assessments. They have endeavored to set the record straight as they see it, with comments praising both Weishaupt and his organization for their work at that convention.

Albert Mackey jumped into the fray and attempted to further explain the Masonic position. He wrote:

> "At first, it [the Illuminati] was totally unconnected with Masonry, of which Order Weishaupt was not at that time a member. It was not until 1777 that he was initiated in the Lodge Theodore of Good Counsel, at Munich [a Masonic Lodge in Germany.] Thenceforward Weishaupt sought to incorporate his system into that of Masonry." [451]

Kenneth MacKenzie added that he considered the efforts of the Illuminati to be:

> "an attempt to purify Masonry, then in much confusion." [452]

318

And Mr. Mackey joined the other Masonic writers when he included a discussion of the Wilhelmsbad convention in his Encyclopedia. He called it:

> ". . . the most important Masonic Congress of the eighteenth century." [453]

> "Its avowed object was the reform of the Masonic system . . . ." [454]

Henry Wilson Coil added his thoughts inside his Encyclopedia:

> ". . . a convent of the *Strict Observance* [of the Masons] . . . was held at Wilhelmsbad for the purpose of reforming the Masonic system and disentangling the confused mass of rites and orders." [455]

One can only wonder why the Masonic Lodge needed "reforming," as these Masonic writers claim.

The word reform is defined as: "to improve by change of form, removal of faults or abuses. Bring from bad to good."

That means that the Illuminati had attempted to bring Masonry from "bad to good." Since Professor Weishaupt was "out to destroy Christianity," one can reasonably conclude that if Masonry was "out to destroy Christianity" at one time, they must have slipped away from that position, and therefore Weishaupt had to "reform it," or bring it back.

That is the only fair interpretation of these comments by the Masonic writers, because at least one of the Masonic writers has stated that the Illuminati was "anti-Christian." That means that these writers know what the Illuminati did for them.

So Masonry was "reformed" by Adam Weishaupt, meaning it was brought back to being an "anti-Christian" movement, because it had previously slipped away.

Albert Pike almost confirmed this interpretation when he wrote the following in his book entitled MAGNUM OPUS:

> ". . . man lost the perfect knowledge of the One True God, the Ancient Absolute Existence, the Infinite Mind and Supreme Intelligence . . . .
> We have returned again to the Primitive Truth [notice that the Masons have "returned again," meaning they had been there once before, and then "returned;"] and that Truth is taught in Masonry." [456]

This comment is consistent with what the other Masons have written about the Professor's "reformation" of the Masonic Lodge. They once believed in something, then had slipped away, and then "returned," meaning they were "reformed," back to their original beliefs.

So the "One True God" has once again revealed himself through Masonry because it had at one time slipped away from man's knowledge. That means that the Masons are acknowledging that Adam and Eve were in the presence of the "one true God" when they were being addressed by Lucifer, in the guise of a serpent. When the two of them and Lucifer were expelled from the Garden of Eden, they no longer knew who this "Supreme Intelligence" was. So Masonry was formed to teach man just who this being was. So, because of Masonry, they "have returned again to the 'Primitive Truth'" that Lucifer is the God who will allow them to use their reason, their wisdom, their intelligence in deciding "right" from "wrong."

And the Masons appear to be grateful that Weishaupt intervened to "reform" their organization and bring it back to its rightful position.

And we have confirmed all of this by reading their own literature.

We have previously discovered that the Masons believe that Lucifer is the "one true God," called by the Masons the Great Architect of the Universe, the Masonic God! The evidence for that conclusion is extensive.

And I have found it in their own literature.

But to close this section, I would like to send this message to Rex Hutchens. You once asked me to "continue seeking the Light." And I have.

I have found the "Light."

The search for everyone is now over.

We now know why Albert Pike wrote that the Adepts "intentionally misled [the initiates] by false interpretations."

I have examined your Masonic works "in depth," as you and other Masons have asked me to do, and I have "not lied about" what you believe in!

The truth is out!

I have found the secret of the "second layer."

It is found in "the Light."

chapter 38
REVOLUTION AND
CONSPIRACY

Albert Mackey was one of the leading Masonic writers of all time. His works have borne up to the test of time, so when he speaks, the world should listen.

The following comments are illustrative of how he addressed the critics of Masonry:

> "There is no charge more frequently made against Freemasonry than that of its tendency to revolution, and conspiracy, and to political organizations which may affect the peace of society or interfere with the rights of governments." [457]

This is a strange statement for him to make, after we have seen that it is not true. The Masons claim to "shape the destinies of worlds" but they have done so without involving themselves in "political organizations;" they have claimed to "hatch no PREMATURE revolutions," yet they "aided in bringing about the French Revolution." And they have done all of this in secret, without identifying themselves to the people of the world, the very definition of a "conspiracy," yet they claim that they are not a "conspiracy."

Mr. Mackey continued:

> ". . . it has been the unjust accusation of every enemy of the Institution in all times past, that its object and aim is the possession of power and control in the affairs of state."

This is even more mysterious, since we have seen that it is the "state" that the Masons have taken oaths to destroy. And they claim to be "the most powerful organization in the land," and we are being asked to believe that they have done so "without getting involved in political organizations."

Returning to Mr. Mackey:

> "It is in vain that history records no instance of this unlawful connection between Freemasonry and politics; it is in vain that the libeler is directed to the Ancient Constitution of the Order, which expressly forbid such connection . . . ." [458]

I hasten to point out that it is the Masonic writer Albert Pike who wrote that the Masons "aided in bringing about the French Revolution." That is the thought of possibly the greatest Mason of all time, yet Mr. Mackey says that history has recorded "no instance" of any such involvement.

And it was Mr. Mackey who unconditionally praised Mr. Pike.

And the student can read my booklet entitled AMERICA'S SECRET DESTINY to learn just how the Masons controlled America's Revolutionary War and how they set this nation up to fail.

I think the reader can now see just who is telling the truth: the "anti-Mason," or the Mason.

chapter 39
SUMMARY

It is now possible to summarize all that we have examined. After reading many of the works of the key Masonic writers, I can now say without reservation that the following is true:

1. The Masons are a secret society.

2. The typical Mason does not know the true nature of the organization he is in.

3. There are two layers inside the Masonic Lodge, a secret one and a visible one.

4. The men in the second layer, meaning the secret one, actually mislead their fellow Masons, meaning the first layer, to keep what they believe in from the average Mason.

5. The Masons lie in their own literature.

    A. They claim not to be involved in politics, yet they "shape the destinies of worlds."

    B. They claim not to be interested in affairs of "the state," yet they take oaths to destroy it.

    C. They claim to "hatch no PREMATURE revolutions," yet the Masons "aided in bringing about the French Revolution."

6. And the secret knowledge, kept from the average Mason, is twofold:

1. The god inside the Lodge that they pray to, called "the Great Architect of the Universe," is Lucifer, also called Satan, the Devil.

2. The single secret inside the Lodge is that the 30th Degree Mason takes an oath "to destroy Christianity," whether the initiate sees it or not.

And the reason we know these conclusions are true is because I have accepted the challenge of the Masons and I have "read, studied and reflected" upon their own material. I have also accepted the challenge of Rex Hutchens, now a 33rd Degree Mason, to "continue to seek the Light."

And when I did, I found the secret of "the world wide Masonic movement."

And now the world can know as well.

chapter 40
WHO THEY ARE

Perhaps the final piece of the puzzle lies in my efforts to iden-tity as many of these "anti-Christians" as I can. And I will do so, as the best I can, from the material I have in my own files. The following list of some of the names of Masons that I was able to locate is certainly not very extensive, but comes from a small amount of documentation that I possess on the subject. However, each source for this information is official, or in the case of several others, from a reputable source, such as the Congressional Record, or from a local newspaper.

Let me advise the reader that I am aware that, if you recognize one of these names on this list, you will probably say some-thing like: "That can't be true. This man is a leader in our community, he sings in the choir in his church and he is a coach of his son's little league team." And I understand why you would say that. It is hard to believe that a man with this type of "All-American" background would actually be in-volved with an "anti-Christian" organization such as the Ma-sons. But he is.

However, one must only look around America and see that there is something very dramatically wrong in this nation. And that the Masons as a group do not seem willing to do anything about it.

The reason I contend that this is so is because they want to change our civilization into what they and others have called THE NEW WORLD ORDER. (For those who want to know just how and why these men want to change our entire civilization, you might read my book entitled THE NEW WORLD ORDER.) So, please do not expect them to directly explain that they are out to destroy "private property, religion and the government."

Because as some of the Masons have taught those who read their literature, they will not conduct their affairs in public, but will do so in secret. However, as we have seen by reading their own literature, sometimes they are very blatant and tell anyone who is interested just who they are.

One of the best sources we have of a list of some of the Masons in the Congress of the United States is the Congressional Record of September 9, 1987. [459] It was on that day that several of the top Masons in the Senate went on record by providing the reader with a list of some of their members.

Senators Strom Thurmond and Jesse Helms, both Masons, rose to endorse the nomination of Federal District Court Judge David Bryan Sentelle to a U.S. Circuit Court position. Senator Thurmond explained that:

> "There were those on the committee [hearing the examination of his qualifications to be a judge] who had concerns regarding his membership in the Masons . . . ."

He added that at another meeting, the committee voted to:

> ". . . favorably report out the nomination of Judge Ronald Lew, of California, to be a U.S. district judge for the Central District of California."

He reported that Judge Lew was also a Mason, and he got his confirmation without any questions being raised about his Masonic affiliation. So the Senator was apparently concerned that the Committee was questioning one potential Judge about his membership, and had not on another.

The Senator then went on to point out that the following Senators were members of the Masonic Lodge:

Senator Charles Grassley
Senator Arlen Specter
Senator Alan Simpson
Senator Strom Thurmond
Senator Harry Byrd
and at least 13 other unspecified Masons in the Senate

That means that there were 18 Senators out of 100 that were publicly acknowledged as being members of the Masons, this "anti-Christian" organization.

The Senator then went on to point out that there were:

". . . 58 Members of the House of Representatives who [were] Masons, including Speaker of the House Jim Wright, Donn Edwards, Claude Pepper, Dan Glickman, William Ford and Trent Lott, to name but a few."

Senator Alan Simpson then rose to confirm that he was a Mason, "since 1959." He went on to be more specific as to who the 18 men in the Senate who were members of the Masons. These are the names he mentioned as being members:

Senator Sam Nunn
Senator Jim McClure
Senator Charles Grassley
Senator Bob Dole

Senator Bennett Johnson
Senator John Stennis
Senator Jim Exon
Senator Jesse Helms
Senator Quentin Burdick
Senator John Glenn
Senator Mark Hatfield
Senator Fritz Hollings
Senator Lloyd Bentzen (the Senator was the Vice-Presidential nominee of the Democratic Party in the 1988 election)
Senator Robert Stafford
Senator Harry Byrd, the majority Leader
Senator Strom Thurmond
and himself, Senator Alan Simpson

According to my count, Senator Simpson only listed 17 Masons. Apparently he missed the name of Arlen Specter who would be the 18th.

He then placed a list of the Presidents of the United States who had been members of the Masons into the Congressional Record:

George Washington
James Buchanan
James Garfield
Warren Harding
Andrew Jackson
Andrew Johnson
William McKinley
James Monroe
James Polk
Teddy Roosevelt

Franklin Delano Roosevelt
William Howard Taft
Harry Truman
and Gerald Ford

Other lists of the Masons, from official sources, have shown that there are at least two additional Presidents who were also members of the Masons:

Thomas Jefferson and
James Madison

It might be appropriate to mention at this time that there are reasons why the Masons are not certain as to whether or not certain early Americans were members of the Masonic Lodge. And the reason is valid. It is because many of the Masonic Lodges and their membership lists were damaged or destroyed during both the American Revolution of around 1776 and the War of 1812. And this must be why lists seem to contradict each other.

Another President, Ronald Reagan, became an "Honorary 33rd Degree Mason" On February 11, 1988. Apparently that means that he did not go through the initiation ceremonies required of other Masons. And also that he is not a "regular Mason," but an "honorary" one. [460] The student of Masonry can see a picture of the President receiving a framed certificate of that "honorary membership" on the cover of the April, 1988 New Age Magazine, published by the 33rd Degree Council.

In addition, Senator Simpson mentioned that:

"Forty-one members of the Federal Judiciary [were] currently Masons."

These Senators then went on to be more specific about the list of 18 Senators who were members of the Masons. They specifically told the nation that these men on the list were 33rd Degree Masons:

Senator Alan Simpson
Senator Harry Byrd
Senator Bob Dole
and Senator Strom Thurmond

The January, 1994 issue of the SCOTTISH RITE JOURNAL, the official magazine of the 33rd Degree Council in Washington, said that Senator Sam Nunn was also a 33rd Degree Mason. [461]

The fact that these Senators mentioned that Senator Bob Dole is a 33rd Degree Mason is extremely interesting.

It will be recalled that he was the Republican Party's nominee for the Presidency of the United States in the 1992 election. It was interesting to note that he asked the Party to nominate Jack Kemp to be his Vice-Presidential running mate and they did. Mr. Kemp also happens to be a 33rd Degree Mason, according to the October 16, 1986 edition of a Buffalo News newspaper. Why this paper made his elevation to the 33rd Degree of Masonry a story in that particular newspaper is not explained, but they did.

That means that both of the Republican nominees for President and Vice President of the United States were 33rd Degree Masons, and both of these men have taken an oath at the 30th Degree to "destroy Christianity." This becomes all the more puzzling when it is remembered that millions of Christians in America voted for these two men.

It is indeed a mystery why these Christians would vote for men who have taken oaths to destroy their faith. But they did.

It is also revealing that when Senator Bob Dole resigned as the Senate Majority Leader, he was replaced by Senator Trent Lott, another member of the Masons. [462]

The Spring, 1963 Royal Arch Mason magazine mentioned that the following justices of the Supreme Court were Masons:

> Earl Warren (later to head the Warren Commission that investigated the assassination of President John Kennedy, not a Mason, but a Catholic)
> Hugo L. Black
> Tom Clark
> William O. Douglas
> and Potter Stewart [463]

Another name connected with the assassination of John Kennedy was J. Edgar Hoover, the head of the F.B.I. at the time. Mr. Hoover was also a 33rd Degree Mason.

That same magazine listed the fact that there were 26 governors in the 50 states that were Masons, and named them. These two names were in the news then, or became news makers later:

> George Wallace of Alabama
> Governor Mark Hatfield of Oregon, later to become a
> U.S. Senator

In addition, the magazine listed the 53 Masons, a majority of the 100 Senators, who were in the Senate of the United States in 1963. These names are important to the student:

Senator Barry Goldwater of Arizona
Senator Carl Hayden of Arizona
Senator Richard Russell of Georgia (later to also sit on the Warren Commission that investigated the assassination of President John Kennedy)
Senator Everett M. Dirkson of Illinois (a powerful leader in the Senate during his time there)
Senator Birch Bayh of Indiana
Senator Hubert Humphrey of Minnesota (later to become the Democratic nominee for the Presidency of the United States)
Senator George McGovern of South Dakota (later to become the Democratic nominee for the Presidency of the United States)
Senator Henry Jackson of Washington (later to become Secretary of Defense)

In addition, the magazine listed the 184 Masons then in the House of Representatives. These names are significant:

John Rhodes of Arizona (the Minority Leader of the House)
Carl Albert of Oklahoma (another Minority Leader of the House)
and Melvin Laird of Wisconsin (later to become Secretary of Defense)

Senators Barry Goldwater and Carl Hayden, and Congressman John Rhodes of my home state of Arizona have been identified as 33rd Degree Masons by official Masonic sources. [464] Senator Goldwater later became the Republican nominee for the Presidency of the United States in 1964. Senator Hayden was the Majority Leader of the Senate for many years. And Congressman Rhodes became the Minority Leader of the

House. So it appears that if you want to run for office in Arizona, it helps to be a member of the Masons. And the other members of the House and Senate will reward you with positions of leadership once you are elected if you are a Mason. It seems like the other Congressmen and Senators, not members of the Lodge, somehow know who are members when they vote for their officers inside both Houses.

It would be appropriate at this point to recall this quotation from Adam Weishaupt, the "Masonic reformer," to the memory of the reader:

> "We must do our utmost to procure the advancement of Illuminati into all important civil [meaning governmental] offices." [465]

It appears as if the Masons have been successful in their endeavors. And the names of the Masons that I just provided is by no means an extensive one.

So it is probably worse than this.

Perhaps the best way to end this chapter is with a story that I found in my research about a meeting between General Gordon Granger, who had an occasion to meet with both Albert Pike, when he was the Sovereign Grand Commander of the worldwide Masonic movement, and then President Andrew Johnson, both of whom were Masons. This event occurred sometime in March of 1867, according to the General, and was later testified to in front of the House Judiciary Committee. They were investigating charges that President Johnson should be impeached, and they felt that the General's recollections of that meeting might be helpful. The General told the committee:

"They talked a great deal about Masonry. More about that than anything else. And from what they talked about between them, I gathered that he [meaning Mr. Pike] was the superior of the President in Masonry. I understood from the conversation that the President was his subordinate in Masonry. That was all there was to it . . . ." [466]

But that wasn't all there was to it.

On June 20, 1867, a few months after this meeting, President Johnson received a delegation of Scottish Rite officials in his bedroom at the White House where he received the 4th through the 32nd Degrees of the Scottish Rite. That means he completed all of the degrees in the White House..

But the important revelation is that the General had testified that the President of the United States was the subordinate to the Sovereign Grand Commander of all of Freemasonry, Albert Pike in this case. And I do not believe that this means just in matters concerning the Masonic Lodge. It could be that the President is subordinate to whatever the 33rd Degree Mason says, including the latter's view on politics, or world affairs.

The reader is asked to recall the oath that the Masons take first at the third Degree, and then at the 18th Degree. First, this is the oath they take at the 3rd Degree:

"Furthermore I DO PROMISE and swear THAT I WILL OBEY ALL regular signs, SUMMONS or to-ens GIVEN, handed, sent, or thrown TO ME FROM THE HAND OF A BROTHER MASTER MASON or from the body of a just and lawfully constituted lodge of such . . . ." [467] (I put the emphasis in the paragraph)

335

The capitalized words when taken together read: "I do promise that I will obey all summonses given to me from the hand of a brother Master Mason." Notice that it reads "all" summonses, including orders on American political affairs. But the oath taken at the 18th Degree is even more compelling. It reads:

"I, [the initiate provides his name] furthermore promise and swear that I will observe and obey all the rules and laws of this order of Knights of the Rose Croix, [the title of the 18th Degree] and the decrees and mandates that may be transmitted to me by the Sov∴ Inspector Gen∴ [apparently means the Sovereign Inspector General] in Sup∴ [means Supreme] Council of the 33rd Degree in whose jurisdiction I may reside . . . ." [468]

So, with those simple oaths taken by all of the Masons in "all important civil offices," all of these men have completely turned their backs on the principles of "government by the people, of the people, and for the people."

We the people elect them, but the Masons control them!

chapter 41
WHY THEY
HAVEN'T SUCCEEDED

It is a fair question to ask why the Masons, who claim to "shape the destinies of worlds," have not succeeded as yet in their grandiose scheme to "destroy Christianity." And there is an answer.

It is simply because they know that they are on a schedule and the time to complete their plans has not yet arrived. And the reason for the delay until the day of reckoning is a very intriguing one. And it involves the way mankind reckons time.

Whenever someone writes down a date on a document, that person should write it with certain letters that stand for Latin words. For example, December 7, 1941 should be written:

"December 7, 1941 A.D." (some people say that the "A.D." should be written before the actual date: "A.D. December 7, 1941.")

According to a dictionary, the two letters stand for the two Latin words: "Anno Domini," meaning: "In the (specified year) of the Christian Era." That means that the year 1941 A.D. would mean that it was 1,941 years since the birth of Jesus. The calendar prior to this date is called B.C., meaning "Before Christ." So the year 1941 B.C. would mean 1,941 years "before the Christian era."

There was no actual B.C. calendar during that time, meaning that the people who lived through parts of those years were not counting backwards each year, for example: 1942 B.C., then 1941 B.C., etc., until they reached the year 0. This calendar was created after the time by men in the A.D. calen-dar period. It never existed while people were living then.

And secondly, and more importantly, Jesus was not born in the year 0. There is some disagreement as to exactly when this was, meaning the exact year he was born, because some are saying now that it was the year 4 B.C., and others have said that it was 6 B.C.

But I believe that we can know for certain what year that birth took place. Gene Faulstich of the Chronology-History Research Institute of Rossie, Iowa has put all of the dates of the Bible into a computer and according to his research, Jesus was born on May 21, 6 B.C.

If Mr. Faulstich is correct, and I believe he is, that means that the entirety of the calendar does not revolve around the birth of Jesus, it revolves around some other date. And it does, because December 7, 1941 A.D. was in fact December 7, 5941 A.L.

Albert Mackey, the Masonic historian frequently quoted in this work, wrote the following in his Encyclopedia, under the heading "Anno Lucis:"

> "*In the Year of Light*; abbreviated A∴L∴ The date used in ancient Craft Masonry; found by adding 4000 to the Vulgar Era [the vulgar era is defined as: "common" era, meaning the date used at the time;] thus [in his example] 1911 [A.D.] + 4000 = 5991 [A∴L∴.]" [469]

The two letters A.L. stand for the two Latin words "Anno," and "Lucis." It is to be remembered that the word "Lucis" is Latin for "Light." So the Masons have created an A.L. calendar, meaning "the year of Light," a "secret," non-public calendar dating back to the year "0," adding one year to their calendar each New Year's day.

It is hoped that the reader is beginning to see that the year "0" in the A.L. calendar is the year that "Lucifer," the "lightbearer," fell to earth after being expelled from heaven. So the Masons reckon time from the beginning of time, the year that God expelled Lucifer from heaven. So ever since that date, the Masons have been adding years to the calendar one at a time.

I can find no attempt by any of the Masonic writers that I read to explain why they have created the A.L. calendar, but my research makes me believe that they have done so for the following reason. They apparently believe in the literal seven days of creation detailed in the Book of Genesis, and because they do, they have created a 7,000 year calender.

It is their contention that man will rule the earth for 6,000 years and then their god, Lucifer, will rule for 1,000.

The Bible records in Genesis Chapter 1 that God created the universe in six days, and then He rested on the seventh. The Masons believe that this conceals a symbolic meaning and that the key to understanding this secret is contained in the Bible where they contend there are two mentions of this mystery. The first is in chapter 90, verse 4 of the Book of Psalms:

"For a thousand years in thy sight are but as yesterday when it is past . . . ."

339

Then the New Testament teaches in 2nd Peter Chapter 3, Verse 8:

> "But, beloved, be not ignorant of this one thing, that one day is with the Lord as a thousand years, and a thousand years as one day."

It appears as if the Masons have taken these three separate Biblical teachings and combined them to mean that their god, the Great Architect of the Universe, meaning Lucifer, will allow man to reign on the earth for 6,000 years, and then he, meaning Lucifer, will reign for the seventh day, the last 1,000 years. It is no coincidence that this 1,000 year period is called "The New World Order." When President George Bush referred to "the 1,000 points of light" during his Presidency, he was referring to "the 1,000 years of light from the Lightbearer," meaning the last 1,000 year period being run by Lucifer, the god who will free man to use his "reason."

They also believe that this thousand year period will start on January 1, 2000 A.D., or January 1, 6000 A∴L∴.

Should anyone wish to study this coming new civilization known as "The New World Order," they might wish to read my book entitled THE NEW WORLD ORDER, and then watch my 14 hour lecture video by the same title. Should they wish to obtain these materials, details on their purchase may be had by writing to the publisher for a catalog.

One of the ways that the reader can confirm that this calendar is being used by the Masons is by seeing the "Distinguished Service Medal" awarded to C. Fred Kleinknecht, the current Sovereign Grand Commander of the 33rd Degree Masonic Council, on May 1, 1990 A.D. (I am certain that the fact that

340

they gave this medal to Mr. Kleinknecht on May 1, the very anniversary date that the Illuminati was founded is just one giant coincidence!)

The front and back sides of the medal were photographically reproduced a short time after he received the medal in the Scottish Rite Journal, the official magazine of the Scottish Rite 33rd Degree Council in Washington D.C. The inscription on the medal reads:

"Awarded to Ill. Bro. [apparently meaning Illustrious Brother] C. Fred Kleinknecht, May 1, 1990, ANNO LUCIS 5990."

Confirmation of the significance of this A∴L∴ calendar can be had by reading just one little article that appeared in the January 3, 1989 edition of the Arizona Daily Star, the morning newspaper in Tucson, Arizona. The article read, in its entirety:

"Millennium [a millennium is 1,000 years long] group expects Bush at '99 Egypt bash

WASHINGTON (AP) [meaning this article was written by the Associated Press in Washington D.C.] -- President-elect [George] Bush is spending this New Year's holiday at Camp David, Md., [Maryland] but in 10 years he may be in Egypt.

Organizers of the Millennium Society say he's already committed to ushering in the next century at the Great Pyramids of Cheops in Giza.

The society holds annual balls in several cities around the world.

341

But those are just a warm-up for the big bash in 1999 at 12 noon, Greenwich Mean Time, outside Cairo.

In 1985, Bush, then the vice-president, prepared a statement that was read at the society's New Year's Eve balls here and in Beijing, China.

'Barbara and I wish you the best of luck in the next year, and we're looking forward to your celebration in Egypt in 1999," Bush said.'"

So "The New World Order" that President Bush mentioned in 1990 is coming to the world sometime after noon on December 31, 1999, A.D., meaning the afternoon and night of New Year's Eve, December 31, 5999 A∴L∴, and the morning of January 1, 2000 A.D., meaning the morning of January 1, 6000 A∴L∴.

It is also interesting to note that Mr. Bush will be joining the others at the site of the Great Pyramid of Cheops near Cairo, Egypt. Those who have noticed the Great Seal on the back of the dollar bill have noted that there is a pyramid on the left hand side, a symbol of the Great Pyramid of Cheops where the party on New Years Eve will be held. That is not a coincidence.

And the reason for this location being chosen appears to be the fact that this pyramid in Egypt was never built as a tomb for a pharaoh. It was built as a temple of initiation into the ancient mystery religion, the one where initiates learn the "true knowledge of god" during an initiation ceremony. I believe that the pyramid will be reopened the night of December 31, 1999 A.D., for initiations once again. And George Bush will be there to see it.

Somehow "the all-seeing eye," the eye of Lucifer, above the pyramid on the dollar bill will somehow land on the top of the pyramid, even though it might well be just a symbolic event.

Something very dramatic is going to happen that night at midnight!

Sometime during that 24 hour period, and I believe it is going to happen at precisely midnight, Egypt time, on January 1, 2000 A.D., the very moment when the new millennium starts in that part of the world, the planet Jupiter will be caused to burn by NASA, the National Aeronautics and Space Administration! The planet Jupiter is going to burn like a star precisely at midnight to herald the "dawn of a new day," the beginning of the "thousand points of light," the moment that Lucifer will symbolically land on the earth to take up residency in the pyramid.

The discussion of the evidence for those statements is in my 14 hour lecture video entitled THE NEW WORLD ORDER.

Because it is that night that they believe Lucifer will usher in the 1,000 year reign of "Light" on the earth and that "Christianity will be destroyed." That means that those who believe in the 6,000 year reign of man before the 1,000 year reign of Lucifer do not need to "destroy Christianity" until that date, and that is why they have not as yet attempted to accomplish that goal.

And that is why they have not succeeded in their plans up to this day. The scheduled day that their goals will be achieved is still in the future.

The very near future.

PART THREE

THE CONCLUSION

chapter 42
THEOLOGY 101

Now that we have seen that the Masons as an organization have only one purpose, and that is the destruction of Christianity, it might be helpful if I explained to you just how I think that fits into the world as we know it.

I would like to start with an examination of my views about Theology [defined as: "the study of God and the relations between God and the universe"] and how I believe the Masons fit in. So I would like to call this chapter THEOLOGY 101, the views of Professor Ralph Epperson, instructor.

Because I believe that my views on Theology will make enormous sense, I am hopeful that the reader will see that what I have discovered about the Masons will completely fit into that world view.

Like many people, I started wondering about what the purpose of life was, and what my role might be in it, about the time I was in college. So what I am about to share with you is the result of many years of thought and reflection. I cannot guarantee that what I believe in is correct, but it is the best that I can do with all of my limited education and research.

So this is my view of Theology.

I believe that the God of the Bible, the God who created the universe, decided, for some reason that I still do not know, to create a class of beings to live with Him for eternity that freely chose to worship Him. As I understand it, the angels were created for that purpose, but they had no choice in the matter. God created angels to live with Him at some point in the past, but they were created the way they were, with no ability to refuse.

Apparently God has chosen to create beings who will have the ability to accept or reject his offer to spend eternity with Him.

So, about 6,000 years ago (I tend to agree with the Masons and the research of Mr. Faulstich that the earth is about 6,000 years old. That means that this decision was made nearly 6,000 years ago) God created the universe out of nothing and then created a race of beings that he called "man" that He put onto the planet earth. He provided each of these beings with a mind, meaning each was provided with the ability to make choices. And then He gave each of them a question to exercise that free choice on.

It is my belief that each man, woman and child on this earth is being asked one simple question, and that each of us has the ability to choose an answer to that question. And so, in my opinion, the sole purpose of life is to make that one decision.

And I think that God has granted man only one life time to make that decision (reincarnation is not a reality.) Also, He has provided all of mankind a certain amount of time to make that decision. He has created this universe for only a certain length of time and then it will cease to exist as we know it. It's end will come when it burns itself out. That means that He will then either replace it or just allow it to exist without life. I do not need to know what decision He will make concerning the destiny of the universe as that question does not need an answer to affect my view on theology either way. In other words, what He does with this universe at that time does not matter to me, because it is of no consequence to my view of the purpose of life.

So I believe that the simple question that all men are to answer was the one asked by Jesus to all of his disciples when He was on the earth. That question is recorded in the book of Matthew, Chapter 16, verse 15:

"He [meaning Jesus] saith to them, [all of his disciples with him then] BUT WHOM SAY YE THAT I AM?"

And the correct answer to that question is the one provided by Peter in the next verse:

". . . Thou art the Christ, the Son of the Living God."

And the reward for the right answer, like the one Peter gave to Jesus, is spelled out in John Chapter 3, Verse 16 (this is the verse that television viewers sometimes see on a banner raised on some National Football League games after an extra point is made):

"For God so loved the world, that he gave his only begotten Son, that whoever believeth in him should not perish, but have everlasting life."

So I believe that each man and woman has but one question to answer during their lifetime, and that there is a reward for those who answer that question correctly.

Each and every man, woman and child was put on this earth to answer but one question, and forgive me for putting it into my own words, but that question is the one that Jesus is asking everyone:

"Whom do you, _____ [fill in your name here] say that I [Jesus] am?

That means that He is asking you, the reader of this book, the same question. Jesus is asking you the only question that matters in this universe.

And if you answer that question correctly, you will receive a gift from the creator God: the gift of eternal life.

And as we have seen, the Masons have but one purpose:

TO KEEP YOU FROM CORRECTLY ANSWERING THAT QUESTION AS PETER DID!

They exist to utterly destroy Christianity so that no one will answer that question correctly.

And now it would be an appropriate place for me to say that the Masons must believe that Jesus is not only real, but that His claim to divinity is genuine as well. If they did not believe this, they would not have devoted all of this energy to keeping the knowledge of Him from the people of the world.

If Jesus is not the "living Son of God," they would just prove it and thereby disprove all of His claims. And they would not have to do this in secret, because all of their efforts could be out in public. So, it is fair to conclude that the Masons believe that Jesus is real.

And their goal is to keep you from knowing that.

This all makes perfect sense to me. It seems to fit with everything my mind has told me for some 40 years. And it seems to fit with everything my research as an historian has shown me for over 30 years. And I am giving you this view of my theology, not as a Christian, but as an historian. I have found this as an historian, even though I have correctly answered the question asked me by Jesus.

I have made my decision in favor of Him.

So, if you have not made that decision yet, may I suggest that you consider whether or not you can see the truth in my view, and then find Jesus.

And may I humbly suggest that you make that decision just as soon as you can.

Because it is the most important answer to the most important question you will be asked in your entire lifetime.

And I am sating these things as an historian. What I have found could be found by anyone who was inspired with a search for the truth.

So, may I suggest that you find the answer to the question.

Because the morning of January 1, 6000 A.L. is fast approaching.

chapter 43
THE BREAD CRUMBS

Somewhere in my memory I can vaguely recall the fairy tale story of Hansel and Gretel. As I remember it, they were on their way to some house, and as they made their way there, they were laying down a trail with bread crumbs.

They were doing this because they wanted a trail they could follow that would take them back to wherever they came from after they had completed their visit.

I must be honest with you and admit that I am following a trail left down by the Masons, and I cannot with certainty state that it leads to the right conclusion. They could be putting down a false trail, or many trails for that matter, to confuse the honest researcher.

So all I can say at this point is that there is no doubt that the Masons have done as Hansel and Gretel have done: they have placed down a trail for the researcher. I have diligently sought out this trail. I have examined it the best way I could by checking out as many credible sources as I could find, and I am saying that I believe that all of the signs are that I have found the correct trail. I have then made those findings public in this book.

I then offer you the question for your final decision: is it possible that I am correct?

It is your decision.

chapter 44
EPILOGUE

Just as in the case of the Abbe Barruel and Professor John Robison, the two writers who also discovered the secret of Masonry, I expect to be attacked for what you have just read, because I too have discovered the secret.

But you, the readers of this work, are not to be dismayed: you can know that I expected it. And the Masons will respond just as I will predict. It is part of their way of dealing with their critics.

The strategy was written down by Adam Weishaupt:

> "If a writer publishes any thing that attracts notice, and is in itself just, but does not accord with our plan, we must endeavor to win him over, or decry him [the word decry means: "to depreciate officially or publicly. To censure freely; clamor against.]" [470]

I can assure you that they will not be able to "win me over,"so they must "decry" me.

And to assist the future Masonic writers who will write the articles that will "decry" me, I have already written a suitable response that they might use in their encyclopedias under the heading of "ANTI-MASONIC BOOKS:"

> "The book by Ralph Epperson, entitled MASONRY: CONSPIRACY AGAINST CHRISTIANITY, is perhaps the most well documented of all the books by any Anti-Masonic writer. He read the works of twelve of the major Masonic writers, including some of the

works of Albert Pike, Albert Mackey, Manly P. Hall, Carl Claudy, Henry Wilson Coil, Kenneth Mackenzie, Henry C. Clausen and Rex Hutchens, all recognized Masonic scholars.

It does not matter that Mr. Epperson used Masonic writers to prove his case; his use of certain quotations and not others proves that he did not care about the quotations he did not use. [Do not expect their efforts to "decry" me to make any sense!]

And the ones he did use, he took them out of context, or mis-quoted them, or mis-interpreted them. [They will not identify which quotations they believe have been incorrectly recorded.]

Secondly, he had the audacity as a non-Mason to use the writings of the Masons to document his case. A non-Mason should only use the works of non-Masons to prove whatever case he believes he has against Masonry. [They will ignore the fact that I believe that only the Masons can speak for the organization. I attempted to do that by quoting only their top writers to prove my case.]

This is the improper use of research, and any honest historian would decry the writer that did."

I will stand duly "decried."

chapter 45
A FINAL STORY

Perhaps I can end this book with this little story.

There once were two men, one very wise, and the other very foolish.

The foolish man decided that he would devise a trick to fool the wise man and convince him that he was not so wise after all.

The foolish man put a peanut in its shell into his hands and cupping it, he took it to the wise man, and said:

"If you are so wise, you should be able to tell me if the shell of the peanut I have in my hands is crushed or whole."

The foolish man knew that if the wise man said that the peanut shell was crushed, he would open up his hands to reveal that the wise man was truly a foolish man.

Or if the wise man said to the foolish man, "the shell is intact," he would crush it and then open his hands to let the wise man see that he was in error.

The wise man thought for a minute and then said:

"The answer is in your hands."

chapter 46
QUESTION ANSWERED

At the end of my two other books, I asked and then answered the final question: "If there is a Conspiracy in the world and if they do not want the truth out, and if the Masons are part of it, and if you are exposing them, why are you still alive?"

Often, those who ask the question cite the deaths of Pope Clement V and Philip le Bel, King of France, apparently murdered by the Knights Templar because they dared confront the organization.

Or maybe they'll say that there are charges that the Masons killed Pope John Paul I, the Pope just before the current Pope John Paul II, or Wolfgang Mozart, the famous composer, or President John Kennedy. Or Grace Kelly of Monaco, the former actress, who was the wife of Prince Rainier. (There have been charges made in Europe that she was murdered because she was a Catholic and knew about the Masonic group known as "Propaganda Due," abbreviated as "P-2," inside the Vatican in Rome and their attempts to withdraw billions of dollars from the church.)

And all I can say is this: I am absolutely convinced that this Conspiracy exists and that the "second layer" inside the Masons are part of it. And I know that they are extremely powerful and that they believe that "the end justifies the means."

And that they have a great deal to gain from the death of anyone attempting to expose them.

I live in Arizona where a few years ago an investigative reporter named Don Bolles died when his car blew-up as he started it. Even to this day, I am not certain why anyone wanted to kill him. It is presumed that he was murdered because he was obtaining information about corruption in our state.

Why his enemies picked on him and why mine have chosen not to pick on me, I do not know.

But I will emphatically say this: if you hear about my car exploding because I rigged it so that it would, or that I suddenly decided to take up bungee jumping from a 200' tower, on a 210 foot elastic cord, because I was told there was a 10' safety factor built in, I want you to know that my car is fine, and I get nose-bleeds from any altitude over 3'!

You can know with absolute certainty: I simply did not do it!

And the reason I will not take my life is because of my conviction that only God can take life! In other words, I cannot commit suicide because of my religious convictions.

So if something happens to me, may I recommend that you double your efforts to expose this Conspiracy, ...

in my memory.

TWO DEMIT LETTERS

I can imagine that many Masons who have read this book will say that they simply do not believe that what I have discovered is true. I have had Masons say this to me already. A typical response goes something like this:

> "This cannot be true. I've been a Mason for 32 years, and I've never heard one word of what you are saying."

I know that what I have uncovered is hard to believe, but notice that I have taken all of the important quotations used in this book from the top Masonic writers. I challenge any skeptic to make the effort and verify that the quotations that I used have been accurately recorded.

But, if you now believe that the Masons are more than what you believed they were when you joined, and are prepared to come out, may I suggest that you read on.

If you are a member of the Masons, or one of their auxiliary organizations such as the Eastern Star, Job's Daughters, Rainbow Girls, or deMolay, and you now wish to resign, you might consider using either of the two "demit" letters that follow that will accomplish that task. One of these is for a Christian Mason, and the other is for the remainder of Masons askin to be removed from their membership lists. It is presumed that these two letters and the instructions that follow will be applicable for all Masonic organizations, although I do not know for certain if either will accomplish the task. These letters were written for the men directly involved in the male only Masonic Lodges who wish to remove their names from their membership lists.

First, I would like to quote from page 153 of the book entitled CHRISTIANITY AND THE SECRET TEACHINGS OF THE MASONIC LODGE, by John Ankerberg and John Weldon:

"As a further help to those of you who have decided to leave the Lodge (whether Christian or non-Christian), we recommend the following instructions, and provide a sample letter. [The letter that can be used for a non-Christian will follow the first one provided by these authors for the Christian.]

The rules and orders of the Lodge specify that if your letter meets the following requirement that it must be read before the members of the Lodge. If done in this fashion, your letter will become a testimony to others in the Lodge concerning the truth of Jesus Christ [if you are a Christian.]

In this way God will use you to help open the eyes of other Masons and lead them to Christ.

In your letter, tell them the reason you are leaving the Lodge is because it conflicts with the teachings of the Bible and especially the teachings of Christ.

Give a few Bible verses to prove where it conflicts [with your Christian views] e.g., you might bring up John 8:12 which asserts the Christian is **not** in darkness apart from Masonry.

You could refer to the nature (deity) and mission (savior) of Christ or to the nature of salvation -- by grace through faith -- not works (Ephesians 2: 8-9).

By writing the letter properly, in this way they must read your testimony and the Bible verses proving why you feel it conflicts with Christianity.

Everybody [in the Lodge] hears it. If the letter is addressed in the following manner, according to Masonic law, it must be read before the Lodge:

The letterhead and envelope must **both** be addressed to the members of the Lodge. Never address your letter to the Lodge Master or merely to "Lodge # - - -" because this refers to the officers who will simply process your request without reading it to the Lodge membership. Again:

1. Your letter must be **addressed** (on the outside of the envelope) "To the members of the Lodge number _____," then give the address.

2. The letter **itself** must begin with "To the members of Lodge number _____," and not to any particular person -- but only to Lodge **members**.

To help you officially sever your ties from the Lodge, we recommend the following sample letter." [It is also recommended that you keep a dated copy of the letter for your own files.]

FOR THE CHRISTIAN MASON WHO WISHES TO DEMIT:

TO THE MEMBERS OF LODGE #_____:

Date: _____

This letter is a formal request for my demit from the Masonic Lodge. Please remove my name from your membership rolls and mail to me a copy of my demit.

Thank you for allowing me an opportunity to express my reasons for withdrawing from the Lodge. Do understand that my withdrawal has no personal bearing upon individual members nor do I have any personal conflicts with members. Those in the Lodge who are my friends know that I still treasure their personal friendships.

However, I am a Christian, and must forsake the Lodge because its teachings are contrary to the true teachings of the Bible. Freemasonry rejects the Lord Jesus Christ Who is the Lord and Master of my life. I cannot with a clear conscience be a Mason because Jesus Christ is not allowed to be named or worshiped in the Lodge as it might offend another Mason.

Masonry's respected authors, Albert Mackey and Albert Pike, openly claim that Masonry is a religion.

They are right!

It is a religion without Christ.

Many of us have heard that the Lodge is based on the Bible. However, in Freemasonry, the Bible is rejected and God's word is misused and misquoted. The Lodge's religion is universalism and the Bible is nothing more than a symbol.

Masonry promises to its members the blessings of Heaven and acceptance before God. But the Masonic plan of salvation is totally contrary to what the Bible teaches. Men cannot be saved apart from Jesus Christ as Savior.

In closing, may I express my love for you as individuals and if you desire, I will gladly share how I became a Christian and help you to understand how you, too, may become a follower of Jesus Christ.

Your friend in Christ,

(Signed)

FOR THE NON-CHRISTIAN MASON WHO WISHES TO DEMIT:

TO THE MEMBERS OF LODGE # _____:

Date: _____

This letter is a formal request for my demit from the Masonic Lodge. Please remove my name from your membership rolls and mail me a copy of my demit.

Thank you for allowing me an opportunity to express my reasons for withdrawing from the Lodge. Do understand that my withdrawal has no personal bearing upon individual members or on any personal conflicts with members. Those in the Lodge who are my friends know that I still treasure their personal friendships.

However, I must forsake the Lodge because I have since discovered that its teachings are contrary to all of the truth that I have discovered since I joined the Lodge. Therefore, I can no longer be a Mason with a clear conscience. Masonry's respected authors, Albert Mackey and Albert Pike, openly claim that Masonry is a religion.

They are right! It is a completely separate religion from the other religions of the world, and I now know that its god is not the god worshiped in any of these religions. Masonry promises to its members the blessings of Heaven and future acceptance before God. But the Masonic plan of salvation is totally contrary to what I believe in now. In closing, may I express my love for you as individuals.

(Signed)

INTRODUCTION TO FOOTNOTES

The author is once again taking an unprecedented step in an attempt to assist the reader.

The following listing of the some of the documentation utilized in this book is different from the majority of listings used by authors in the past.

First of all, I have not used the traditional words "op cit," and "ibid," to show references to a previously cited book. I have also altered somewhat the lengthy reference information traditionally used by authors in the past. What I have done is to list the major works cited in this book first, with all of the information normally placed there. In addition, I have provided a brief introduction to the contents of the book, in an attempt to induce the reader to read the book themselves.

Then I have simply listed the book by title, and the page where the reference in my book may be found. I have only used this method where the book is cited more than once, or where the book cited is important enough for the reader to know about it and its contents.

This list of books will also serve as a bibliography.

It is hoped that these changes will meet with the approval of those who read this book.

A PARTIAL LISTING
OF BOOKS UTILIZED

A BRIDGE TO LIGHT by Rex R. Hutchens

The Masons believe that "the publication of this work could truly be the dawning of a new day in our [meaning the Southern] Jurisdiction" of Freemasonry. An important esoteric" book, written by a 32nd degree Mason.

Published by the Supreme Council in 1988.

AMERICA'S ASSIGNMENT WITH DESTINY, by Manly P. Hall

"This book presents the unfolding esoteric tradition of the Western Hemisphere," meaning that this nation has a "secret," Masonic destiny.

Published by the Philosophical Research Society, Inc., Los Angeles, California 1979

AN ENCYCLOPAEDIA OF FREEMASONRY by Albert G. Mackey, M.D., 33°

This two volume encyclopaedia is described by the publisher as "a work which would furnish every Freemason . . . the means of acquiring a knowledge of all matters connected with the science, the philosophy, and the history of his Order."

Published by The Masonic History Company, New York, 1873.

A NEW ENCYCLOPAEDIA OF FREEMASONRY by Arthur Edward Waite

The Preface to this book claims that Mr. Waite "endeavours [their spelling] to represent the latest knowledge and to be the spokesman of the latest research," because Masonry is a "part of a Divine Quest."

Published by Weathervane Books, New York, 1970, but originally published in 1920

A PILGRIM'S PATH by John Robinson
The dust cover explains that Mr. Robinson "combines scholarly research and entertaining storytelling in tracing Freemasonry as a worldwide political, religious, economic and social body dedicated to self-improvement and charity . . . ."
Published by M. Evans and Company, Inc., 1993

BORN IN BLOOD by John Robinson
The dust covers states that the author "persuasively links Freemasonry's origins and goals to the once powerful and wealthy Knights Templar Order."
Published by M. Evans and Company, Inc., 1989

CLAUSEN'S COMMENTARIES ON MORALS AND DOG-
MA by Henry C. Clausen
"For years each new member of the Scottish Rite of the Southern Jurisdiction was presented with a copy of MORALS AND DOGMA, by Albert Pike. The supply of the volumes being exhausted, and recognizing that today few members would tackle the reading of so formidable a volume, Henry C. Clausen, grand commander of the Scottish Rite, Southern Jurisdiction, wrote a fine book entitled COMMENTARIES ON MORALS AND DOGMA."
Published by The Supreme Council, 33°, Ancient and Accepted Scottish Rite of Freemasonry, Southern Jurisdiction, U.S.A., 1976

COIL'S MASONIC ENCYCLOPEDIA by Henry Wilson
Coil, 33°
". . . none can equal the factual, unbiased and informative work" of Coil's Encyclopedia.
Published by the Macoy Publishing & Masonic Supply Company, 1961

DUNCAN'S RITUAL OF FREEMASONRY by Malcolm C. Duncan

"The purpose of this work is . . . to furnish a guide for the neophytes of the Order, by means of which their progress from grade to grade may be facilitated."

Published by David McKay Company, no date of publication shown

HISTORY OF FREEMASONRY AND CONCORDANT ORDERS, written by a Board of Editors

"The purpose of this work is to furnish an outline History of Freemasonry, including many facts not before published."

Published by the Fraternity Publishing Company, London, England, 1891

INTRODUCTION TO FREEMASONRY, by Carl H. Claudy

This is a series of three books given by the Grand Lodge of Massachusetts to "all candidates as an important part of their initiation into the Masonic Fraternity."

Published by the Temple Publishers, Washington D.C., in 1931.

IS IT TRUE WHAT THEY SAY ABOUT FREEMASONRY by Art deHoyos & S. Brent Morris

The authors contend that "some reasoned reply is needed . . ." to the charges of "recent critics" of Freemasonry.

Published by the Masonic Service Association of the United States, Silver Springs, Maryland, 1994

LECTURES ON ANCIENT PHILOSOPHY, by Manly P. Hall

This book is a "commentary and expansion" of Mr.Hall's book entitled THE SECRET TEACHINGS OF ALL AGES.

Published by The Philosophical Research Society, Inc., of Los Angeles, in 1984.

LEGENDA OF THE ANCIENT AND ACCEPTED SCOT-
TISH RITE OF FREEMASONRY, by Albert Pike

"There are other things that you [the Mason] should hear
said now, and without which you will not be fully in possession of this degree . . . ."

Reprinted by Kessinger Publishing Company, Kila, Montana

LITURGY OF THE ANCIENT AND ACCEPTED SCOT-
TISH RITE OF FREEMASONRY by Albert Pike

"The present work includes all of the Liturgies [defined as:
"a rite or body of rites"]" Pike prepared for the current high-
degree rituals of the Scottish Rite."

Reprinted by kessinger Publishing Company, Kila, Montana

THE LOST KEYS OF FREEMASONRY, by Manly P. Hall

The foreword to this book reports that "the leading Masonic scholars have agreed that the symbols of the Fraternity
are susceptible of the most profound interpretation and thus
reveal to the truly initiated certain secrets concerning the spiritual realities of life." One of those "secrets" is revealed to the
reader on page 48: "The seething energies of Lucifer are in his
hands . . . ."

Published by the Macoy Publishing and Masonic Supply
Company, Inc., Richmond, Virginia, in 1976.

THE MAGNUM OPUS OR GREAT WORK by Albert Pike

"One of the rarest and most important books ever published on the Ancient and Accepted (Scottish) Rite of Freemasonry . . . ."

Reprinted by Kessinger Publishing Company, Kila, Montana

MARX AND SATAN by Richard Wurmbrand

This book examines the evidence that Karl Marx was "led to a deep personal rebellion against God and all Christian values." That anger led him to a Satanic cult.

Published by Crossway Books, Westchester, Illinois, in 1986.

MASONIC INITIATION by W.L. Wilmshurst
The author claims that his book was "an amplification" "in the deeper and philosophic aspect of Freemasonry."

Re-printed by Kissinger Publishing Company, Kila, Montana

MEMOIRS ILLUSTRATING THE HISTORY OF JACOBINISM, by A. Barruel
One of the earliest works exposing the connection beween the Illuminati of 1776 and the Masonic Lodge.

Published by American Council on Economics and Safety, Fraser, Michigan, 1995, but originally published in 1789

MORALS AND DOGMA by Albert Pike
This "esoteric" book [it has secret meanings] is specially intended to be read and studied by the Brethern" of the Scottish Rite of Freemasonry. It was written by the Sovereign Grand Commander of the Scottish Rite from 1859 to 1891.

Published by The Supreme Council of the Southern Jurisdiction of the Scottish Rite of Freemasonry in Washington D.C. in 1871.

OCCULT THEOCRASY by Lady Queenborough, Edith Starr Miller
The author attempts to "research into the causes of social unrest," by exposing "some of the means and methods used by a secret world." She connects the Illuminati and Freemasonry, and releases the "Official ritual of the 33rd degree," and Albert Pike's alleged letter of July 14, 1889.

Republished by The Christian Book Club of America, Hawthorne, California, originally published in 1933

OLD CAHIER OF THE 33D DEGREE, by Albert Pike
This book provides the reader with "The Complete Text of Albert Pike's translation of a 33° Ritual discovered in Louisiana in 1860."
Published by Poemandres Press, Masonic Publishers, Boston & New York, 1996

THE PORCH AND THE MIDDLE CHAMBER, THE BOOK OF THE LODGE by Albert Pike
This book, which is the "Secret Work" that "is true to the intent of Pike's Ritual," was "to be studied and understood before investiture with the fourth degree."
Reprinted by Kessinger Publishing Company, Kila, Montana

PROOFS OF A CONSPIRACY by John Robison
This is possibly the finest book ever written on the secret society known as the Illuminati, by a professor who was asked to join the organization. This book was read by President George Washington in 1798.
Originally published in 1798, but it was republished in 1967 by Western Islands, now in Appleton, Wisconsin.

ROYAL MASONIC CYCLOPAEDIA, THE, by Kenneth Mackenzie
This encyclopaedia has been "highly esteemed by occultists."
Published by The Aquarian Press, Wellingborough, Northamptonshire, England in 1987.

SECRET TEACHINGS OF ALL AGES, THE, by Manly P. Hall

The book is described as "an Encyclopedic Outline of Masonic, Hermetic, Qabbalistic and Rosicrucian Symbolical Philosophy," and "an Interpretation of the Secret Teachings concealed within the Rituals, Allegories and Mysteries of all Ages."

Published by The Philosophical Research Society, Inc., Los Angeles, in 1977.

THE SPIRIT OF MASONRY by William Hutchinson

"For more than two centuries, [this book] has been the essential source for anyone exploring the inner mysteries of the Masonic Fraternity."

Published by the Bell Publishing Co., New York, in 1982, but originally published in 1775

SYMBOLISM OF FREEMASONRY by Albert G. Mackey

Contains "Its Science, Philosophy, Legends, Myths, and Symbolism."

Reprinted by Kessinger Publishing Company, Kila, Montana

WAS KARL MARX A SATANIST? by Richard Wurmbrand

The earliest book of the two written by Reverend Wurmbrand. It first exposed the evidence that Karl Marx had joined a Satanic cult when he went away to college.

Published by Diane Publishing Co., Glendale, California, 1976

WHAT THE ANCIENT WISDOM EXPECTS OF ITS DISCIPLES by Manly P. Hall

This book is a "study concerning the mystery schools," "a road leading to the understanding of life's purpose."

Published by The Philosophical Research Society, Inc., Los Angeles, 1982.

FOOTNOTES

1. Henry C. Clausen, 33°, What is the Scottish Rite, an 8 page pamph-let published by the Supreme Council, 33° (Washington D.C., 1973) page 4
2 . The Arizona Daily Star, April 25, 1983, page 6A
3. The New Age Magazine, June 1986, page 34
4. Scottish Rite Journal, November, 1990, page 22
5. LECTURES ON ANCIENT PHILOSOPHY, page 433
6. Secret Societies and the New World Order, a 90 minute lecture video, available through the catalog from the publisher
7. A BRIDGE TO LIGHT, pages 330 and 331. Mr. Hutchens lists several of Mr. Pike's books on these two pages.
8. THE LOST KEYS OF FREEMASONRY, pages 13-14
9. A REVIEW OF MORALS AND DOGMA, by A. Ralph Epperson, a 72 page booklet, available through the catalog from the publisher
10. The New Yorker magazine, June 7, 1993, article: "The Hearts and Minds of City College," starts on page 42; the two references to my book entitled THE UNSEEN HAND are on page 52
11. THE NEW WORLD ORDER, by A. Ralph Epperson. A 357 page book, available through the catalog available from the publisher
12. Northern Light magazine published by the Supreme Council, 33°, of the Northern Jurisdiction, Scottish Rite of Freemasonry, February, 1993. The quote is part of a review by Thomas W. Jackson, 33°, of the book entitled The New World Order by Pat Robertson, pages 20-21 of the magazine
13. PROOFS OF A CONSPIRACY, page 111
14. LEGENDA, Twenty-eighth degree, page 132
15. LEGENDA, Twenty-fifth degree, page 39
16. THE LOST KEYS OF FREEMASONRY, pages 13-14
17. LITURGY, Eighth degree, page 75-76
18. THE PORCH AND THE MIDDLE CHAMBER, page 269
19. MAGNUM OPUS, XXIV degree, page 3
20. LEGENDA, thirty-second degree, page 17
21. James L. Gould, M.A., 33° in his book entitled Guide to the Royal Arch Chapter, (New York:Masonic Publishing and Manufacturing Company, 1867) 46
22. W.L. Wilmshurst, Masonic Initiation, (Kila, Montana: reprinted by Kessinger Publishing Company, year not shown) pages 4-5
23. MAGNUM OPUS, XIV degree, page 20
24. LITURGY, Fourteenth Degree, page 198

25. LEGENDA, Thirty-second Degree, page 32
26. LEGENDA, Thirty-second Degree, page 53
27. LEGENDA 1, page 6
28. LEGENDA, The Enigma of the Sphinx, pages 27, 36
29. LEGENDA, Thirty-second degree, page 17
30. LITURGY, Fourth degree, page 19
31. LEGENDA, "Of Ineffable Words," page 51
32. A NEW ENCYCLOPAEDIA OF FREEMASONRY, Volume 1, page 395 under "Initiation"
33. COIL'S MASONIC ENCYCLOPEDIA, page 620
34. A. Ralph Epperson; Jesse James, U.S. Senator (Tucson, Arizona: Publius Press, 1992) available through catalog from publisher
35. Henry C. Clausen, What is the Scottish Rite (Washington D.C.: published by the Supreme Council, 33rd Degree, unknown date of publication) page 4
36. Vietnam, America's Betrayal and Treason, a 3 hour video, The Kennedy Assassination, a two hour video, and The New World Order, a 14 hour video series, are all available through a catalog from the publisher
37. COIL'S MASONIC ENCYCLOPEDIA, page 616
38. CLAUSEN'S COMMENTARIES ON MORALS AND DOGMA, page xvii
39. MAGNUM OPUS, XVIII degree, page 9
40. MACKEY'S ENCYCLOPEDIA, inside cover
41. MACKEY'S ENCYCLOPEDIA, on ALBERT PIKE, pages 563-564
42. A NEW ENCYCLOPAEDIA OF FREEMASONRY, on ALBERT PIKE, Volume II, page 278
43. INTRODUCTION TO FREEMASONRY, II Fellowcraft, pages 104-105
44. A BRIDGE TO LIGHT, page 2
45. A BRIDGE TO LIGHT, page 2
46. A BRIDGE TO LIGHT, page vii
47. A BRIDGE TO LIGHT, page 2
48. "Devilish Danger," a pamphlet published by the Supreme Council, 33°, Washington D.C. Written by Henry C. Clausen, 33°
49. A BRIDGE TO LIGHT, page vii
50. A BRIDGE TO LIGHT, page 2
51. COIL'S MASONIC ENCYCLOPEDIA, page 472
52. MAGNUM OPUS, unnumbered page at the beginning of the book
53. MAGNUM OPUS, unnumbered page at the beginning of the book
54. MORALS AND DOGMA, page 293
55. MORALS AND DOGMA, page 297

56. MORALS AND DOGMA, page 330
57. MORALS AND DOGMA, page 24
58. THE ROYAL MASONIC CYCLOPAEDIA, page 658
59. MASONIC INITIATION, page 34
60. LECTURES ON ANCIENT PHILOSOPHY, page 451
61. THE LOST KEYS OF FREEMASONRY, page I 00
62. WHAT THE ANCIENT WISDOM EXPECTS OF ITS DIS-
     CÍPLES, page 58
63. MORALS AND DOGMA, page 815
64. MORALS AND DOGMA, page 817
65. LEGENDA, Thirty-second Degree, page 12
66. MORALS AND DOGMA, page 849
67. MORALS AND DOGMA, page 772
68. MORALS AND DOGMA, page 781
69. MORALS AND DOGMA, page 370
70. MORALS AND DOGMA, page 218
71. MORALS AND DOGMA, page 219
72. MORALS AND DOGMA, page 224
73. MORALS AND DOGMA, page 225
74. MORALS AND DOGMA, page 104
75. MORALS AND DOGMA, page 819
76. LEGENDA, page 53
77. LEGENDA, Thirty-second Degree, page 21
78. MORALS AND DOGMA, page 817
79. MORALS AND DOGMA, page 324
80. LEGENDA, XXIX Degree, page 10
81. MAGNUM OPUS, XVIII Degree, page 5
82. MAGNUM OPUS, XXVIIII Degree, page 13
83. MORALS AND DOGMA, page 213
84. LEGENDA, Thirty-second Degree, pages 3-4
85. MAGNUM OPUS, XIV Degree, page 20
86. SECRET TEACHINGS OF ALL AGES, page LXXX
87. MORALS AND DOGMA, page 7
88. MAGNUM OPUS, XIII Degree, page 16
89. MAGNUM OPUS, XXVIII Degree, page 42
90. COIL'S ENCYCLOPEDIA, page 494
91. MORALS AND DOGMA, page 352
92. LOST KEYS OF FREEMASONRY, page [v]
93. SECRET TEACHINGS OF ALL AGES, page CLXIX
94. SECRET TEACHINGS OF ALL AGES, page XX
95. MORALS AND DOGMA, page 483
96. MORALS AND DOGMA, page 624

97.   James L. Gould, 33°, Guide to the Royal Arch Chapter (New York: Masonic Publishing and Manufacturing, Co., 1867) page 1 of the Introduction. Mr. Gould quotes "Webb's Monitor" as the source of this quotation

98.   SECRET TEACHINGS OF ALL AGES, page XX

99.   MORALS AND DOGMA, page 205

100. MORALS AND DOGMA, page 35

101. MORALS AND DOGMA, page 37

102. MORALS AND DOGMA, page 52

103. MORALS AND DOGMA, page 160

104. MORALS AND DOGMA, page 163

105. MORALS AND DOGMA, page 165

106. MORALS AND DOGMA, page 166

107. MORALS AND DOGMA, page 167

108. MORALS AND DOGMA, page 833

109. MORALS AND DOGMA, page 834

110. MORALS AND DOGMA, page 833

111. MORALS AND DOGMA, page 834

112. CLAUSEN'S COMMENTARIES, page 214

113. MAGNUM OPUS, 15th Degree, page 10

114. MAGNUM OPUS, XVl Degree, page 7

115. MAGNUM OPUS, XVII Degree, page 8

116. MAGNUM OPUS, XXVIII Degree, page 7

117. MAGNUM OPUS, XXIX Degree, page 7

118. MORALS AND DOGMA, page 169

119. MORALS AND DOGMA, page 366

120. MORALS AND DOGMA, page 12

121. MORALS AND DOGMA, page 13

122. MORALS AND DOGMA, page 15

123. MORALS AND DOGMA, page 697

124. MORALS AND DOGMA, page 776

125. MORALS AND DOGMA, page 32

126. LITURGY, Twenty-ninth Degree, page 210

127. THE ROYAL MASONIC CYCLOPAEDIA, page 659

128. COIL'S ENCYCLOPEDIA, page 375 under the heading LIGHT, BRING TO LIGHT

129. SYMBOLISM OF FREEMASONRY, page 148

130. SYMBOLISM OF FREEMASONRY, page 148

131. LITURGY, Twenty-fourth Degree, page 99

132. LITURGY, Eighteenth Degree, page 169

133. MORALS AND DOGMA, page 77

134. MORALS AND DOGMA, page 593

135. THE SECRET TEACHINGS OF ALL AGES, pages XXI-XXII

136. Both of these materials are available through the catalog provided by the publisher

137. MORALS AND DOGMA, page 477

138. Available through the catalog from the publisher

139. Available through the catalog from the publisher

140. MORALS AND DOGMA, page 495

141. MORALS AND DOGMA, page 506

142. MORALS AND DOGMA, page 254, and MAGNUM OPUS, History section, page 15

143. MACKEY'S ENCYCLOPEDIA, page 310, under heading GREAT ARCHITECT OF THE UNIVERSE

144. MAGNUM OPUS, 28th Degree, "Lecture" section, page 42

145. DUNCAN'S RITUAL OF FREEMASONRY, Preface, unnumbered page, but would be page 3

146. DUNCAN'S RITUAL OF FREEMASONRY, Preface, unnumbered page, but would be page 3

147. Morgan, Captain William, Freemasonry Exposed, (Batavia, New York: Col. David C. Miller, publisher, 1826)

148. THE PORCH AND THE MIDDLE CHAMBER, pages 115-116

149. MACKEY'S ENCYCLOPAEDIA, Volume 1, page 446

150. MACKEY'S ENCYCLOPAEDIA, Volume 1, page 446

151. MORALS AND DOGMA, page 321

152. MORALS AND DOGMA, page 324

153. THE LOST KEYS OF FREEMASONRY, page 48

154. HISTORY OF FREEMASONRY AND CONCORDANT ORDERS, page 49

155. HISTORY OF FREEMASONRY AND CONCORDANT ORDERS, page 101

156. MORALS AND DOGMA, page 592

157. MORALS AND DOGMA, page 287

158. MORALS AND DOGMA, page 660

159. MORALS AND DOGMA, page 567

160. From the entry on Mr. Levi's book entitled THE HISTORY OF MAGIC in Roger Kessinger's catalog

161. Eliphas Levi, The Mysteries of Magic (Kila, Montana: reprinted by Kessinger Publishing Co., unknown year) page 428

162. Arthur Edward Waite; Some Deeper Aspects of Masonic Symbolism (Kila, Montana: reprinted by Kessinger Publishing Co., unknown year) page 5

163. COIL'S ENCYCLOPEDIA, page 374

164. THE ROYAL MASONIC CYCLOPAEDIA, page 450

165. Doreen Valiente; An ABC of Witchcraft Past & Present (New York: St. Martin's Press, 1973) page 19

166. Doreen Valiente; An ABC of Witchcraft Past & Present (New York: St. Martin's Press, 1973) page 33
167. MACKEY'S ENCYCLOPEDIA, page 97
168. MORALS AND DOGMA, page 324
169. MORALS AND DOGMA, page 294
170. MORALS AND DOGMA, page 32
171. AMERICA'S ASSIGNMENT WITH DESTINY, page 32
172. MORALS AND DOGMA, page 275
173. MORALS AND DOGMA, page 287
174. THE ROYAL MASONIC CYCLOPAEDIA, page 659
175. MORALS AND DOGMA, page 715
176. MORALS AND DOGMA, page 718
177. MORALS AND DOGMA, pages 737-738
178. MORALS AND DOGMA, page 296
179. MORALS AND DOGMA, page 305
180. MORALS AND DOGMA, page 810
181. MACKEY'S ENCYCLOPAEDIA, page 5 3 7
182. MACKEY'S ENCYCLOPAEDIA, Volume 2, page 537
183. MACKEY'S ENCYCLOPAEDIA, Volume 1, page 455
184. MACKEY'S ENCYCLOPAEDIA, Volume 1, page 455
185. MORALS AND DOGMA, page 102
186. MORALS AND DOGMA, page 94
187. MORALS AND DOGMA, page 274
188. LEGENDA, Thirty-second Degree, page 7
189. LEGENDA, Thirty-second Degree, pages 38-39
190. LEGENDA, Thirty-second Degree, page 27
191. LEGENDA, Thirty-second Degree, page 31
192. SECRET TEACHINGS OF ALL AGES, page LXXX
193. MAGNUM OPUS, IX Degree, page 7
194. MORALS AND DOGMA, page 530
195. LEGENDA, page 109
196. MAGNUM OPUS, XXXII Degree, page 18
197. LEGENDA, 32nd Degree, page 66
198. Annotations prepared by Henry M. Morris, Ph.D., The Defender's Study Bible (Grand Rapids, Michigan: World Publishing, 1995) page 3
199. MORALS AND DOGMA, page 293
200. LITURGY, page 210
201. LITURGY, Fourth Degree, page 19
202. LITURGY, Fourteenth Degree, page 198
203. MAGNUM OPUS, XIV Degree, page 20
204. MAGNUM OPUS, XXIV Degree, page 3
205. THE PORCH AND THE MIDDLE CHAMBER, page 269

206. LITURGY, Eighth Degree, pages 75-76
207. MAGNUM OPUS, XII Degree, page 6
208. MAGNUM OPUS, IV Degree, page 9
209. MAGNUM OPUS, X Degree, page 8
210. LITURGY, Eighteenth Degree, page 169
211. LITURGY, 17th Degree, page I 00
212. MAGNUM OPUS, IV Degree, page 7
213. MAGNUM OPUS, XXVIII Degree, page 6
214. MAGNUM OPUS, XIII Degree, page 14
215. MAGNUM OPUS, XVI Degree, page 2
216. LITURGY, Fourteenth Degree, page 199
217. THE LOST KEYS OF FREEMASONRY, pages 13-14
218. MAGNUM OPUS, XXIX Degree, page 10
219. THE SECRET TEACHINGS OF ALL AGES, page LXXX
220. LITURGY, Thirteenth Degree, page 167
221. MAGNUM OPUS, XVIII Degree, page 5
222. MAGNUM OPUS, XIII Degree, page 16
223. MAGNUM OPUS, XVIII Degree, page 8
224. MAGNUM OPUS, XXIX Degree, page 12
225. MAGNUM OPUS, XIV Degree, page 3
226. MAGNUM OPUS, XVIII Degree, page 19
227. MAGNUM OPUS, XVIII Degree, page IO
228. MAGNUM OPUS, XVIII Degree, page 7
229. MAGNUM OPUS, XXX Degree, page 2
230. CLAUSEN'S COMMENTARIES, Thirtieth Degree, page 184
231. MAGNUM OPUS, XVII Degree, page 25
232. LITURGY, Thirtieth Degree, page 272
233. LITURGY, Thirtieth Degree, page 243
234. LITURGY, Thirtieth Degree, page 237
235. MAGNUM OPUS, VI Degree, page 6
236. A BRIDGE TO LIGHT, page 188
237. LEGENDA, Thirty second Degree, page 12
238. MAGNUM OPUS, XIX Degree, page 8
239. Annotations by Henry M. Morris, Ph. D., The Defender's Study Bible (Grand Rapids, Michigan: World Publishing Co., 1995) page 13
240. MAGNUM OPUS, XIX Degree, page 8
241. MORALS AND DOGMA, page 324
242. MAGNUM OPUS, XIX Degree, page 8
243. LEGENDA, Thirtieth Degree, page 156
244. LEGENDA, Thirtieth Degree, page 151
245. MAGNUM OPUS, IX Degree, page 7
246. MACKEY'S ENCYCLOPAEDIA, Volume 1, page 239, "Elus"

247. MAGNUM OPUS, IX Degree, page 11
248. LITURGY, Fifteenth Degree, page 32
249. LITURGY, 15th Degree, pages 41-42
250. LITURGY, Twentieth Degree, page 30
251. AMERICA'S SECRET DESTINY, page 69
252. MAGNUM OPUS, XXXII Degree, page 54
253. MAGNUM OPUS, XXIX Degree, page 13
254. MAGNUM OPUS, XVII Degree, page 26
255. LITURGY, Thirtieth Degree, page 273
256. LITURGY, Seventeenth Degree, page II 7
257. LITURGY, Eighteenth Degree, page 190
258. MAGNUM OPUS, XXV Degree, page 7
259. LEGENDA, Thirty-second Degree, page 33
260. AMERICA'S ASSIGNMENT WITH DESTINY, page 114
261. PROOFS OF A CONSPIRACY, page 129
262. THE SECRET TEACHINGS OF ALL AGES, page CLXIX
263. THE LOST KEYS OF FREEMASONRY, page v
264. THE PORCH AND THE MIDDLE CHAMBER, page 128
265. THE PORCH AND THE MIDDLE CHAMBER, page 84
266. LITURGY, Thirtieth Degree, page 236
267. THE PORCH AND THE MIDDLE CHAMBER, page 261
268. A BRIDGE TO LIGHT, page 104
269. LITURGY, 17th Degree, page 100
270. LITURGY, 15th Degree, pages 41-42
271. MAGNUM OPUS, XXX Degree, page 3
272. MACKEY'S ENCYCLOPAEDIA, Volume 2, page 489, under Molay, James de
273. COIL'S ENCYCLOPEDIA, page 420, under Molai, Jacques De
274. MAGNUM OPUS, XXX Degree, page 14
275. THE ROYAL MACONIS CYCLOPAEDIA, page 493, under Demolay, Jacques de
276. THE ROYAL MASONIC CYCLOPAEDIA, page 758, under Vengeance
277. LITURGY, Seventeenth Degree, pages 114-115
278. MORALS AND DOGMA, page 324
279. LEGENDA, Thirty-second Degree, page 23
280. MAGNUM OPUS, XVIII Degree, page 9
281. THE PORCH AND THE MIDDLE CHAMBER, page 319
282. MAGNUM OPUS, VI Degree, page 3
283. A BRIDGE TO LIGHT, page 10
284. A BRIDGE TO LIGHT, page 82
285. MACKEY'S ENCYCLOPAEDIA, Volume 1, page 83
286. LITURGY, Thirtieth Degree, pages 240-241

287.   A BRIDGE TO LIGHT, page 73

288.   INTRODUCTION TO FREEMASONRY, page 131

289.   MACKEY'S ENCYCLOPAEDIA, Volume 1, page 4, under Abif

290.   MAGNUM OPUS, XXVIII, page 38

291.   A BRIDGE TO LIGHT, page 10

292.   THE PORCH AND THE MIDDLE CHAMBER, page 322

293.   LEGENDA, Chapter 1, page 11

294.   SYMBOLISM OF FREEMASONRY, page 343

295.   MACKEY'S ENCYCLOPAEDIA, Volume 1, page 83

296.   COIL'S MASONIC ENCYCLOPEDIA, page 307, under Hiram Abif

297.   MACKEY'S ENCYCLOPAEDIA, Volume 1, page 373 under Jubela-o-m

298.   THE PORCH AND THE MIDDLE CHAMBER, page 293

299.   LITURGY, Eleventh Degree, page 114

300.   LITURGY, Eleventh Degree, pages 101- 102

301.   A BRIDGE TO LIGHT, page 66

302.   A BRIDGE TO LIGHT, page 66

303.   A BRIDGE TO LIGHT, page 66

304.   THE SECRET TEACHINGS OF ALL AGES, page LXXX

305.   MAGNUM OPUS, X Degree, page 7

306.   LITURGY, Tenth Degree, page 96

307.   LITURGY, Eighth Degree, page 76

308.   LITURGY, Fourth Degree, pages 17-18

309.   LITURGY, 18th Degree, page 180

310.   A PILGRIM'S PATH, dust cover

311.   A PILGRIM'S PATH, pages 71-72

312.   A PILGRIM'S PATH, page 166

313.   A PILGRIM'S PATH, page 178

314.   Macoy Publishing & Masonic Supply Co., Inc., Richmond, Virginia, catalog, September 1, 1994, page 10

315.   BORN IN BLOOD, page 337

316.   Flick-Reedy Education Enterprises; Two Worlds (Bensenville, Illinois: Flick Reedy Corp., 1966) page 107

317.   Macoy Publishing & Masonic Supply Co., Inc., Richmond, Virginia, catalog, September 1, 1994, page 10

318.   A PIILGRIM'S PATH, page 102

319.   The two booklets, AMERICA'S SECRET DESTINY and THE U.C.C. CONNECT1ON are available through the catalog from the publisher

320.   MORALS AND DOGMA, page 324

321.   A BRIDGE TO LIGHT, page 284

322.   LITURGY, XXX Degree, pages 225-226

323. MAGNUM OPUS, XVIII Degree, page 19
324. LITURGY, XXX Degree, page 227
325. LEGENDA, Chapter 1, page 19
326. LEGENDA, Chapter 1, page 19
327. A BRIDGE TO LIGHT, page 287
328. MAGNUM OPUS, XXXII Degree, page 12
329. MAGNUM OPUS, XXXII Degree, page I 1
330. MAGNUM OPUS, XXX Degree, page 17
331. MAGNUM OPUS, XV Degree, page 16
332. MAGNUM OPUS, X Degree, page 2
333. MAGNUM OPUS, XXX Degree, pages 17-18
334. MAGNUM OPUS, XXVIII, pages 38-39
335. A BRIDGE TO LIGHT, page 73
336. OLD CAHIER OF THE 33d DEGREE, page 10
337. MAGNUM OPUS, XXII Degree, page 1
338. THE PORCH AND THE MIDDLE CHAMBER, page 322
339. MAGNUM OPUS, XX Degree, page 11
340. MAGNUM OPUS, XIX Degree, page 8
341. MAGNUM OPUS, IX Degree, pages 2-3
342. LITURGY, Tenth Degree, pages 101 - 102
343. A BRIDGE TO LIGHT, page 283
344. LITURGY, Eleventh Degree, page 114
345. A BRIDGE TO LIGHT, page 63
346. Thomas Paine, The Age of Reason (New York: Thomas Paine Foundation, Inc., 1794) page 135
347. OCCULT THEOCRASY, pages 363-364
348. OCCULT THEOCRASY, pages 220-221
349. MAGNUM OPUS, XXXII Degree, page 22
350. IS IT TRUE WHAT THAT THEY SAY ABOUT FREEMASON-RY?, page x
351. Pope Leo XIII, The Church Speaks to the Modern World (Garden City, New York: Image Books, 19S4) page 117
352. Pope Leo XIII, The Church Speaks to the Modern World (Garden City, New York: Image Books, 1954) pages 122-123
353. Pope Leo XIII, The Church Speaks to the Modern World (Garden City, New York: Image Books, 1954) pages 128-129
354. Rev. Clarence Kelly, Conspiracy against God and Man (Boston: Western Islands, 1974) pages 57-58
355. Jack Harris, Freemasonry, The Invisible Cult In Our Midst (Chatta-nooga, Tennessee: Global Publishers, 1983) pages 126-127
356. Pamphlet, Presidents United States, (Chicago: National Christian Association, 1953) p. 6

357. Pamphlet, Presidents United States, (Chicago: National Christian Association, 1953) page 7

358. Pamphlet, Presidents United States, (Chicago: National Christian Association, 1953) page 8

359. Everett C. DeVelde, Jr., A Reformed View of Freemasonry, in Christianity and Civilization, page 278

360. William Preston Vaughn, The Anti-Masonic Party in the United States (Kentucky: University Press of Kentucky, 1983) page 29

361. MORALS AND DOGMA, page 817

362. Bernard Fay, Revolution and Freemasonry (Boston: Little, Brown, and Company, 1935) page 111

363. Christ of The Lodge, (Philadelphia: Great Commission Publications, undated), pages 22-23

364. The Arizona Daily Star, July 14, 1987, page 8-a

365. Edward Ronayne, The Master's Carpet (publisher and date of publishing not shown) page 25

366. Karl Marx and Frederick Engels, The Communist Manifesto (Brooklyn, New York: New York Labor News, 1968) page 35

367. Karl Marx and Frederick Engels, The Communist Manifesto (Brooklyn, New York: New York Labor News, 1968) page 38

368. Edited by Max Eastman, Capital and Other Writings by Karl Marx (New York: The Modern Library, 1952) page ix

369. Committee on the Judiciary of the United States Senate, Contradictions of Communism (Washington D.C.: U. S. Government Printing Office, 1964) pages 39-40

370. Rabbi Marvin S. Antelman, To Eliminate the Opiate (New York: Zahavia Ltd, 1974) unnumbered page that would be page 2

371. Committee on the Judiciary of the United States Senate, Contradictions of Communism (Washington D.C.: U.S. Government Printing Office, 1964) page 40

372. Richard Wurmbrand, Marx & Satan (Westchester, Illinois: Crossway Books, 1986) page 59

373. Committee on the Judiciary of the United States Senate, Contradictions of Communism (Washington D.C.: U.S. Government Printing Office, 1964) page 40

374. Rev. Richard Wurmbrand, Marx & Satan (Westchester, Illinois: Crossway Books, 1986) page 49

375. Committee on the Judiciary of the United States Senate, Contradictions of Communism (Washington D.C.: U.S. Government Printing Office, 1964) page 40

376. Edited by Max Eastman, Capital and Other Writings By Karl Marx (New York: The Modern Library, 1932) page xi

377. Committee on the Judiciary of the United States Senate, Contradictions of Communism (Washington D.C.: U.S. Government Printing Office) page 54

378. Committee on the Judiciary of the United States Senate, Contradictions of Communism (Washington D.C.: U.S. Government Printing Office) page 54

379. Committee on the Judiciary of the United States Senate, Contradictions of Communism (Washington D.C.: U.S. Government Printing Office) pages 54-55

380. Rev. Richard Wurmbrand, Was Karl Marx A Satanist? (Glendale, California: Diane Books, 1976) page 4

381. Rev. Richard Wurmbrand, Marx & Satan (Westchester, Illinois: Crossway Books, 1986) page 59

382. Rev. Richard Wurmbrand, Was Karl Marx A Satanist? (Glendale, California: Diane Books, 1976) page 7

383. Rev. Richard Wurmbrand, Was Karl Marx A Satanist? (Glendale, California: Diane Books, 1976) page 19

384. Rev. Richard Wurmbrand, Was Karl Marx A Satanist? (Glendale, California: Diane Books, 1976) page 20

385. Rev. Richard Wurmbrand, Was Karl Marx A Satanist? (Glendale, California: Diane Books, 1976) pages 20-21

386. Rev. Richard Wurmbrand, Marx & Satan (Westchester, Illinois: Crossway Books, 1986) page 25

387. Rev. Richard Wurmbrand, Marx & Satan (Westchester, Illinois: Crossway Books, 1986) page 31

388. Karl Marx and Frederick Engels, The Communist Manifesto (Brooklyn, New York: New York Labor News, 1968) pages xii-xiii

389. London, England Illustrated Sunday Herald newspaper, February 8, 1920

390. MACKEY'S ENCYCLOPAEDIA, Volume 1, page 346, under Illuminati Of Bavaria

391. MACKEY'S ENCYCLOPAEDIA, Volume 11, page 843, under Weishaupt, Adam

392. PROOFS OF A CONSPIRACY, page 129

393. PROOFS OF A CONSPIRACY, page 112

394. PROOFS OF A CONSPIRACY, unnumbered page, but would be page 7

395. Alan Stang, Illuminism (American Opinion magazine, June, 1976) page 45

396. PROOFS OF A CONSPIRACY, page 115

397. PROOFS OF A CONSPIRACY, page 92

398. PROOFS OF A CONSPIRACY, unnumbered page but would be page 2

399. PROOFS OF A CONSPIRACY, page 119
400. PROOFS OF A CONSPIRACY, page 7
401. PROOFS OF A CONSPIRACY, page 7
402. PROOFS OF A CONSPIRACY, page 121
403. PROOFS OF A CONSPIRACY, page 124
404. Alan Stang, The Manifesto (American Opinion magazine: February, 1972) page 57
405. PROOFS OF A CONSPIRACY, page 84
406. PROOFS OF A CONSPIRACY, page 85
407. MEMOIRS ILLUSTRATING THE HISTORY OF JACOBINISM, page 393
408. MEMOIRS ILLUSTRATING THE HISTORY OF JACOBINISM, frontispiece
409. MEMOIRS ILLUSTRATING THE HISTORY OF JACOBINISM, page 7
410. MEMOIRS ILLUSTRATING THE HISTORY OF JACOBINISM, page 19
411. MEMOIRS ILLUSTRATING THE HISTORY OF JACOBINISM, page 80
412. MEMOIRS ILLUSTRATING THE HISTORY OF JACOBINISM, page 320
413. MEMOIRS ILLUSTRATING THE HISTORY OF JACOBINISM, page 509
414. A NEW ENCYCYCLOPAEDIA OF FREEMASONRY, Volume l, page 386 on Illuminati of Bavaria
415. MEMOIRS ILLUSTRATING THE HISTORY OF JACOBINISM, page 319
416. PROOFS OF A CONSPIRACY, page 55
417. Gary Allen, Illuminism, the Great Conspiracy, 1776-1848 (American Opinion magazine June, 1976) oage 49
418. PROOFS OF A CONSPIRACY, pages 60-61
419. Alan Stang, The Manifesto (American Opinion magazine, February, 1972) page 57
420. PROOFS OF A CONSPIRACY, page iv
421. MEMOIRS ILLUSTRATING THE HISTORY OF JACOBINISM, page 300
422. MEMOIRS ILLUSTRATING THE HISTORY OF JACOBINISM, page 320
423. PROOFS OF A CONSPIRACY, page 102
424. PROOFS OF A CONSPIRACY, page 63
425. Macoy Publishing & Masonic Supply Co., Inc., September 1, 1994 catalog, page 73

426.   Sabbar Temple, Pictorial History from 1966-1977 (Tucson, Arizona: presented by R & R Publishing Co., Inc., 1977) unnumbered page, but would be page 4

427.   From a newsletter published by Mick Oxley, Route 1, Box 257E, Crescent City, Florida, 32112

428.   A NEW ENCYCLOPAEDIA OF FREEMASONRY, Volume 1, page 64, on Abbe Augustin Barruel

429.   MACKEY'S ENCYCLOPAEDIA, Volume 1, pages 62-63, on Anti-Masonic books

430.   THE ROYAL MASONIC CYCLOPAEDIA, pages 607-608, on John Robison

431.   THE ROYAL MASONIC CYCLOPAEDIA, page 608, on John Robison

432.   THE SPIRIT OF MASONRY, page 177

433.   MACKEY'S ENCYCLOPAEDIA, Volume 1, pages 98-99

434.   MACKEY'S ENCYCLOPAEDIA, Volume 1, page 64

435.   THE ROYAL MASONIC CYCLOPAEDIA, page 68

436.   MACKEY'S ENCYCLOPAEDIA, Volume 1, page 347 on Illuminism

437.   MACKEY'S ENCYCLOPAEDIA, Volume 1, page 347 on Illuminism

438.   MACKEY'S ENCYCLOPAEDIA, Volume 1, page 64 on Anti-Masonic books

439.   THE ROYAL MASONIC CYCLOPAEDIA, page 766 on Adam Weishaupt

440.   THE ROYAL MASONIC CYCLOPAEDIA, pages 328-330 on Illuminati of Bavaria

441.   THE ROYAL MASONIC CYCLOPAEDIA, page 18

442.   MORALS AND DOGMA, page 849

443.   COIL'S MASONIC ENCYCLOPEDIA, page 681

444.   MACKEY'S ENCYCLOPAEDIA, Volume 2, page 842 on Adam Weishaupt

445.   MACKEY'S ENCYCLOPAEDIA, Volume 2, page 843 on Adam Weishaupt

446.   MACKEY'S ENCYCLOPAEDIA, Volume 2, page 843 on Adam Weishaupt

447.   MACKEY'S ENCYCLOPAEDIA, Volume 2, pages 843-844 on Adam Weishaupt

448.   MACKEY'S ENCYCLOPAEDIA, Volume 1, page 347 on Illuminati of Bavaria

449.   Gary Allen, Illuminism, the Great Conspiracy (June 1976 American Opinion magazine) pages 47-49

450. Alan Stang, The Manifesto (February, 1972 American Opinion magazine) page 50

451. MACKEY'S ENCYCLOPAEDIA, Volume 2, page 843, on Adam Weishaupt

452. THE ROYAL MASONIC CYCLOPEDIA, page 68 on Augustin Barruel

453. MACKEY'S ENCYCLOPAEDIA, Volume 2, page 849, on Congress of Wilhelmsbad

454. MACKEY'S ENCYCLOPAEDIA, Volume 2, page 849, on Congress of Wilhelmsbad

455. COIL'S MASONIC ENCYCLOPEDIA, page 146

456. MAGNUM OPUS, XXVIII Degree, page 6

457. MACKEY'S ENCYCLOPAEDIA, Volume 2, page 574 on Politics

458. MACKEY'S ENCYCLOPAEDIA, Volume 2, page 574 on Politics

459. Congressional Record -- Senate, September 9, 1987, pages 11868-11870

460. The New Age Magazine, published by the 33rd Degree Council, April 1988, Volume XCVI, Number 4

461. The Scottish Rite Magazine, published by the 33rd Degree Council, January, 1994 issue, pages 30-31

462. From an official biography of Senator Lott in the possession of this author, taken from what appears to be an official U.S. Senate report

463. The Royal Arch Mason, Volume VII, Spring, 1963, No. 9, page 259

464. The Royal Arch Mason, Volume XI, No. 8, Winter, 1974-75, page 252

465. PROOFS OF A CONSPIRACY, unnumbered page but would be page VII

466. BEHIND THE LODGE DOOR, page 210

467. FREEMASONRY EXPOSED, page 75

468. MAGNUM OPUS, XVIII Degree, page 9

469. MACKEY'S ENCYCLOPAEDIA, Volume 1, pages 60-61 under Anno Lucis

470. PROOFS OF A CONSPIRACY, page 111

INDEX

-A-

391